Jane Anderson graduated with an Honours degree in Zoology from the University of Glasgow, Scotland, later specialising in developmental neurophysiology before leaving the world of formal scientifc research to follow her dreams. After living in Africa and South America, she arrived in Australia in 1984, some twenty-five years later than her childhood attempts to dig an antipodean tunnel from her English back garden with an old dessert spoon. Settling in Queensland in 1992, Jane began her self-funded research into dreams and moved full-time into the professional world of writing, radio broadcasting and public speaking.

From 1992 to 1997, Jane worked with various ABC radio stations, broadcasting her popular weekly *Dream Talkback* programs. In 1996 Queensland's ABC radio broadcast her forty-two part series *Reality Matters,* co-presented with Chris Welsh. Jane is a regular guest on ABC radio's nationally broadcast shows and is looking forward to a new adventure in bringing *The Shape of Things to Come* to television. This is her third book.

By the same author

Sleep On It and Change Your life
Dream It: Do It!

Jane Anderson

the shape of things to come

A scientist explains how it is possible
to predict – and change – the future.

RANDOM HOUSE
AUSTRALIA

Jane Anderson communicates through her informative
and interactive web site at http://www.janeanderson.com.au

Published by
Random House Australia Pty Ltd
20 Alfred Street, Milsons Point, NSW 2061
http://www.randomhouse.com.au

Sydney New York Toronto
London Auckland Johannesburg
and agencies throughout the world

First published in 1998

National Library of Australia
Cataloguing-in-Publication Data

Anderson, Jane, 1954- .
   The shape of things to come : predicting the future.

   ISBN 0 09 183667 0.

   1. Dreams. 2. Dream interpretation. 3. Dream
   interpretation – Case studies. 4. Precognition. 5.
   Precognition – Case studies. I. Title.

154.634

Design by Luisa Laino
Typeset by Asset Typesetting Pty Ltd, Sydney
Printed by Griffin Press Pty Ltd, South Australia

10 9 8 7 6 5 4 3 2 1

Dedication

To my husband, Glen, for courageously choosing to dream your life with me.

To my daughter, Rowan, for letting your dreams teach us all the freedom in choice.

To my son, Euan, for dreaming the soul music of life.

And to my baby godson, Emryn, for the love you inspire through simply being.

Contents

Part Three
The Soul Searches for Meaning

Epilogue

Index

Postscript

Acknowledgments

Two hundred people contributed towards this research by answering questionnaires and entering into private correspondence through the Dream Research Bank. Fifty of these completed the lengthy and detailed precognitive dreaming questionnaire and many continued to update me on their precognitive experiences and thoughts for up to three years. Some have been mentioned by name, or by pen-name, in this book, but while others have not been named, their input has shaped both the book and my conclusions. To all these very special people who have given so much time, effort and thought, I extend my deepest thanks.

Some experiences in this book resulted from 'Reality Matters', the radio series which I co-presented with Chris Welsh on Queensland's ABC radio station 612:4QR. Thank you, Chris, for the part you played in encouraging people to tune into what really matters and to become involved in my research. Thank you also to our listeners who took the plunge and carried out some of the experiments with us.

Thank you to the four clairvoyants whose stories appear in this book: Margaret Stuart, the Reverend Ruth Bennett, Saanthi and Bruce Way. Apart from giving me their time and energy during the initial interviews, each read their individual stories and gave me permission to publish. Thank you especially for being frank and honest in expressing your individual concerns about the nature of your work.

Seven members of the Dream Research Bank became special project researchers, organising and collecting survey material: Pat Collis, Sue Coulston, Jaquie Grewar, Barbara Hughes, Kerry Kroesen, Anita Mudge and Celine Richardson. Thank you all for your wonderful dedication and work.

The Hypnosis Project with hypnotherapist John Suess was a turning point in this research. Thank you, John, for all the hours you donated towards this research, for your interest in investigating such an unusual field, for your trust in carrying out my experiments and for your support, encouragement and discussion.

Finally, thank you to everyone who has discussed this subject with me during the years, in particular to dream analyst Kerry Kroesen, dream and subconscious mind therapist Beth Richardson and, of course, the greatest sounding board of all, my family.

Introduction
What If?

How would you feel if you found yourself reliving one of your dreams, detail for detail? Would you dismiss it as a strange coincidence, or question your sanity perhaps? You might conclude that your memory had played tricks on you, that there had been no such dream in the first place. Maybe the whole experience was an intense deja vu, an imbalance of brain chemistry leaving you certain that you had dreamed this very occasion before.

Or maybe the experience was genuine, leaving you questioning whether free will exists. If you can see your future before it happens, is it, after all, predetermined? Or did you create your future by seeing it in the first place? How would you feel if you dreamed or had a vision of a fatal accident, only to walk into the identical scene the next day? Was it an inevitable accident? Should you have warned the person concerned? Why did you get to preview it? What does it all mean?

The implications of each of these questions are huge, particularly in the areas of personal freedom, power and responsibility. Many precognitive dreamers and visionaries wrestle with these questions throughout their lives, not knowing where to turn for social acceptance, let alone explanation.

Being a scientist, my reaction to these kind of experiences in my own life has been to record all my dreams shortly after waking, a discipline I have continued for six years. My family and those who know me well often witness my excited flourishing of my dream journal in evidence that some event we have all shared has been documented in advance. The awe never dwindles, even though I have now reached an understanding of the hows and whys behind the dramas of precognition. For that is where I now stand, paused at the milestone which marks not the end of my travels, but the conclusion of a three-year research quest which has led me on the most extraordinary journey.

There were many facets to this quest and I approached it from a variety of angles. While my own story interweaves the pages of this book, you will also meet others whose dreams have previewed specific future events, as well as those whose future insights have been received while awake. The stories of four esteemed professional clairvoyants are presented, documenting their experiences, hopes, fears and philosophies of precognition. All these people were questioned in depth and many contributed additional experiences and thoughts during the three-year period. Each has read and edited his or her story as it appears in this book and each has agreed to publication, although some have chosen pen-names to maintain confidentiality. Several experiences were retold from my radio talkback programmes using transcribed tapes and these are acknowledged as they occur.

The most extraordinary part of the quest for me was the Hypnosis Project in which I was hypnotised into the future six times by John Suess, a well-regarded professional hypnotherapist. Going under hypnosis as a scientist, recording and transcribing the sessions in secrecy and then living through the unfolding scenarios as objectively as I could, was exhilarating yet traumatic. The results of my experiments challenged me way beyond the boundaries of my previous thinking. I emerged from those months of headaches, confusion and disbelief with a completely new, yet rational, understanding of the way life is.

You will also travel, through these pages, the dimensions of quantum physics and relativity where reality as you think you know it will never be the same again. Imagery leads you over the bumpy bits to impart clear understanding of these insights without losing scientific accuracy.

The book is structured in three parts. The first 'The Body of Evidence', presents the evidence for precognition (the 'what?'), through precognitive dreams, visions, professional clairvoyancy and the Hypnosis Project. The intention is to keep you questioning at this stage, to lead you along a similar journey to my own and to give you the opportunity to assess the evidence, reminisce your own experiences and come up with your own theories. Part One threads questions throughout the evidence, much as you might encounter when reading a detective novel. Indeed that was the idea behind this structure, to let you enjoy the book as a great mystery, allowing your conscious and unconscious mind to simmer and brew over the possibilities and the huge implications of areas of this research. While you might find the questioning frustrating and the evidence at times contradictory, you will enjoy the journey best if you enter into the 'detective' frame of mind.

The second part, 'The Mind Questions "How?"', introduces science into the arena to answer some of the 'hows' and then progresses through further extraordinary experiences to arrive at a complete understanding of how precognition works. The only question then remaining is whether our ability to experience the future and then live through it again is merely a fantastic mechanism explicable by science and theory, or whether there is a deeper spiritual meaning behind it all.

And so the third part of the book ponders 'The Soul Searches for Meaning', completing the 'what?' and the 'how?' with the 'why?'. Spirituality enters the picture, highlighting meaning, purpose and the role of personal power in addressing our individual responsibilities towards our personal and collective futures. The final practical component shows you how to apply the results of this research to gain maximum insight into the what, how and why of the shape of things to come.

part one

the body
the body of evidence
of evidence

when
dreams 1
come
true

Anna's second marriage had broken up and she had returned home to her mother's house. Her husband would not move out of their home and she couldn't get access to collect sentimental gifts or to retrieve the Siamese cat which had been a present from her first husband. Her dream therefore occurred at a time of great stress.

'I dreamed I was walking around the house, which had been stripped bare of all its furniture. My husband had left taking everything but my orange cat which I found in the wardrobe with its head off. As I walked around I heard a voice say, "It's okay, you can come back now."'

The next day Anna returned to her house and it was indeed empty. She found the decapitated cat in the wardrobe.

Anna felt that the preview offered by her precognitive dream helped her handle the event the following day. 'Because I came to terms with having no furniture and my cat destroyed *before* it actually occurred, I was prepared, so it was not such a shock.'

What was happening here? Was Anna seeing the future before

it happened, or was the cat already dead at the time of the dream? Did she inadvertently tune into the thoughts of her husband as he left the house for the last time, incorporating the precognitive information into her dream?

The dictionary defines telepathy as 'the supposed communication of thoughts or ideas otherwise than by the known senses'; in other words, picking up someone else's thoughts. If you have never experienced telepathy you will find this book extremely challenging. I laughed to myself as I sat down to write the opening paragraph of this chapter and realised that throughout my research into precognition I have made the basic assumption that telepathy is an accepted phenomenon of daily life. I'm not referring to the endless parapsychology papers on ESP and card guessing. Neither am I endorsing well-known entertainers who profess mind-reading skills while deluding their audiences with magic illusion tricks. While some people may well have developed telepathic skills to the level where they can 'tune in and out' at will, I don't believe this is the case for most of us. The usual experience is more often a fleeting 'knowing', a moment's insight instantly chased away by the following thought. Looking back we say, 'I knew that was Mary on the phone' or 'I was just thinking about that!' We might put the kettle on an instant before our 'unexpected' visitor drives into the street, or converge on the same shop at the same moment as our partner to buy some obscure item that has not been discussed. Serve a cynic a bottle of wine and even they will have at least one strange story to tell, even if they prefer to sweep it away as a good yarn based on coincidence.

That analytical left brain takes its repose at night while our dreams are freely orchestrated by the more creative, intuitive right brain. Here, I believe, with the guard off duty, we are more receptive to the thoughts of others, which intermingle uncensored among the symbolism of our own personally meaningful dreams.

In my own case I often dream that I press the replay button on a telephone answering machine, hear a message, then continue with the main storyline of my dream. That message frequently surfaces the next day. For example, in one dream I received an answering machine message from a male real estate agent telling me that the house we rented would be put on the market before the end of our lease and that we would need to move out in three months' time. In the dream I told him three months was plenty of notice, so he must mean either three days or three weeks.

The next morning the phone rang and, yes, it was a male real estate agent. Guess what? Right again! When the agent, Andrew Degn, arrived, suitably accompanied by a back-up in case the tenants revolted, I made them a cup of tea and said, 'That's fine. Don't ask me why I say this, but I bet you the house sells in either three days or three weeks,' and we all laughed politely. It sold three weeks later, to the exact day. The dream was precognitive because it contained accurate foreknowledge of the sale, but how did I gain this information? At the time I was dreaming, the decision to put the house up for sale must have already been made. The note to phone me would have been marked in Andrew's diary. To that extent the precognition was perhaps based on telepathy. In fact the number of precognitive dreams which involve letters in the mail, articles appearing in the next day's newspapers, or items on tomorrow's television news are manifold and may all be explained in this way (how telepathy occurs is discussed in Part Two of this book).

My interest, however, is more in the kind of dreams which cannot be explained in such terms. My quest, prompted by the stranger experiences of my life, is to explain apparent precognition of future events which have not been set in motion.

Returning to my 'house for sale' dream, the more interesting question is the accuracy of the three weeks' notice reasoned during the dream. Did I pinpoint a sale in three weeks' time because that was when it was going to occur, or did Andrew get really motivated at my three week suggestion and perform accordingly? Or, or, or … There are a million questions in between. I'm sure you're already asking them.

I entered the world of dream research full-time six years ago, blending my scientific background with my passion for understanding dreams, perception and reality. I was sure that my curiosity, my need to know and my own unusual life experiences would ultimately lead me to write this book. Firstly, though, I felt I needed to carry out some groundwork in the field of dreams. Somewhere between the symbolism of dreams and our constantly shifting perception of the reality of life is an understanding of precognition and here I hoped to find an explanation as to why so many events in my life were preseen in my dreams or previewed in the strangeness of some memorable days. With the conviction that I might somehow bring rational light into the shaded borderline territory where 'weird things' are left untouched, I marched forward.

My work in dream research has been wholly satisfying on a personal level. I have learned to analyse and comprehend the symbolism of dreams, drawing out the physical, emotional, psychological, spiritual and metaphysical relevance, as appropriate, for the dreamer. My basic catchphrase is 'Turning the nonsense of dreams into common sense'. The only sticky bit in the whole analytical process is the precognitive dream. My getaway explanation is always, 'Look, 99.9 per cent of our dreams are symbolic, so let's analyse your dream and make sense of it. Let's see if it relates to your life and what you are going through at the moment. If you're worried that your dream about your toddler getting knocked down and killed by a truck falls into the itsy-bitsy category of precognitive dreaming, then heed the warning and watch your child at all times. Meantime, let's analyse!' I still believe this to be the best approach.

I cannot emphasise enough, before you delve further into this chapter, that most dreams are symbolic and have very little chance of playing out as actual events in your waking life. If you are not familiar with meaningful dream analysis, I suggest you become so in order to balance what you will read in this book. Okay, warnings complete, let's leave the analytical to one side for a while and look at the evidence for precognitive dreaming.

Precognition, according to the dictionary, is 'supposed foreknowledge, especially of a supernatural kind'; whereas 'premonition' is defined as 'a forewarning'. While many of the examples here could be described as premonitions, I prefer to use precognition to cover all 'supposed foreknowledge', whether or not it seems to carry warning.

The dreams presented in this chapter are examples either from my own dreaming life or from some of the fifty dreamers who responded to the detailed research questionnaire or who contributed their experiences through my research network, the Dream Research Bank. (The full precognitive dreaming questionnaire is presented in Appendix 1.) In search of the evidence for glimpsing future events or details through precognitive dreaming, this chapter raises many questions. Since Part One of this book is dedicated to presenting the evidence for precognition, I suggest you let the questions trickle through you as you read, feel the nature of enquiry but immerse yourself in the experiences. Parts Two and Three focus on answers. To understand the answers, we need to know the nature and breadth of the questions. The evidence acquaints us with the questions.

Foreknowledge through Telepathy?

The following examples, I believe, may incorporate elements of telepathy.

Lorna: *'I have, on several occasions, dreamed that someone I know is involved in the death of someone I do not know. For example, I woke one night, almost forty years ago, in severe distress. I told my husband that something had happened to my brother, that someone was dead and my brother was involved but safe. In the morning news broadcast there was a report of two student teachers who died when their motorcycle collided with a bus. My brother was driving the bus.'*

Cynthia: *'Some years ago I had a cat who was due to have kittens any day. One night I had a very clear dream that the cat had four kittens; two lay dead and the other two were missing. Next morning, after telling my husband about the dream, we went outside and found the cat had two dead kittens. After an hour we found another two chewed up.'*

Paddie was living in Wangaratta when she received word that her father was dying of cancer back home in the States, so she flew over immediately, staying there for the next six weeks. It was a traumatic time as she had been unaware of her father's illness. While there, she dreamed she saw her house in Wangaratta being restumped, and was amazed because her landlords had not given notice of any renovation. Nevertheless, she felt sure the house had actually been restumped. In the end she decided her friend must have told her so on the phone, and that she had only absorbed it subconsciously due to her overriding grief for her father.

On her return to Australia, Paddie was met by her friend, who avidly brought her up to date with all the news, including the restumping of the house. Paddie reminded her that she had already told her about it on the phone, but her friend was quite sure that the phone contact had been prior to the work being notified or carried out. With this confirmation that she had on some level 'seen' the restumping taking place, and that the dream was not simply the surfacing of unprocessed information from a telephone conversation, Paddie felt frightened. Looking back now, however, she sees her father's death as the beginning of a 'psychic opening', and her initial fear of her dream experience has become, instead, amazement.

Many years ago **Heather** was awakened at ten p.m. by the sound of a loud shot.

'Thinking it to be in the neighbourhood, I got up and looked outside for signs of the disturbance, but saw nothing. I prayed that help would come to whoever had been shot. Still feeling very disturbed, I went back to sleep at eleven p.m.

'I dreamed of receiving a long letter from my former husband, in which he had written several pages of vitriolic accusations about myself. I read the letter through but didn't wake up. At midnight I was roused in a state of such terror that I still wonder why the shock didn't cause a heart attack or death. I felt that some evil presence was trying to take my soul. I was awake and physically paralysed. I couldn't move to turn on the bed light. I was praying to God to save me from this evil.

'After some minutes I was able to turn on the light, get out of bed and go to the phone to ring a counselling agency where I worked as a volunteer counsellor. I was sitting with my back to the wall, but still looking over my shoulder, such was my terror. We talked for four-and-a-half hours after which I relaxed and became very warm and drowsy. I went back to sleep and slept until the phone rang at eleven in the morning. It was my former husband's second wife with the news that he had shot and killed himself. "The police say that it happened yesterday evening," she explained. That is when I heard the shot, yet they lived over 1000 kilometres away from me. I later asked my mother-in-law if there had been a letter, "Yes," she confirmed. "The police destroyed it."'

I have many examples on file of people who have dreamed of the death of someone they know, woken up, noted the time and later discovered this to be the precise moment of death. Although a relatively common experience, it is no less overwhelming for the fact that it is shared by many. Does the dreamer tune into the dying person's thoughts, the thoughts of the hospital staff or carers, or the essence of the person's released spirit? Across the range of possibilities, the explanation is most likely telepathy at one of these levels.

I have not macabrely picked death dreams for this section, but they do seem to make up a large proportion of precognitive dreams. This observation is, in fact, a vital clue to the nature of precognition. But more of that later.

The unit next door to **Linda** had become vacant and she had no idea who would be moving in when she had this dream.

'We were having a very loud party. I saw this elderly man walking towards me with a walking stick and he had a most peculiar gait. He seemed to be walking like an automaton or a wind-up toy. Anyway, I was really worried as I thought he was not very well and he would think he had moved next door to a very noisy crowd and wouldn't know that this was the first noisy party we had ever had. (In fact, we've never had one!)'

Two or three days after the dream, Linda was talking on the phone to the lady who had previously occupied the unit next door, and discovered that the new neighbour would be moving in later that day. The new occupant, she learned, was an elderly gentleman who was unwell due to a hip replacement operation which had gone wrong. Apparently he had some wire protruding through his skin.

'When I heard about the man's hip problem, I immediately understood why, in my dream, he was walking in a strange way, which involved a mechanical aspect to do with the hips. I can't describe it, but I can see it in my mind.'

Although there were no noisy parties to upset the elderly gentleman, the unit did prove unsatisfactory to him and he moved out within six months.

If this dream is explicable in terms of telepathy, Linda may have tuned in to the elderly man's thoughts as he contemplated the move and his health.

Louise: *'Ray and I decided to have a short holiday so we headed off to Byron Bay. We both love this area with its beautiful beaches and wonderful array of wildlife. Every morning, just after daylight, we would walk the miles of almost deserted beach. We saw dolphins so close to the shore that we could see their eyes, and the seabirds busily searching for breakfast were a delight. All this and the magnificent power and beauty of the ocean were pure magic.*

'I was happy and relaxed when I went to bed on the Tuesday night and slept soundly until three a.m. when I awoke from a strange dream. In the dream, Ray and I were standing in front of a low-set house, observing the house at eye level. The roof and walls appeared to be normal, but there were ugly, black, gaping holes where the windows should have been. Inside the house was totally black. It was an eerie feeling looking into these desolate holes. My attention returned to what I was doing, which was stroking a very large, fluffy, long-haired cat. The cat was looking at the house and it was very upset about something. I continued to stroke and soothe it, and could feel its soft fur. I spoke to it in a calming way.

'Over to my left I could see Ray who was stroking and soothing a different cat. His cat was sleek and short haired and a different colour, but it was equally upset and looking towards the house. Something about the house had unnerved the cats and I felt it had to do with the awful black interior. We continued to reassure the cats because we didn't want them to go near the house. Then I woke up.'

On the Friday Louise and Ray drove home feeling good after their break and vowing to go back soon. When they arrived home they found the house next door had been completely burned out, though the occupants had escaped safely.

'The roof and walls were intact but the inside was a totally blackened ruin. When I looked in through the nonexistent windows, it was exactly as I had seen it in the dream. The dream showed the house as it is now: black, empty and desolate. We then discovered that the fire had occurred on the Wednesday at around three a.m. To say that I was amazed would be an understatement, but what word could I use that would describe the feeling? Even though I have had this type of experience before, it still always amazes me.'

Louise has often watched waking life events echo her dreams, and each time she questions the experience from many angles.

'Did I receive a telepathic message when the firemen and TV news crews were asking about us? (They did ask because our house is very close on that side.) Did a telepathic message enter my subconscious mind and become my dream? Was I there in spirit, checking things out? Were the cats not to go near the house because it was still too hot? Or were the cats symbolic of my psychic, inquisitive self needing to be calmed and reassured? There is no doubt in my mind that I did tune in to this fire, or the aftermath of it, and this shows me, again, the incredible power of the subconscious mind, that it allows us to tune in to things in dreams that we may doubt in reality … whatever that is! I don't think it matters if I had this dream before, during or after the fire. That I had it at all is the really incredible thing.'

No matter how many times we experience precognition, it generally inspires a deep sense of wonder. Even now that I believe I understand the process, I am still in awe. Perhaps more so. Maybe it is this sense of the extraordinary, no matter how palpable, that holds some people back from integrating it into their perception of the reality of life.

The precognitive dreams presented in the rest of this chapter all mirror future events which cannot be explained by telepathy alone.

Precognitive Warning Dreams
Changing the Future by Taking Action

Living through a situation which was once a dream may empower the dreamer to change the outcome. In doing so, of course, the dreamer never knows whether the original dream outcome would have come to pass; but in some cases, such as **Rowyn's**, action seems the sensible course to take. While holidaying in the South of France in 1988, Rowyn had a dream which recurred several times during the same week.

'I was a passenger in a car which was travelling along a mountain road. I was seated in the middle of the back seat minus a seat belt, a position I never sit in because I get car sick. A red car came towards us on the wrong side of the road and hit us head on. I flew through the windscreen, dying instantly.'

The dream unsettled Rowyn sufficiently to cause her to mention it to one of the other dream passengers who was also sharing the holiday. The two children on the vacation were restless and grumpy, unable to sleep because of their own persistent nightmares, so a daytrip was arranged to cheer everyone up. It was a week after the first occurrence of the dream.

'We set out for a picnic on the Italian–French border. I was hesitant about going, but not because of the dream. I just had a nagging doubt that I couldn't explain and I wanted to stay behind. Eventually, though, I was persuaded to go. When we got into the car, the two children had to sit by the windows in the back because there was no seat belt in the middle. I sat there so the boys could be buckled in. At no time did I think of the dream which had occurred prior. It just didn't enter my mind.

'Halfway up the mountain I was busy reading, not watching where we were going, totally oblivious to passing traffic. I felt the urge to look up as we approached the tunnel. Coming out of the tunnel was a car and as it came closer I registered that it was on the wrong side of the road and travelling extremely fast and erratic. At that time Mary, who was a passenger in the front, noted the same thing and cried out "It's going to hit us!" I thought the exact same thing at that moment, her cry mirroring mine in my mind.

'It was in this split second that I thought of the dream for the first time that day and so I immediately threw up my hands and brought my leg up and across my body. As we collided I was thrown forward. Had my arms and legs not blocked my passage, I would have ended up going through the windscreen onto the road. The car which had hit us was red.'

The event was identical to the dream except for the ending. Should we assume that Rowyn's recognition of the unfolding dream, which caused her to brace herself against the force of the headlong crash, saved her life? Certainly the waking life event broke away from the dream pattern at the moment she took evasive action. On reflection Rowyn recorded that she felt relieved and grateful that she had been warned and was allowed sufficient time to change events. She said she felt she had been able to choose life or death.

Libby decided her dream was a warning and took preventative action.

'I dreamed that my parents stopped at a corner store petrol station at Coober Pedy, South Australia, where my father filled up his car with petrol and had a conversation with an old Aboriginal lady who was standing outside. He went inside, paid for the petrol and left. Approximately one and a half miles down the road, I could see he was having difficulty driving because of the dust and the sun glaring in his face. He failed to

see a hole in the road and hit it, causing their white four-wheel drive vehicle to roll. My mother died in the crash.'

Libby's parents were in Coober Pedy at the time and, believing her dream to be precognitive, Libby felt both scared and relieved. At least, she thought, she could warn her parents in advance so they could be aware of the danger and avoid an accident. She gave them a call.

Two to three weeks later newspaper headlines reported that a bus, approximately the same size as Libby's parents' white four-wheel drive vehicle, hit a pothole approximately three kilometres down the road from Coober Pedy. The bus rolled and a lady in her fifties died. When interviewed, the driver revealed that the sun and dust were so bad that he hadn't seen the pothole in the road.

When her parents heard the news and realised the similarities to Libby's dream, they phoned her immediately to let her know they were safe.

By taking action, did Libby change the outcome of her dream? Would her parents have been involved in the accident had she not taken action? Would it have been their accident, or would they have been on the scene and witnessed the one which did eventuate? Or was Libby's dream slightly inaccurate? Or was it totally coincidental?

Geographical locations beyond the dreamer's home often feature in precognitive dreams, particularly when travel of a friend or relative is involved. I believe this is a further clue to the nature of precognition.

Glenys took action on a dream she believed to be precognitive, although she will never know what the outcome would have been had she not done so. The mother of three children under the age of ten, Glenys was in full-time employment when her mother-in-law suggested sending the children down to her by bus for the school holidays. Three weeks before they were due to leave, Glenys had a dream—a nightmare.

'I dreamed that the bus with my children on board overturned on the journey. It caught on fire and I could see my middle child enveloped in flames and screaming. I woke in a cold sweat.'

Glenys cancelled the holiday immediately. A month later her usual babysitter was taken sick and sent her daughter around to look after the children in her place.

'The daughter was giving them a picnic in the back yard and boiled the kettle on the portable spirit stove. To make a long story short, my middle child was horribly burned. Two long years were spent in and out of hospitals and plastic surgery ensued. My in-laws have always maintained that if I had not cancelled the holiday, this accident would never have occurred. I have agonised over this for many years.

'I tell no-one about my precognitive dreams now, because everyone I know believes that if you do predict things correctly you have actually caused them to happen. I even stopped writing them down last year when a friend's father died exactly as I'd dreamed, but I couldn't prepare her and I couldn't show her the dream after the event, as it was, by then, unhelpful to her.'

Did Glenys save her middle child by cancelling the holiday? The bus did not crash, but without the child on board perhaps the whole future had been changed. Or did she foresee, in her dream, a burning accident occurring during the holidays, but in an inaccurate context? Are some events in our future unavoidable in the grander plan of things, while precognitive dreams help to prepare us to cope with the inevitable? Or do we indeed cause our futures through our dreams, and if so, why is it that only some of our dreams eventuate? Glenys's anxieties and concerns are shared by many precognitive dreamers: these will be addressed in Parts Two and Three of this book.

Precognitive Warning Dreams
No Action Taken

How can you take action on a dream if you don't know it is precognitive? From all the answers given in the precognitive dreaming questionnaires and despite continual searching, I have not been able to identify a consistent description of a precognitive dream. Some say they recognise their precognitive dreams because they are 'vivid', 'real' or have 'clarity', but many other people experience all their dreams as vivid, real and clear. For most people the factors seemed individual and specific, like my telephone answering machines, for example. It may be a case of 'know thyself and thy dreams'.

I have often had dreams that have been full of accurate details about the future except for the identification of the person involved. I have found this to be particularly true with dreams warning of death. In my dreams the person who is about to die may be a different person but have the same first name as the person in the dream, or may be a relative of the dream character. Also I don't see the actual death, but I am given notice of it, or I feel an exhilarating sensation of casting off the heaviness of a physical body. I have come to accept this, in my life, as meaning that I am not supposed to take any action on behalf of, or towards, another person. How can I if I don't know whom the dream concerns? The only action I can take is to prepare myself or to learn from the positive experiences these dreams impart.

Ken's dream left him in the same quandary. He did not know what action to take as a result of his strange dream until he was living the reality of it—when it was too late.

'I was driving along in the car. My wife, Beth, was sitting in the passenger seat. To my alarm I noticed, lying on the road ahead, a decapitated head. In that instant I noticed there was a steel plate on the left-hand side of the head. I remember thinking that it was a baby, but it didn't look like a baby. I didn't recognise the face. I swerved sharply to miss it, thinking at the same time that it was dead already anyway. Then Beth yelled "Look out or you'll hit the tree!" I woke up feeling sad.'

Over breakfast Beth set about helping Ken look at his dream symbolically, but no matter how relevant she felt her analysis to be, Ken disagreed. Beth takes up the story at this point.

'At eleven o'clock that evening a car drove into our driveway and Ken went out to meet it. It was the father of one of my nephew's friends. He told us to contact my brother and get down to the hospital immediately because my nephew Ricky was critically injured. "Dying," he whispered to Ken. Ricky had been a front-seat passenger in a friend's car, returning home from band practice. The driver was driving too fast approaching a series of S-bends on a narrow road. The car went out of control at high speed, slewed across the road and hit a tree. The tree hit Ricky. He died in hospital shortly after arrival, due to massive brain injury to the left side of his head. When my parents, Ken and my brother arrived at the hospital they were met by a doctor and a counsellor. They were told that Ricky was dead. Mum cried out, "But he was only a baby." He was nineteen years old.'

Beth's interest in dreams and her accomplishment as an interpreter had led to her making a personal study of her family's dreams, and relatives often confided in her. A few days after Ricky's death, she remembered his phone call, back in February that year, following a worrying dream he had just experienced.

'Ricky dreamed he was living back at the caravan park and he was sitting outside with his friends, having a gig. He was feeling good, happy. But then he left them and found himself struggling up a steep hill. Finally he

got to the top and there was this guy he used to know who, in waking life, had died from taking drugs. He said something to Ricky. He couldn't remember what was said, but it worried him sufficiently to phone me and ask my opinion.'

A month before his death Ricky did move back to the caravan park to be close to his musician friends. On the day of the accident he had been practising all day with a band he had just joined. They had had their first professional gig the weekend prior, and Ricky was over the moon about it. Apparently he'd had a wonderful day. They were returning home from this band practice when the accident happened. As Beth observed, 'It was almost like the dream, apart from going up the hill to be met by a dead friend.'

Rebekah didn't realise her dream was precognitive until she was living it either.

'Sixteen years ago I dreamed that my daughter came to me and said, "This is Tony and I'm going to marry him." He was very short, that was my first reaction, as our daughter is tall and quite big. He was thin and dark and Welsh. I remember feeling appalled and totally rejecting, for he was the antithesis of everything we had visualised for her, especially educationwise.'

Six months passed between the dream and the event, which played out in its entirety. When Rebekah was introduced to the short, thin, dark, Tony who was to marry her daughter, the intervening months had done nothing to mellow her emotional response. As the scene unfolded before her Rebekah realised her dream had been accurately precognitive. Had she recognised this beforehand, she might have prepared herself to give Tony a better reception or to discuss her expectations with her daughter. Instead, the sudden impact of living a dream was so strong that she wonders, looking back, whether she might have overreacted as a result. Certainly she did not welcome the news at the time and it took several rocky years before mother and son-in-law finally became close friends.

In contrast to Rebekah's and Ken's experiences, some dreamers recognise certain dreams as precognitive. When they predict sickness or death, they often feel an emotional burden as they await the unfolding of the event.

Carol has an active dream life and records many dreams, both symbolic and precognitive. She can usually identify a precognitive dream by a 'heavy feeling' experienced in the dream, which then stays with her for days, leaving her unsettled. Such dreams are also always in vivid black and white, and her recall of details is usually very clear. The following seemed to be such a dream and she knew it was a preview of something which would run its course naturally. One August, several years ago, Carol recorded in her dream journal:

'I dreamed that my mother-in-law would have four squares of skin removed from her leg. She was lying on a lounge rather than a hospital bed. The first three squares were okay, but the fourth contained what looked like a black cauliflower.'

Carol's mother-in-law lived overseas and the family had received no warning from her that she was unwell. Then, two or three weeks after the dream, Carol's mother-in-law had a melanoma removed from her leg, which involved cutting one square from her leg and a second for a skin graft. At this point Carol began to feel uneasy. A third square was removed a little later. Carol was hopeful but unconvinced when the doctors told her mother-in-law she was okay. When a fourth square was removed, cancer of the lymph glands of the groin was diagnosed. She died in March, seven months after the dream.

Cynthia *felt a similar burden in the face of her precognitive dream. 'The daughter of a close friend was expecting her first child. I had a dream that my friend came running up to greet me at her front gate and said, "The baby—the baby, it's not there any more." Two weeks later I had a call to say the baby had died at birth. I felt awful.'*

Sometimes the opportunity to take action on a warning dream is missed because the dream is so symbolic that it's overlooked until the event occurs and the connection becomes obvious. **Cheryl's** dream involving a big black rhino definitely seemed symbolic.

'I was sitting behind glass in an old house that had been turned into a restaurant. Jed, our dog, was outside laying on the grass looking at me. Behind him was a big black rhino. Its right feet were churning the ground and its head was down. I screamed at Jed to get out of the way but he couldn't hear me.'

Less than a week later Cheryl was heading out of the house with her daughter.

'We were going out. Jed was asleep in the garage. I told him to get out of the way, then went back inside the house because I'd forgotten something. Returning to the car, I reversed out of the garage. The car didn't want to move as if something was holding it. I realised the handbrake was still on, so I released it and accelerated, running over Jed with the right-hand wheels in the process.'

Cheryl had run over Jed's head, breaking his jaw. The vet wasn't sure that the sixteen-year-old dog would survive the necessary operation but, happily, he did. As far as the dream was concerned, Cheryl felt it was related to the accident the very moment it happened. With further thought, she linked her four-wheel-drive with its big black tyres to the dream vision of the big black rhino churning the ground with its right feet. As for being behind glass in the dream, Cheryl noted that she observed the scene through the glass of her car window, which was up at the time of the accident.

Was the symbolism in Cheryl's dream a case of substitution (the rhino for the car, for example) due to inaccurate recall or to being unable to get the full picture? Or was the theme, or idea, inherent in the symbolism a precursor to the actual event?

Precognitive Winning Dreams

Not all precognitive dreams are so heavy. Changing the mood from warnings to winnings and from death to new beginnings illustrates the fuller range of precognition. While precognitive dreams about birth are commonly reported, descriptions such as 'a beautiful dark-haired boy' are not really detailed enough to qualify for the definitely precognitive category! Here's an identifiable, quirky one from **Cynthia** though.

'When I was two months pregnant with my second child I had a crystal-clear dream of the baby's face. In the left eye there were three dots in the position of five o' clock from the pupil. When my son was born the marks in the left eye were there, in exactly the same position.'

Once I dreamed of a job advertised in the small classifieds of the *Sydney Morning Herald*, under W for Writer (which is a rare classification in Australian newspapers!). I tested the dream and bought the paper. The advert was there and I got the job. It led to a whole new future, though I didn't realise it at the time. The point is that if I hadn't checked out the dream by buying the paper, I would never have known that it was a precognitive dream, and I would also have missed out on a very positive, life-changing opportunity. I wonder how many positive life experiences pass us by because we miss or dismiss the associated dreams?

When I admit to experiencing precognitive dreams, people usually ask, 'Can you dream the Lotto numbers?' Although at this point I have not had much success with purposively inducing precognitive dreams, I did have a great Lotto dream once. It was the morning of 8 December 1992.

In the dream I visited an old lady who had four large cards face down on a grass verge. She challenged me to read the numbers on the cards without turning them over. I looked at the first one and said, '23,' then I said, 'No, I always say 23.' I looked closer and saw a 16. The next two were easy: 4, 19. The fourth card was hard so the woman gave me a clue from which I deduced, 'Ace,' meaning 1. She said this was the most important card. I woke up and wrote down the five numbers: 23, 16, 4, 19, 1. I rarely enter Lotto but was struck that these looked like Lotto numbers, except that I needed six numbers to try. I went back to sleep purposively seeking another number and had a dream featuring an 8.

I asked my husband, Glen, to put these numbers in the next day, but he forgot, and anyway they didn't come up. A few days later he decided to enter them for the Saturday draw instead. As we sat and watched the results on television, the first number to come up was 1, then 4, by which time Glen hid in the kitchen! The third number was 43, then came 28 (not my 23, but not far from it, a 3 looking like half an 8). Two teens came next: 13 and 14, not my two teens which had been 16 and 19. One of the supplementaries was 8, as in my return to sleep to get the last number. If I had noticed the hint in my dream to look closer at what I saw to be 23 we would have had a win. Unfortunately I haven't had another Lotto dream since!

What are the chances of dreaming six Lotto numbers, three accurately (one as one of the supplementaries), one visually similar, and two getting the teens bit right? I did pursue this question, but it's not easy to answer in a few lines. In formal statistical terms, the first Lotto ball drawn is the result of a 1:46 chance, the second a 1:45 chance and so on. Such an approach does not make a distinction between a 16, a 19 or a 42: they're all just balls. In dream terms we see the 16 and 19 as more similar than a 16 and a 42. In dreams the right brain is more active than the left. While the left brain sees mathematical meaning in 19, the right brain sees 19 as a 1 and a 9, or 19 years old or a symbol associated with the twentieth century or a teen, to name but a few examples. So it can be argued that in dream terms, my teen numbers, although they were the wrong teen number balls as far as the Lotto results were concerned, were rather more accurate than a statistician would pronounce through formal mathematical (left brain) analysis.

Similar quandaries exist in applying statistical formulae to other aspects of my dream Lotto selection. Intuitively, and simply, it's a pretty good result, considering it was my one and only Lotto dream, although a statistician would argue that we face exactly the same chances of winning each time we enter the Lotto, regardless of how many times we have done so before.

Apart from the insight into how the dreaming brain handles numbers, the challenging part of this precognition, as I see it, is its timing. We missed the first chance to put the numbers in and they didn't come up. We put them in at the next opportunity and got a good match. Was the dream partly precognitive of the Saturday's draw, a fact which Glen unconsciously knew and responded to by delaying entering the numbers? This seems unlikely given that it was my dream, not Glen's! Or did the dream, and our discussion about it, cause the numbers to come up once we entered the draw and believed we had a chance? Did I sway the selection of the Lotto balls as I watched them on the television? Somewhere perhaps, lost between the Wednesday and the Saturday, is another major clue about the nature of precognition. The Lotto dream will be further addressed later in this book.

Trivialities or Major Clues?
The Importance of Keeping a Dream Journal

Dedicated dreamers aside, most people recall only their most vivid, bizarre or emotionally charged dreams, tossing those which register less impact into waking oblivion. With practice it is possible to recall up to five detailed dreams each night. Once you start to record this level of detail, you will discover that precognitive dreaming covers a whole range of events, not just the 'biggies' of major consequence to our everyday lives. To understand the nature of precognition, it is just as important to investigate clues provided by apparently trivial precognitive dreams as it is to ponder the heavily consequential ones.

So deeply ingrained is this idea that precognitive dreaming equips us with knowledge of great significance or urgency, that seemingly trivial experiences such as **HM's** can be totally bewildering.

'I dreamed that I was standing facing my Year 6 class and the children were laughing. I looked down and saw that I was wearing my pale blue checked shorts. I knew the children were laughing at them, but I could see nothing wrong.'

The next morning HM did not recall the dream until he went to select a pair of shorts for the school day.

'I came across the pale blue pair and the sudden thought hit me: "This is the pair the dream said I'd have trouble with!" I then thought, "What superstitious nonsense!" and wore them as if to prove the point. I'd never had any problem with these shorts before!

'At eleven-forty that morning I turned my back on the class to write something on the board, when several children began to laugh. I turned to face the class and asked what the problem was, receiving the reply that my shorts had split at the back! Sure enough, the stitching at the seam had

completely given way. Luckily the next period at midday was taken by another teacher, so I was able to drop back home and change. I was obviously rather amazed, as I subsequently told the full story to the Principal and my wife. The Principal made no comment, but I'm sure he thought I was a bit crazy.'

Asked whether he felt he handled the waking life event any differently because of the dream, HM explained,

'I had absolutely no control over the situation, nor did I influence it in any way. I could not understand why the dream did not reveal to me what was actually wrong with the shorts. It ended with me looking down, but as it was in the front I saw nothing amiss. The incident did not really embarrass me, so in fact I had not foreseen anything that would have a great impact on me.'

HM was deeply perplexed. He had experienced a few precognitive dreams over the years, but this one bewildered him; it was as if the dream's very insignificance was the most significant factor of all.

Louise noted a whole series of precognitive dreams that predicted such inconsequential details that she didn't even recognise the events when they occurred. An active member of the Dream Research Bank, she was avidly searching back through her dream journals as part of an exercise for another project. In so doing she found what appeared to be seven such 'lost' precognitive dreams. For example:

'I dreamed that my daughter was visiting us with her dog, P, which she often does. P and our dog L were doing what they normally do, which is playing and tailing each other about. Bringing up the rear was the cutest, black and white, roly-poly puppy who was trying to get into the action. I remember wondering in the dream where this puppy could have come from.

'Some ten months later this puppy became a reality, although he wasn't even thought about at the time of the dream, and the people who now own him had no plans to get a dog at all. Now when my daughter brings him over to visit and I watch him trailing along behind P and L or trying to get into their game, I am amazed because it's exactly as I saw it in the dream.'

In my own case I made the commitment to myself years ago to record every dream, no matter how small or apparently inconsequential. Such is the life of a dream researcher! I find trivial precognitions occur very frequently and often grouped in the same night, as this little snippet trio illustrates.

These dreams occurred on the night of Monday 17 March 1997, flowing into the morning of Tuesday 18.

The first dream involved a plane flight to Perth with a friend, Martin. The second dream was centred outside a coffee shop in Park Road, Brisbane, where I met and mingled with a large group of friends. This seemed to take place after a concert where, my dream journal records, 'a woman a bit like Caro was singing'. I saw an old friend, Brian, in the distance. He was happy chatting to others, and I was busy too, so our paths didn't cross. I noticed the distance between us, as if we were now following different paths. Martin was close by. In the third dream I was busy washing loads of other people's laundry, most of which had been flung into muddy piles throughout a field. I had worked through most of it and was scrounging about underneath an old house to extract the very last load, when a young Aboriginal girl came up and warned me of the spiders among the clothes. I looked at my hands and saw that I had one large spider bite on each palm.

Tuesday morning's scribblings in the dream journal were rewarding once I got down to the job, reminding me yet again never to dismiss the smallest dream as invaluable. The interpretations were clear and easy and the resulting observations on how

I had been handling those last few days were worthwhile. That, I thought, was that: analysed, understood, absorbed, completed.

I find it helpful to organise my dream journal to allow for daily observations to be recorded. I write my dreams on the right-hand pages only, then divide the left-hand page into three columns. One column records a very brief diary of my day, including any insights, thoughts, questions or conflicts. Since dreams often reflect or comment upon such things, it is vital to be able to compare day with night, waking events and thoughts with dreams. The second column is for my interpretation of each dream. The third column is for recording things which happen *after* a dream, but which seem linked to it in some way.

In the third column I recorded the following observations. On that Tuesday a friend phoned to say a dinner party was being organised. He gave the list of guests, one of which was Brian from my dream. (A few days later the event was cancelled, so we didn't get to meet up, as in my second dream.) The next day, on Wednesday, Caro phoned from Perth. Caro phones perhaps two or three times a year. I had not been thinking of her prior to my dream and there was no special reason to expect her to call. She is not a singer.

That afternoon Glen arrived home with a new washing machine. We had been struggling with our old machine for months and had been talking about buying a new one for about the same length of time. It was one of those mañana items and if Glen had plans at the time of my dream, I certainly didn't know about them. The trials and tribulations of washing with an exhausted old machine were discussed with regularity, but the fact was no great issue at that particular time. Although I had been happy with my analysis of the dream and the role played by the Aboriginal girl, I did vaguely mumble something about the Simpson Desert and Aboriginal tribes when I noted the brand of the machine: a Simpson.

The beauty of keeping a dream journal, especially if you make the effort to keep it updated, is that it can be brought out in evidence, a regular occurrence in our house, to which my family will no doubt yawningly attest. Struck by the apparent inconsequentiality of these waking life similarities to my dream, I trundled out the diary and told my tale over a gin and tonic. The family were largely unimpressed since my stories are generally far more goose bumpy and persuasive.

This, however, is the point: in endeavouring to understand how waking life events can follow dreams, we need to include a look at the multiple small, baffling, yet seemingly insignificant happenings as well as the big mind-blowing epics. Oh, and to finish the story, the spiders did appear, although I escaped the bites. Our house had been thoroughly cleaned that day, and as we were switching off the lights to go to bed, I saw wispy spider threads, backlit by moonlight, embroidered over my two new carved ducks, which had certainly been dusted during the morning. As if on highwires, hundreds of tiny newborn spiders tottered along in single file, following the threads laid before them. I hadn't seen a spider explosion before and Glen told me, as he sucked them up the vacuum nozzle, that spiders often hatch on a such a full moon night. Which, I thought, added a bedtime touch of magic to a rather analytical day!

There was an aftermath to this story. Remember Martin from the first and second dreams? He phoned me in late April and told me about his overseas holiday. He had taken in a return trip to the UK and gone in search of a house he lived in as a child. He found it. The name of the street? Park. I told him about my dream and seeing him in Park Road and he worked out from his diary that he was most probably standing outside the house at the time of my dream.

Apart from the spider episode, all my 'third column' notes could be explained by telepathy, picking up thoughts from as close as Glen sleeping beside me, to Caro on the other side of the continent and Martin on the far side of the world! But why these people on that particular night, and why did the spiders explode from the dream into reality too? Wait! The hows and whys belong to Part Two, but trivial precognitive series like these are crucial to answering these questions. For the moment, just remember the questions while we continue with the evidence.

Get the Meaning?
Thinking symbolically

So far the evidence has concentrated on precognitive dreams foreshadowing literal events to come. The focus has been on the outer world events, rather than contemplation of any personally meaningful echo. The following two examples introduce the dimension of meaningfulness, an important consideration in understanding the nature of precognition. **Lorna's** story derives meaning from the event which followed the dream, whereas mine extracts meaning from the dream, which then accelerates the previewed event. The two experiences are different sides of the same coin. The currency is symbolic meaning.

Now in her early sixties, Lorna's recurring precognitive dream started when she was fifteen and at high school in Sydney.

'It frightened me then and sobers me now. There was a girl in our class who was a member of the Exclusive Brethren. She never travelled to school by public transport like most of us: her father used to drop her off at the nearest intersection. I travelled by train to Central and walked from there to school. I had never seen her crossing the Elizabeth Street intersection with George Street on the Treasury side. Yet that is where she was in my dream. That was the only comfort I could draw from the repeated dream. The events it contained were not possible because she never travelled the route in the dream.

'In the dream I saw her killed in a traffic accident while she was crossing the intersection. A Jackson & O'Sullivan truck, red with black trim and lettering as all that company's vehicles were, came up George Street from the Gardens and turned into Elizabeth Street, travelling towards William Street. It came rather fast considering the geography of the corner and the number of pedestrians using it. As the truck made its turn, the other pedestrians jumped out of the way. My classmate, however, was struck. Her body was squashed on the road. Her suitcase burst open and her books were scattered. The truck did not stop.

'Then the macabre and, I later realised, the strong symbolic element of the dream occurred. The books gathered themselves back together and poured neatly back into the port which had somehow mended itself. She became unsquashed, got up, her port floated up into her hand, and she went on her way as if nothing had happened.

'Each time I had the dream I felt sick and dreaded the walk down George Street. If I could have changed my route, I would, but the school did not permit us to use either Albert Street, because of the brothels, or Edward Street because there were boys by the hundreds, students at another high school. I kept telling myself the dream meant nothing. Nothing could happen because the lass did not use that route and did not travel by public transport.

'One morning, about two months after the first dream, I turned out of Queen Street into George Street and saw her on the opposite footpath, about a street width ahead of me. She was exactly where the dream said she would be. There was no mistake about identity, the slender build, the long dark plaits and our school's uniform. It's hard to describe the feelings I experienced: horror, dread, guilt, expectation, denial.

'I could see a red truck approaching from the Gardens end, too far away to see which firm owned it but I was certain it would be a Jackson & O'Sullivan vehicle. As I approached the intersection, she was about three-quarters of the way across. The truck came quickly round the corner. It was a Jackson & O'Sullivan's. People scattered. The truck clipped her suitcase, burst it open and books spilled across the street. She jumped aside,

unhurt. Others rushed to help gather her books. She was probably shaken but she continued down George Street. I stood where I was, frozen, still horrified but relieved, incapable of moving but already beginning to assess why I had dreamed the broad shape of the event.

'Two teachers escorted me down to the school and asked several times what was wrong, but I could not tell them. I did not even speak of my dreams at home let alone to a teacher we called the death adder. It was roughly ten years before I told anyone about the dream which was as vivid then as it was when it occurred. It is still vivid.'

Although the event differed from the dream in that the girl was not killed, Lorna's overriding medium-term response was,

'A feeling of guilt resulting in a lot of introspection for motives. I felt variously that I had wished her dead but could not understand why when I did not dislike her; or that I had in some way been reprieved because she had not only not been killed, but was also unhurt; or that the dream was a warning of some kind.'

As time passed Lorna was able to piece together some of the symbolic meaning within her dream.

'It took a long time to put the dream into real perspective. She had been on the receiving end of some nasty teasing about religion. In my local area, I had been savagely teased, on religious grounds mostly, so I had some idea how she must have felt. I gradually found myself stepping in and defending her when the teasing became vicious.

'I grew to the conclusion that the dream was probably more symbolic than literal, that it was meant to make me realise that we all have a responsibility for the way we treat others, or allow them to be treated. It was meant to make me see how we "kill" others in many ways, and that by changing our behaviour towards or among others, or by stopping others from being cruel, we can prevent some "deaths".'

Lorna's story is enlightening because she was able, years after the event, to look back and see double meaning. On the surface was the precognitive dream and the subsequent event, although the endings were different. On a deeper level Lorna was able to touch meaning.

By the end of December 1996 my work path seemed to be changing course. I had been researching this book for over three years and knew that I would be writing the final manuscript during the first half of 1997. I had a few loose ends to tie, such as finishing the Hypnotism Project I was engaged in and choosing which publisher to sign with. Of that much I was sure. I had no other definite plans.

My broadcasting career with ABC radio seemed to be coming to an end. My weekly 'Dream Talkback' had been established for four years and in the past year, 1996, I had created and copresented a new weekly ABC radio series entitled 'Reality Matters'. When the ABC was called upon to rip millions of dollars from its budget, each of the copresenters who had incorporated my programmes into their shows was made redundant. I followed my dreams which suggested 'out with the old, on with the new', and did not present myself for consideration as part of the new Queensland line-up. I knew my life was changing, but I was unsure which direction to follow.

A dream on 5 January 1997 seemed, at first glance, to reinforce the feeling that my work plans were left hanging in the balance and that it was time to watch the flow of life from an objective distance with total trust. The flow of my future work, I felt from this dream, would take its natural course if I just let it happen. There are always surprises if you create space in your life to let them in. This reasoning is easy to see from my dream.

I dreamed the Brisbane River was the centre of a huge on-the-water festival, a really good and successful idea. I had moved back from the celebrations for a while, but then returned to watch

('watch the river flow') from a viewing grandstand high in the sky. There were no seats. Instead I dangled from an overhead loop, clutching on with my left hand in much the same way as you steady yourself when standing in a tube on the London Underground. My son was hooked onto my right hand. We were aware of the delicate balance ('hanging in the balance') but we were absolutely certain that we'd be safe ('trusted the process').

Then, overhead, Glen flew past in a motorised hang-glider, carrying a walkie-talkie. He was communicating with the crew or organisers on the river, in the heart of the celebrations, who also had walkie-talkies. Glen had kept his important involvement a secret specially to surprise me, which he did!

There was a lot more to the dream, but that is enough to illustrate this story. Avid dream interpreters will already have noted the deeper meanings which pervade the dream, but for the sake of simplicity, let it be said that I understood the full symbolic meaning of the dream and its relevance to my life, and I acted upon it.

Ten days later I had a very short dream which I recorded in my journal as 'The Z Contract'. In this dream my daughter and I had each been given a book contract from a country which, in the dream, began with a Z and was in South America. In the dream I thought it was Brazil. (Dream logic!) My daughter was filling her contract in, but I didn't, as something about it made me feel uneasy.

Three days after this dream a friend, Sue Manger, phoned to invite me to complete a team of people she had chosen to be interviewed on community television station Briz 31. I had a function I wanted to advertise and so it seemed a good idea and I went along to prerecord the interview on 22 January.

A day after the prerecording, Sue and Glen hatched a plan and returned to Briz 31 to look at some options. During the discussions, and in my absence, the station offered me the opportunity to take over as host of the show. As my life was indeed 'hanging in the balance' at the time, I decided to do it for a trial period and watch the way 'the river flowed'. The studios were in the heart of the city on the riverbank, and after each programme I went outside to let the peace of the river wash away the rush of the recording. The production was largely left in our own hands, so Glen ended up taking on a producing role and spent much of his time coordinating the team on the studio floor, reminding me of his dream role as walkie-talkie co-ordinator of the Brisbane River celebrations. He had surprised me in the dream in just the same way as he surprised me when he came home with the offer to host the show and then surprised me again with his production abilities.

Four weeks later I perused the Briz 31 contract which was then formally on offer, but for personal reasons I felt uncomfortable with it. I didn't sign. It was weeks later that I looked back through my dream journal and saw 'The Z Contract' (Brazil/Briz 31?) dream. It was not in my conscious memory at the time we were contemplating the contract.

In truth there was more to the original dream, which came to pass in much the same fashion as the elements described above. These included attitudes, feelings, reference to particular people and reasons for leaving. To elaborate these details could lead you, the reader, into such complicated corners of the puzzle-maze which links dreams to waking life that you may no longer see the trees for the wood. The whole episode remained, for me, a clear case of dream symbolism and meaning appropriate to my personal development and daily decision making, reinforced by elements of that symbolism surfacing in my everyday waking life. This is where our dreaming and waking worlds overlap.

Where did 'hanging in the balance', 'watching the river flow', 'trusting the process' and 'leaving room in my life for surprises to enter' get me, I hear you ask? Well, I learned a lot personally from these experiences and I certainly did discover how to make life slow down in order to let surprises climb on board. In trusting the process I discovered new skills and in contemplating the contract I realised what kind of deal it would take to make me feel comfortable. At the time of writing Glen has gone on to form a production company and is now producing a show for someone else.

(*Postscript*: Little did I realise the full implication of my future in television when I was writing this chapter. When the manuscript was completed it excited sufficient key people that the material is now being prepared as a documentary series for international distribution. Perhaps you will witness with me the final outcome, the 'Shape of Things to Come', via a television channel near you.)

Foreseeing the Future or Previewing the Past?

Basic assumptions can lead us into quagmires of confusion. I'm not at ease with our day-to-day assumption of linear time: that the future follows the present and the present trails the past. Consider the following.

On 17 November 1996 I had a powerful dream that I was in a park where huge explosions were expected and people were covering their heads. The explosion was loud. On the next night I dreamed I was killed because my murderers said I knew too much about a cover-up. They hit me on the back of the head as I lay on my tummy on the floor. I was not dead and I was torn between wishing I had died and the fear of them discovering I was still alive and having to bear the dreadful pain of another hit.

The next month, on Christmas Eve, I received a letter from a close friend, **Mike**, who was travelling with his wife, **Elizabeth**, in Central America while writing a book about their journey. He described how, on 15 November, he had found himself in a park in the middle of gunshots. Everyone cowered and hid their heads. As the robbers ran away, they realised that one of the locals in the party recognised them, so they shot him in the back of the head as he lay on his tummy. My friend went over to him and found that he was not yet dead. He died in his arms.

The following extracts from Mike's letter illustrate the similarities between his experiences and my dreams two and three days later.

> *I saw the gun swinging from his hand as he approached someone lying flat, face down and absolutely still on the ground ... the bandit pointed the gun towards the back of the person's head from behind. The gun fired ... he was breathing ... I held his shoulder and rubbed his back and chatted to him in a mixture of English and Spanish. After a few moments the sound of his breathing stopped, for good ... I kept stroking his back to let him know that he wasn't alone.*
>
> *The question of 'Why?' was soon answered, as people nearby related hearing distinct threats directed at him during the robbery. The threats were personal and indicated that at least one of the bandits knew him. Just before he was killed, the bandit asked the man if he recognised him. He replied it wasn't a problem. The bandit told him it was and then executed him.*

Was it just coincidence that I experienced similar circumstances in my dreams two and three days after this event? If not coincidence, it would be easy to argue that I was picking up on Mike's distress telepathically as he relived the terrible events in his mind. Yet again, in my dream I experienced the incredible pain of being hit on the back of the head, just as the dying man must have felt the gunshot wounds which did not immediately kill him. Did I tune into the thoughts and pain of the dying man, or was this a case of projection of Mike's feelings about the man's pain mingling into my dream via telepathy? Or was it all pure dream symbolism, relevant to my personal life alone?

I was aware that I had dreamed of Mike and Elizabeth on three or four occasions since they had left Australia so I decided to look back over my journals and examine those dreams. The details I discovered were uncannily pertinent to the whole episode and to the developments which followed, but these were dreamed up to six weeks before the murder! The dreams themselves were long and detailed and contained whole sequences which seemed to bear no relevance to the event we are discussing here. I have isolated some of the sentences which stood out to me as I reviewed the dreams. Realise that they are extracts only, but notice how much impact they deliver. Remember also that these were the only dreams in which Mike and Elizabeth appeared, and yet each one has at least one item of interest to observe.

JANE'S DREAM 1, 26 SEPTEMBER 1996
'I have a gun *made of wrought iron metal, fashioned in circular fretwork —more a piece of art for targeting than a destruction weapon ... I was experimenting with focusing on targets and shooting at them. Precision and focus were the keynotes and it felt powerful.'*

'... the dangers of "modern" travel which we forget. I think of Mike and Elizabeth and their flight to America and travelling and I realise that there is always danger in adventure—if you want to adventure, you have to face that. The risks go with it.'

Extract from Mike's account (received Christmas Eve, 1996)
'... the barrel of a gun was then shoved into my face. I focused on the muzzle and had an absurd thought that it was probably a 32 mm and noticed that it was being held straight and perfectly steadily ... kept the gun pointed straight into my eyes.'

JANE'S DREAM 2, SAME NIGHT AS DREAM 1
'We hear Mike and Elizabeth are back in Australia and I am getting ready to go and meet them at a restaurant but they turn up at home instead

saying they're fed up (pun!) with restaurants. They seem quiet (low) but say they have not given up their journey, just decided to make a flying visit home before continuing. Later Mike says we knew that he had to come back for the cancer test: cancer in the abdominal *region. He thought he could get the test done in America, but he had to come home. Now it was okay.'*

Extract from Mike's account (received Christmas Eve, 1996)
'We considered giving South America the flick and, at one time, just coming home ... Two days after the incident I contracted a mean dose of amoebic dysentery. It has gone on for over a week and left me a shadow of my former self.'

JANE'S DREAM 1, 24 OCTOBER 1996
'I have both arms in the air signalling 'surrender'. *A* camera *moves in closely to film my face.* This is all being documented. *I sit behind a man who I seem to know—perhaps he is a* journalist, *and I'm chatting to him. I think this is maybe where Mike comes in.'*

Mike's letter described how they had to 'surrender' when faced with the guns and machetes. Among other things, his prized camera was stolen. They later obtained statutory declarations (documents) from the Central American authorities and copies of the articles which appeared about the murder in the local papers (journalists) and sent duplicate copies of these documents for their insurance claim to us for safe keeping. The newspaper cuttings included photos of the huge funeral procession which I assume was also covered on television.

JANE'S DREAM 2, SAME NIGHT AS DREAM 1
'I think Mike and Elizabeth have had enough of travelling, or are avoiding it, and I ask Elizabeth if they are going to get to South America. After all, it is nearly November and they should be near the border by now. Mike has taken a job for a while as some kind of financial adviser/

insurance *job in an office. I am talking to him on the phone but I can tell by his answers that* someone is listening, so he is giving "work" answers to give me the clue that he is not telling it how it is. *Later I meet Mike.* He is thin and not looking well, *although he thinks he is healthy and slim. I imagine his rounder face and bigger body which exuded vitality and wonder what has happened.'*

It's interesting to note the sense of urgency in my dream, the feeling that Mike and Elizabeth should be leaving Central America and moving on to South America by now, considering the murder was still three weeks in the future. The reference to insurance could be seen as recognition of the forthcoming danger or could also foreshadow the insurance claim for the camera they would eventually lodge.

In the event Mike and Elizabeth were concerned that the news did not reach their family and other friends until they were safely back in Australia, when they could physically comfort them and prove they had lived to tell the tale of their whole journey. My dream reference to 'not telling it how it is' came to be reality in the weeks that followed, where a softer version of the camera theft, revolving around a street robbery, was sent home instead. Mike also told us in his letter about the sickness and weight loss that followed the murder.

Remember, these dreams occurred *before* the murder, and did not involve my immediate life—or did they? One of the beauties of this example is that the dreams straddle the time before and after the event. Also the symbols or correlations get stronger as the date of the actual event is approached. These observations form more vital clues in uncovering the nature of precognition which will become apparent as our discussion unfolds.

Moving past the date of the murder and past the two dreams opening this account, I had a third dream. Again this was only three days after the murder, and I was still in conscious ignorance of the event. I dreamed of running to Mount Kilimanjaro. As my dream journal records:

'I'll just go so far and then stop. No point aiming for the full distance unprepared *and I don't* have *to anyway. I* climb a steep but easy path *and come to the* top of a stunning lookout. *Three men are talking on what appears to be the edge and I feel the* fear *of heights in the* pit of my stomach.'*

In the letter I received from Mike on Christmas Eve he described the murder site as being 'up the hill' at a 'lookout'. He and Elizabeth had climbed a path to a hilltop lookout and that was where the murder took place. The fear in the pit of the stomach needs no explanation, but again mirrors Mike's ensuing stomach upsets. The dream also questions the need to finish the whole journey and brings up the notion of being unprepared (for what is to follow?). Best of all, I like the pun in the name of the mountain. In best dream language: 'Kill the Man' hums loud and clear in both shape and sound from the word Kilimanjaro.

Put this Mike and Elizabeth sequence of dreams and events to the back of your mind for a while, we'll return to it later. Turn your attention instead away from the evidence presented by precognitive dreams and walk with me into the next chapter to sample the evidence provided by the waking world of precognitive visions.

Summary Memo

- 1/1 Accurate information about a future event, of which the dreamer has no prior conscious knowledge, can appear in a dream. *E.g. Anna's decapitated cat, page 3*.

- 1/2 The future event for the dreamer may be the *discovery* of an event which occurred just before, or at the same time as, the dream. This is commonly referred to as telepathy. *E.g. Heather's ex-husband's suicide, page 9.*

- 1/3 The future event for the dreamer may be the *end product* of the thought or action of another person which occurred just before or during the dream, and of which the dreamer had no prior conscious knowledge. This is another example of telepathy. *E.g. Our rented house being put up for sale, page 5.*

- 1/4 Future events previewed in dreams frequently appear to concern events which have not been set in motion at the time of the dream. *E.g. Rebekah's Tony dream, pages 19–20.*

- 1/5 Future events commonly concern:

  * illness, accident and death (most commonly reported); *E.g. Ken's dream of Ricky's death, pages 17–18;*

  * travel or distance (second most commonly reported); *E.g. Several of my Mike & Elizabeth dreams, pages 36–41;*

  * change (third most commonly reported); *E.g. My Brisbane River dream, pages 33–36.*

- 1/6 A dreamer may discover, in retrospect, a series of dreams over a period of time, which all contain information relating to the same future event. In such cases the amount or accuracy of the information often increases towards the date of the actual event. *E.g. My Mike & Elizabeth dream series, pages 36–41.*

- 1/7 A dreamer may discover, in retrospect, a series of dreams related to a future event occurring for a person known to them. In the absence of conscious knowledge that the event has taken place for that other person, the dreamer may continue to receive information about the (now past) event in their dreams. If the level of detail is beyond coincidence, such dream series suggest that 'time hopping' (dreams referring to past, present and future around a consciously unknown event) is more the case than 'foreseeing' an event. *E.g. My Mike & Elizabeth dream series, pages 36–41.*

- 1/8 Very few dreams, on the surface, contain information about future events. Those which do, however, often show a level of detail beyond coincidence. *E.g. My Lotto dream, page 23.*

- 1/9 Some precognitive dreams are literal. That is, the future event takes place exactly as previewed in the dream. *E.g. Rebekah's Tony dream, pages 19–20.*

- 1/10 Some precognitive dreams are symbolic (or a mixture of symbolic and literal). Unless the dreamer is conversant with dream symbolism, it is not until after the actual event has occurred that the dreamer looks back and sees the connection. *E.g. Cheryl's dream of Jed's accident, pages 21–22.*

- 1/11 A dreamer who understands dream symbolism often sees valid personal meaningfulness in a dream and subsequently acts on the meaning, only to discover at a later date that the dream was *also* symbolically or literally precognitive. *E.g. My Brisbane River dream, pages 33–36.*

- 1/12 A dreamer, believing a dream to be precognitive, may take action to prevent the previewed event. If completely successful, of course, the future event will not occur, so the dreamer will never know for sure whether the original dream was precognitive. *E.g. Glenys's dream of child being burned, pages 15–16.*

- 1/13 A dreamer, believing a dream to be precognitive, may take action to prevent the previewed event. The event may then unfold to a degree, but with a changed ending, appearing attributable to the dreamer's preventative measures. That is, the dreamer may apparently change the future outcome of an event because of advance knowledge received in a precognitive dream. *E.g. Rowyn's car accident, pages 13–14.*

- 1/14 Some precognitive dreams concerning events which later occur to other people (e.g. death), appear unpreventable to the dreamer. In some cases the dreamer may take comfort from the dream, being able to prepare emotionally for the future event. In some sense this action changes the future in that it changes the dreamer's coping ability, the dreamer's attitude towards the other person, or the relationship between the two. *E.g. Carol's cancer dream, page 20.*

- 1/15 Many precognitive dreams may be overlooked because they are not acted upon, or because the dreamer considers them insignificant. Some dreams, or series of dreams, highlight significant detailed precognition of small, insignificant (in the dreamer's opinion) events. *E.g. HM's split shorts, pages 25–26.*

- 1/16 Identifiable characteristics of precognitive dreams were more individual than shared (*page 17*).

visions
of the   2
future

I was in Quito, Ecuador, sitting in a garden with friends who were farewelling me after a year of living the high life in the Andes. We had packed up our house and despatched our furniture to Australia where we planned to live for the next three years. One of the women asked me how my family back in the UK were. 'Dad's in hospital, but he's okay now,' I replied quickly. I didn't hear the next part of the conversation. I was too shocked. I had no idea why I had said that because it just wasn't true! Suddenly I realised someone was asking me why my father had gone into hospital. How do you answer a question like that when you've just heard yourself tell a lie? I muttered something like 'I don't really know' and changed the subject as quickly as I could.

At the time it didn't even occur to me that Dad might have been ill. We left South America within the week, spent a few days in San Francisco and then flew on to Australia. The letter from my mother was waiting for us there. Dad had had a minor heart attack and had been hospitalised for a few days, but he was okay. She hadn't sent word to Ecuador because she didn't want me to be worried or to fly to Britain before going to Australia. I didn't ever discover which came first: the heart attack or my announcement of it. I suspect the attack came first and someone did send a message to me, though not in the form of a letter. It was probably a case of a telepathic message received while awake and inadvertently spoken aloud. I don't recall any visual component befitting the common notion of precognitive visions.

In the previous chapter on precognitive dreaming, many dream senses were employed in capturing the future events: the sight of Anna's decapitated cat, the voice on my dream answering machine and the pain of being hit on the head, for example. Other senses such as taste, smell and 'knowing' come into dreams, although with less frequency. However, all the dream messages or experiences are perceived silently, in sleep. In comparing stories of waking precognitive experiences, I immediately noticed how much emphasis people put on the senses they use to receive or deliver the information. Automatic verbal deliveries, like mine, were quite common.

Kelly is completely aware that she is being given a message, although she has no control over the contents she speaks. She is comfortable with this, feeling the messages are delivered through her for a specific purpose, as in this case.

'I was enjoying a moment at an old familiar country pub when a man I vaguely knew walked in with his lady friend. We exchanged greetings and I was introduced to his companion. She would have been in her forties, and I took an immediate liking to her. When she said she was going home to Europe to visit her mother in roughly three months time, I began to have a fuzzy vision. I replied, "Too late, too late, she's dead!"

'Taken aback, she told me her mother was not dead, but I told her I could see her in bed near death, and that she was not frightened of death, only the dying part. I relayed that her two brothers were at her bedside, both *with brown hair, one noticeably taller than the other and that she was not terribly close to them. Also, that the brothers did not get on very well either. I described the room where there was much dark wood and I pushed the seriousness of the matter, telling her to go before it was too late. The final part of the vision, before I was interrupted, was of a small fountain with golden water spraying from it. I told her that it would end well, that there was good feeling surrounding everything. I was not completely aware of what I had relayed until the lady repeated the message after I had finished. In less than two weeks she was with her mother and they talked about many things. She died four or five days later.'*

Harry's ability to foresee or foretell the future surfaced at the age of nine and has continued unabated throughout his life. Now into his seventies, he describes his experience of the 'automatic voice':

'Each incident seems to occur suddenly and without forethought. From time to time an involuntary thought enters my mind and occasionally I give expression to it, to my own surprise.'

As a child in the early 1930s, Harry expressed his precognitive visions through art. Once, for example, he drew pictures of four-lane highways with stop and go lights at the intersections.

'Red for stop and green for go. When my brother and his friend insisted on seeing what I was drawing, it was pointed out to me that an accident could occur between vehicles while the lights were changing from one colour to another. I immediately said I would include an intermediary light, the exact colour not then decided upon. My interjectors said there would never be enough traffic on the road to warrant traffic lights. In those days we were lucky to see half a dozen cars on the roads in a week.'

Frequently Harry's precognitions took the shape of visions.

'Unfortunately for me, at age nine one vision concerned two of my primary school mates. Without duly causing any show of alarm I desperately tried

to guide each of them from danger. Each of them on separate occasions chose not to accept my suggestions. Ivan died in a car accident by acting irresponsibly the next year. Geoff, who had a badly lacerated knee one Friday after school, refused my plea to bathe it. Two other boys present had earlier spoken out against me in this regard. Realising there was nothing more I could do and that my prediction for Geoff seemed inevitable, I slowly walked the mile home with a heavy heart. Geoff died of a tetanus disease the following week.'

As with many of the precognitive dream experiences, death and sickness visions seemed to dominate in this survey. **Heather's** vision remains vividly in her memory fifty years after the event. She was nineteen at the time.

'I was on night duty in a Sydney hospital. At about three a.m. I became very drowsy so left the ward to prepare coffee. As I proceeded to the day room, I glanced along the hallway and saw an elderly patient walk through the outside wall of the building. Since the patient's door was locked, because of the habit of wandering at night, I decided that I was seeing things.

'After having the coffee, I returned to the ward but couldn't shake off the feeling that I should check the patient's room. I would have done so on my normal four a.m. rounds, but felt compelled to go immediately, which I did. I found that the patient had died, and since her body was still warm, I must have seen her at the moment she was leaving her body.'

Anna's vision gave her sufficient warning, not to change the predicted death, but to make the necessary preparations.

'I was sitting on my bed, awake, when all at once I saw my sister, who died ten years ago, in front of me. I asked, "What is it really like, Jenny, where you are?" She answered, "You think you can't know, so I can't tell you!" I did not take this up at the time because her appearance so much surprised me. She went on to say she was waiting for my dad, saying, "It won't be long," then vanished. Dad had been sick, but not that sick.

'The next month I made sure I flew down and stayed with him even though my mother kept saying he was okay. He became ill and died while I was there.'

The questions raised by most of the examples given in this chapter are identical to those posed in Chapter 1, so I will not repeat them here. They will be addressed at a later stage. What is important here is to demonstrate the evidence for waking precognition and to note the circumstances under which they occur, the nature of the predicted events and the senses used in receiving the messages.

Some visions occur moments before the event. **Cheryl** was bushwalking while on a camp.

'In my head I saw a girlfriend bouncing down a small waterfall. I turned around to see where she was. Suddenly she lost her footing and slipped and came bouncing down a small waterfall.'

Other predictions can be many years ahead, yet equally as detailed. At the age of nine, **Harry** accurately described his own future as a young adult.

'I predicted that I would be called up for army service and would go to the States of Western Australia, Queensland and the Northern Territory, in that order, and that, despite all my attempts, I would not leave Australia. I determined that this would not be so.

'At age seventeen I sought enlistment in the Australian navy, but for some unaccountable reason was rejected. I next applied to the air force and was accepted as a fighter pilot, but this acceptance arrived eight days too late. I had been inducted by a call-up from the army and was already in training with that organisation.

'On arrival in Western Australia in 1942 I eventually managed to join the Australian Imperial Force with the intention of going overseas. However, after qualifying as a signals instrument mechanic at the Perth

Technical College, I eventually arrived in North Queensland. It was while I was stationed within three miles of the tip of Cape York Peninsula that I was advised that I should attend another signals school.'

While here, Harry was heard to make a further prediction.

'When the instructing lieutenant at Jacky Jacky stated that we were to embark by boat to Horn Island and from there be flown by plane direct to Townsville, I involuntarily said, in a quiet voice, that the plane would come down about half way. After being roundly criticised, I said it would not be serious. This evoked further criticism from the lieutenant who said if it was his choice I wouldn't be going!

'The plane, a Douglas DC-3 piloted by two Americans, for some reason made what I believe was an unscheduled stop at Cooktown. An attempt was made to leave the Cooktown airport an hour or two later but one of the two engines failed to start. A DC-3 plane from Townsville delivered another starter motor for the failed one. However it was a different model, not designed for the plane we were in. After being accommodated in Cooktown for the night, a further DC-3 from Townsville finally carried us to our destination.'

A frequently expressed concern is that the predicted future is caused by the visions or verbal deliverances which define them. The Aboriginal 'pointing of the bone' is oft quoted in evidence. While the argument initially seems logical, I noticed how often statements such as Harry's 'I determined that this would not be so' came up. In many cases we can act on a precognitive insight to change an envisioned outcome, but other foretold details, such as Harry's future career travels, seem to occur despite all conscious intention to divert the course of the future away from the predicted path.

Although Harry has such a store of precognitive experiences to share, he finds he has little control over the process, an observation made by several people in this survey.

Cynthia: *'I can't predict the future or lotteries or tell people what is going to happen, neither do I want to. These things happen usually in crystal-clear dreams or appear in my head during my waking hours. I can't tell when they will happen.'*

Neither do visions necessarily relate to the future. Cynthia said,

'I always was able to see a room that I was very familiar with. On describing the room to my mother, it was the room that I was born in.'

Was Cynthia able to access the past? Was this a visual memory of the room she saw at birth, or was it an impression gained through telepathy with her mother?

On another occasion she apparently experienced the room from the perceptual angle of a second person. Although this is less verifiable in the sense that there was no definite outcome to suggest the vision was accurate and not imagined, Cynthia describes the sensation convincingly.

'My aunty had a sudden heart attack when I visited her in hospital. She was hooked up to all kinds of machines. I had my four-month-old daughter over my shoulder when a strange thing happened that I can't explain. I had a view from my aunty's eyes of the back of my jacket as I was walking out of the room. I saw my baby smiling at Aunty and I saw the pattern that was only on the back of my jacket. I didn't see Aunty alive again.'

Most people can probably relate to **Diwata's** precognitive experience, which can perhaps be explained by telepathy.

'All of a sudden I pictured the face of a man I knew four years ago. All sorts of questions came to mind. How did he look now? Where was he now? The next day I went to lunch with my friend and someone opened the doors of the cafeteria for us. Believe it or not, he was the man on my mind the previous day. I was shocked!'

Anna's case is less clear cut.

'I was awake but thinking of my father who was asleep as he worked night shift at the airport on security. I kept seeing this huge engine exploding and knew my father was in danger as this was a plane engine. That was it.

'I felt very panicky but rang my mother to make sure Dad was asleep. He wasn't. He had been called back to work because someone was ill. I was then frantic as he would have been near the hangars.

'My mother rang the airport and my dad, forewarned, checked the hangars for planes taking off or being overhauled. Eventually he rang to tell me to relax. It had happened. An engine had exploded as they wheeled the aeroplane onto the tarmac, but he had stood well back. He wasn't injured and neither were the mechanics, thank God.'

Over the years I have experimented with giving readings for people. When relaxed, I found it easy to 'see' visions in my mind that often related to the person's life. On occasions I could build an awareness of another person, or an object as if it were in front of me, though I couldn't actually *see* anything in the usual visual way. In most cases these visions confirmed some degree of telepathy, as in, for example, being able to describe the house the person lived in, objects they worked with or plans they had been discussing. Occasionally, however, these visions related more to the person's future.

According to the dictionary, clairvoyance is 'the supposed faculty of perceiving things or events in the future or beyond normal sensual contact'. In other words, clairvoyance, by definition, is not necessarily visual and does not relate specifically to future events, despite common usage which generally embraces a notion of prediction.

Many psychic readers hear voices and then relay the messages. Unlike the automatic speech described at the beginning of this chapter, the spoken words are heard and then consciously repeated. This is known as clairaudience, defined as 'the supposed faculty of perceiving, as if by hearing, what is inaudible'. Although commonly reported by professional psychics, not one of the precognitive experiences sent to me for this survey described this. Since hearing voices is commonly associated with schizophrenia, it may be that people held back from describing the phenomenon. In my own case, as with visual clairvoyance, my experience in readings was of feeling the shape of the words in my head, rather than hearing any audible tones. In that way I found I was often able to feed back particular phrases or catchwords either used by the person I was attempting to read, or by people close to them in a meaningful way.

Clairsentience

Clairsentience is a term used by many people to describe a third sense modality for tuning in on a telepathic or, perhaps, precognitive basis to another person. People on the survey described clairsentience variously as 'a knowing', 'intuition' or 'a sensing'. Some described it in the way that I understood it. For me, during that period of reading, this was the easiest and most identifiable sensation associated with linking up in either a past, present or future way, with the mind of the person sitting with me. I would feel either a sharp pain or a tingling in an area of my body that related to the other person. I found that pain often related to pain the person had experienced in the past on a physical level, while tingling tended to indicate an underuse either of that part of the body or of skills or emotions symbolically connected with that body part in dream symbolism. Occasionally I would feel the numbness of a past stroke (while not visible on the physical level) or muscular tension which I could directly interpret according to where the tension was held. I'm not aware that I used these senses to accurately predict the future health or wellbeing of the people I was reading at the time, but I suspect my current knowledge of symbolism would equip me to do that, if I wished. But I do not wish.

The clairsentience aspect of precognitive visions was reported in my survey.

Julie often feels the body pain of another person. She felt pain, for example, when her friend went into hospital.

'He had an operation on his right shoulder and hardly experienced any pain at all. I told him it was because I had most of it! My pain began when he had his operation and I even lost sleep over it. He only spent a couple of days in hospital and when I saw him the following day, he looked great.

'I had made a card to give him and on this card I drew an operating theatre with doctors working on his shoulder. I also drew (in the same card) them operating on his left leg. I had no idea why I drew that part at the time, but I thought I'd leave it there anyway.

My friend hadn't noticed this at first, but the next time I saw him he took me aside and asked me, "How did you know that they operated on my left leg at the same time as my shoulder?" No one knew about that part of his operation.'

Rebekah's clairsentience is a blend of the physical and the emotional.

'In 1989 I was building sandcastles with our grandchildren at our local beach when suddenly I felt as if somebody had pulled out the plug. I was totally drained of energy, so much so that I had to tell the children to go ahead across the park to the house. I then literally had to crawl home. I sat, too weak to move, for over an hour. Soon after I had a telephone call from another city that my mother had died at that exact time. She and I had always been very close. I knew she was afraid of death and am sure she would have been calling on me at that time.'

At other times it is a 'compulsion', as Rebekah explained: 'One night I had a compulsion to go to the neighbour's over the road, even though I had not met her. She was going to commit suicide.'

Paddie describes her precognitive clairsentient sense as 'sadness'.

'My father warns me of death. Usually I get a very sad feeling about my dad, often while showering. No matter how I feel prior to getting into the shower, my mind will think about my dad. I become so sad, extremely rueful. It usually isn't family, but the death of the relative of a close friend. This has happened on numerous occasions.'

Coming Out

Coming out as a person who experiences precognitive visions takes courage. Friends, colleagues and acquaintances quickly shuffle themselves into distinct groups. Some feel relieved to find someone with whom they can confide their own experiences. Some can't wait to ask you for personal predictions. Some will ask you caring questions to check your stress level and psychological stability. Some will disappear from your life, either because, in their eyes, you have lost credibility, or because they feel the fear of the unknown. The most vociferous may well be those with fundamentalist religious beliefs who are taught that precognition, despite the many instances cited in the Bible, is the work of the devil. **Harry**, a devout Christian, describes his experience of this.

'In the early 1950s, while at a workers' club dance, four cards representing four suits were placed face down on the dance floor during a Monte Carlo dance. Each time the music stopped the cards on the floor were replaced by four other suits or, on one or more occasions, rearranged. By some means that I do not understand, I found myself able to see not only which suit was represented on each of the four cards, but also what number or picture was indicated.

'On each occasion I communicated this knowledge to my girl partner. At first she asked me if it was some trick. I assured her it was not. When I continued to do it for eight or more times, she became alarmed and claimed I was an agent of the devil. She then backed away from me saying, with a look of horror in her face, "No, you are Satan himself" and wanted nothing more to do with me.'

Since physical manifestations of precognition were a common occurrence in Harry's life, he couldn't deny their existence. However, he did feel a need to turn his head in the other direction and look not at the end product, the predicted event itself, but towards its source. He firmly believed each manifestation had a source outside himself and so, in 1963, in silent prayer, he consulted God.

'I was standing on the pavement in silent prayer to God, and I asked whether the source of the numerous predictions of future events was from that deity. In my prayer I wished to know by a manner other than a physical manifestation which I could explain away. I was fully prepared that nothing untoward would happen but nevertheless debated with myself whether God in His wisdom would give some sort of reply. God's action was totally beyond my greatest expectation.'

There followed what Harry believed to be his greatest experience to date: a resplendent vision of Heaven. It could be argued, because this place has not yet manifested in physical form for Harry (unlike the outcome of many of his prior predictive visions), that the experience was a convincing imaginative delight whipped up from years of religious devotion and in retaliation to his 'work of Satan' critics. In this way it could have been a perfect example of a hypnopompic hallucination in which a visual perception, such as a dream image normally located in the brain, is perceived to be at a location outside the head and is therefore superimposed on the surrounding environment. It could also be argued, though, that Harry's vision was indeed the answer to his prayer.

In fact, all sorts of arguments could be made from this point, and this may be one of the many jumping off places for some readers whose credibility is exhausted. It is important to remember, however, that Harry shares an ability, apparently common to many others, to accurately envision the future and, according to his reports, the outcomes of his predictive visions have been witnessed by other people on numerous occasions.

Harry's logical questioning of his experience endorses his objectivity.

'Even though I looked away to see the traffic in the avenue, the vision was maintained. There was no sign of any sort of photographic projection in the vicinity to account for the vision and I felt perfectly normal. That was, until I became intensely afraid when I became conscious that my mind or soul was moving through space to a point behind the nearby St Andrews Presbyterian Church. The fear I experienced only lasted a split second before a great calmness settled over my mind. Somehow I was still enabled to perceive the earlier vision but from a different angle.'

He finally encapsulated his understanding of this experience.

'There was an exhilarating sense of freedom as I came to understand that I was one with space and time, although neither space nor time seemed to exist. This may seem a contradiction but at this juncture I am unable to express myself otherwise. I saw God as a radiance where it is impossible for evil to exist. I seemed to have retained my individuality, personality and character and could see with my mind or soul as if I had eyes.'

Harry felt that, for a moment, he had a clear option. He could stay in this heaven, or 'fourth dimension' as he also referred to it, or he could return.

'Even though the exceedingly beautiful heaven enthralled me, I felt a sense

of responsibility to return to the physical world of earth and await my future there. It was at this juncture that a voice I recognised said from behind me, "What are you staring at, Harry?" With a mild sense of dismay I was fully aware I was no longer in Heaven.'

Harry maintains an active interest in the Church, but his experiences have shaped his beliefs away from some of the more mainstream views, and vehemently against the fundamentalist line.

'Since my retirement I have come into contact with ministers or pastors and lay members of differing religious denominations. I became, in the absence of another word, annoyed at what I perceive as undue emphasis on Satan, the Devil and demons, none of which I have any credence for. If people have free will, then they have the opportunity to follow the path enunciated by Jesus Christ, or be separated from God, even to deny Him, and go their own way.'

Harry's belief in free will was shared by most of the contributors to this research. Not only has this belief survived despite the precognitive experience but, paradoxically, in most cases it has been strengthened.

And so this chapter has gathered along its journey an appreciation of the sensual components of waking precognition, which brings us to the borderline where apparently involuntary visions cross into the territory of conscious formal prediction: the land of the professional psychic. Which is where we head next.

Summary Memo

Most of the evidence summarised for Chapter 1 also applies here, substituting vision for dream in each case. Additional evidence from this chapter includes:

- 2/1 Senses receiving or relaying the precognitive information are:

automatic speech

thought

vision

pain

emotions/feelings

hearing

knowing/intuition

- 2/2 People accustomed to experiencing precognitive visions, but who are not working as professional clairvoyants are generally unable to control the visions or produce them at will. *E.g. Cynthia, page 51.*

- 2/3 The time scale between the vision and the event seems variable, accuracy being observed in both short- and long-term predictions. *E.g. short-term: Cheryl's waterfall trip, page 49; long-term: Harry's future career travels, page 49.*

- 2/4 Along with the precognitive dreamers, most contributors to this research expressed a belief in free will, either because of or despite their precognitive experiences. *E.g. Harry, pages 55–58.*

3 meet the professionals

Professional predictions support our decision making in many everyday situations. We plan tomorrow's events by listening to the weather forecast, change political tactics according to polling predictions, make financial investments based on market trends and maintain an awareness of earthquake and natural disaster probabilities. Most of these forecasts are based on the accumulation and interpretation of hard data, though professionals at the top of their fields probably acknowledge an extra touch of intuition, a certain 'nose for the job'. The business of prediction is certainly a potentially lucrative one for those who get results for their clients.

Professional clairvoyants, or psychics, make predictions based on extrasensory input, not on hard data. They may specialise in various fields, from business to finance, health, politics, the global economy or earth changes, but they are popularly consulted for insights into people's personal futures. They may use a variety of prompts, including tarot cards, playing cards, crystals, the client's jewellery, or nothing visual at all. They may talk directly with you or communicate through spirits or guides. They may work through advertisement or through word of mouth and operate from alternative centres, markets, fairs, tea rooms, spiritualist churches, offices or their own homes. There are those who prefer to work at a distance, consulting via the telephone, internet or by mail. Some answer questions, some prefer their clients to remain silent and others choose to have nothing more than a name and address to work on. They vary from the genuinely accurate to the well intentioned but inaccurate, and from the fraudulently brilliant to the fraudulently carefree.

My research interest was to meet and interview in depth four clairvoyants with a popular reputation for accuracy, to discover what light their experiences could throw on the nature of precognition. I made it known that I was looking for recommendations of accurate psychics and kept a list, finally narrowing it down by focusing on their differences. Each answered a preprepared questionnaire (see Appendix 2) and also agreed to an interview.

Margaret Stuart, BA, Dip Ed, Dip Crim
Problem Solver, Clairvoyant, Author and Speaker

I slowed the car to a crawl as I inspected the house numbers adorning the mail boxes, finally stopping outside number thirty-two. A woman sat at her desk, phone in hand, cameoed in the bay window of her home which is also her consultation office. Margaret Stuart's reputation as a seer and problem solver is international and with a list of regular overseas clients willing to pay the costs of lengthy phone conversations on top of her professional reading fees, this woman's story begged my attention.

Margaret welcomed me with a businesslike handshake and showed me towards a big comfortable armchair, while she settled herself into its partner and tilted her head towards me expectantly. 'It's going to be interesting to be interviewed by someone who knows something about precognition and can talk my language,' she said excitedly. Her tailored jacket, her spectacles and the piles of paper on her large antique desk defined a corporate businesswoman with an intellectual bent. Although she had been working as a full-time clairvoyant problem solver for sixteen years, Margaret had also found the time to write several internationally successful books, including *Switch on Your Brain, How to Write Essays* and *Release the Genius.* She has several degrees to her name, including a Diploma in Criminology and was once head of the English department at an exclusive secondary school.

A well-known name on the public speaking circuit, Margaret was, in former years, treated as a bit of a guru, being a regular guest on the national television chat shows.

'From when I was born, I've always been aware of being psychic, clairvoyant or clairaudient,' Margaret started. *'Mum and I used to carry on conversations sitting at the dinner table and we'd only realise at the end of the conversation that we had never verbalised anything. She was telepathic too. Because she never ridiculed it or denied it, I was free to explore it. We never called it clairvoyance or anything like that, it was just "Mum and Margaret talking".'*

Margaret works with people to help them solve the subconscious problems which are holding them back from achieving their full potential. Some people would rather avoid looking at their difficulties and just shoot to the bottom line, especially if it's a rosy one. If pressed, Margaret will supply; for example,

'One lady rang and she said, "Can you just do a reading for me?" I scanned her and I said, "Within eight weeks you're going to marry a dark-haired fellow who comes from South America and he's got eight brothers and sisters." Six or seven weeks later she phoned again and said, "I've just got married. He's South American, he's got dark hair and he has eight

brothers and sisters." Since she hadn't known him at the time of the reading I hoped that she hadn't met him, seen that everything fitted into line, and therefore married him. During the reading I had warned her: "You've still got your own free will, your own choice at any stage." '

Recognition of free will is the crux of Margaret's approach to her work.

'I don't believe there's anything that's absolutely immutable. My method teaches self-responsibility. The person is always responsible for whatever occurs in his life. Once the person accepts this, then he can change his life.'

The old image of a genuine clairvoyant as being someone who has open access to all the details of a predetermined, fixed future does not fit Margaret. Yet here is a lady who can give an accurate description of an unlikely marriage in six or seven weeks time to a client who has no man in her life at the time of her reading! What kind of future was this? 'I believe I see possible futures,' Margaret explained.

Margaret's marketed ability is that she can hear her client's subconscious thoughts as clearly as if they were speaking aloud. She will only tune in with her client's permission but, once given, she believes she can access all subconscious thought on a time line from before birth to death. Before birth can include, in Margaret's opinion, information imprinted on the subconscious from past lives. The subconscious, according to Margaret, not only carries detailed information about the past but is already at work determining the future. Our past experiences, fears, thoughts and programming affect how we approach our future, so Margaret can get a good picture of the client's future based on where his subconscious is at now. If something happens to alter that subconscious programming, then the whole future picture shifts and the client finds himself on a different path. This is a relatively rational line of thought. Few people would disagree with the idea that our subconscious thoughts greatly affect how we approach our lives. What is more difficult to grasp is how Margaret can project ahead from a present subconscious mindset to see specific details unfolding within specific time frames such as her client's surprise wedding to an unknown South American.

Before continuing, Margaret paused to show me how she questions her clients' subconscious minds directly. As well as hearing subconscious messages, she tests the subconscious to target precise information. Usually she is after details such as age, emotions, names and places. With my permission to access my subconscious, her fingers began to tap furiously, as if of their own accord. Occasionally her whole arm agitated in circles or swung back and forth as if angrily crossing out a page of writing: she had apparently picked up on a thought pattern and was silently consulting my subconscious as to how old I was when this particular thought was lodged. Her rapid finger movements were giving her quick-fire yes and no answers as she ran through possible ages and emotions connected with this thought pattern. She ran, she told me later, the gamut of selected emotions in her mind: fear, love, forgiveness, guilt ... until the finger tapped a resolute positive response, and so it continued. The violent scribbling movements were associated with anger at four years of age, she said, which needed releasing. Each movement led to a deeper level of emotion, somewhat like peeling back the layers of an onion until the whole pattern was revealed. The demonstration came to an end as Margaret turned towards me and resumed interviewee pose.

I asked Margaret how much work her clients needed to do once a subconscious block was identified, in order to set their future on a more desirable path.

'Once you've hit the actual block, it takes just a second. The subconscious mind deals only with "now" and has no judgement of right or wrong, so once an emotion is recognised and no longer needed, it erases it, like pushing an erase key on a computer. With the subconscious programming out of the way, the person can see the problem more clearly and logically and see what needs to be changed.'

Margaret gave an example of a client who was involved in multi-level marketing.

'He had got as far as "emerald" level, which gives an income of about $160 000 a year, when everything, including each leg of his downline, collapsed. It seemed inexplicable. He was still working in the same way but not getting anywhere, until I discovered the block. When he was single he had been really poor and he had struggled to pay off an emerald engagement ring over a long period of time. As soon as he hit emerald level his subconscious mind triggered his belief in being poor and struggling, and so he became poor and struggling. What he had to do was mentally think back to nineteen when he bought the ring and release the conditioning that emerald meant poor and struggling. That done, the fifty year old was instantly released too. Now the emerald level is no problem to him.'

One woman flew over to Australia to consult Margaret face to face. She'd had diarrhoea for years and was unable to cure it or find a cause.

'In the first ten minutes of the consultation I said to her, "This is related to your daughter." She said, "No, it's not. My daughter's happily married ..." Half an hour later I said, "This is still related to your daughter." "No, there's nothing. We get on wonderfully well. Very happily married, everything's going wonderfully." Again much later I said, "It is related to your daughter. Describe her husband to me." "Oh, she's not *married to a man, she married another woman,"* she replied. *"It's enough to give you the shits!"* I said, *"Did you hear what you just said?"* '

The woman, Margaret inferred, had told herself so often that her daughter's lesbian relationship gave her the shits, that her physical body simply followed the plan and delivered.

The most important aspect of her work, Margaret says, is giving people options to let go of their illnesses, their problems and their hurts. 'I'd say I spend most of my time in a reading dealing with the past and the present because once you've cleared up those two, the future is assured.'

This work can get pretty complicated once you start to look at the dynamics between two or more people, in a personal relationship or, say, within a business structure.

'For example, three or four partners might have formed a business together because they all have experienced some loss in life that draws them together on a subconscious level. What you find is that the business will be held back because of their shared belief in loss. They'll go up several million, but they'll lose it again, and so it goes up and down until something changes. My job is to help them release their belief in loss so they can change their shared future through to successful business.'

If Margaret is right and one's past, present and future are largely the result of subconscious conditioning, we need to consider group dynamics from a different angle. Put simply, if Bob's subconscious conditioning has attracted him to Mary and, by the same argument, Mary's conditioning has attracted her to Bob, what happens when one of them identifies a crucial block and releases it? What if that just happens to be the 'attracted to Mary' block that Bob has released? Suddenly the relationship is not as fulfilling for either of them and the future of the partnership is under question.

Margaret suggests family relationships often operate on such a delicate interconnected web of blocks and reactions to other people's blocks. One family, for example, might come to Margaret because the child seems to need help.

'I may find I don't need to work with the child but with the grandmother. The grandmother will release something from her life which releases the mother and that releases the child.'

Projecting this idea forward, just how much effect might the release of one woman's block have, not only on her own future, but on the futures of all those people associated with her in one way or another? Is it really possible for Margaret to see the reverberating patterns of new futures and predict, for example, the appearance of the hitherto unknown South American husband, wedding ring in hand?

It emerges that Margaret's approach to problem solving is distinctly based on psychological theory. All things are possible, all people have all potential and all futures exist. All you have to do is make your choice and then release any subconscious blocks in your way. Her added appeal is that she demonstrates an ability to read your subconscious for you and identify the blocks that you, as an individual, cannot see. If her method is to predict outcomes through projecting a situation ahead, while her philosophy of life is one of total free will and choice, what can her insight offer our study of precognition?

For one, her ability to predict detailed future outcomes seems astonishing. It may be fairly logical, in theory, to predict general changes within a business structure or a personal relationship based on one individual's choice to release a subconscious block. To be able to do it with specific accuracy would be akin to predicting all possible ripple patterns generated by throwing a pebble into a pond, the surface of which is being constantly broken by the activity of a huge population of jumping fish and a crowd of another one hundred pebble throwers in the vicinity, and then selecting the pattern that will actually be seen by an observer from above! Has Margaret's brain developed this degree of pattern recognition? Or is her theory only partially right? Are our choices only apparent, were Margaret's clients destined to go and consult her and release a certain block on a certain date all along? While Margaret may be able to see all combinations and permutations resulting from her clients' apparent choices, was the 'chosen' path always the only option, the choice itself an illusion? Is Margaret able to see a predestined future, despite the illusion of alternatives and choice?

There is an oft-quoted scientific principle known as Occam's Razor which, in everyday language, states that the simplest theory is probably the correct one. It is easier for many people to explain a skill such as Margaret claims as an ability to see a fixed future or one of a limited range of alternative futures, than as an ability to perform mathematical computations beyond the scope of present day computers.

I shifted the angle of my questioning to discover Margaret's view on the nature of time.

'It's only now. There's no time. I think there's a false linear time but overall there's only now. So if you could stand at the top of where time is, you'd be able to see past, present and future. You'd be able to see everything that's occurring everywhere in the one dimension, in the one time, yet going along the ground you're in what we call a linear time pace. It's as though if you could look down on the world like an astronaut looks down on the world, and sees all the things that are happening there, past, present and future are just all encapsulated in that one little ball.'

Now this, of course, is the central paradox in my work, and one which will reappear in many forms and guises throughout this book until I pin it down. So I was eager to ask Margaret how she worked her view of 'no time' into her theory of choice and the ability of her clients to change their futures within that 'no time, one little ball' framework. As a seer of future detail and yet a believer in free will, could she reconcile these two modes of time?

'It's very hard to explain,' she started. Her argument seemed to come down to the fact that people have a belief in linear time, so that is what she deals with when she's working with them. At the same time Margaret noted that, on the little ball side of things, she's able to see a person's past lives, plus their present life right up to death, but never future lives. I noted that I'd never read or heard of anyone who claims to be able to predict future incarnations even though plenty of clairvoyants are happy making predictions about their clients' present lives. Surely, if past lives exist, then future lives should also be predictable based on the little ball theory of no time.

I took another tack and asked Margaret whether she ever had precognitive dreams.

'Yes. It's a funny sort of dream. It takes a strange shape. It's the feel more than the actual scene of the dream and when I get that, I know a relative is about to pass. It happened in 1964 and my brother died in 1965. He wasn't ill in 1964. It happened again in 1976 and my father died six months afterwards. Later I went to New Zealand and all of a sudden I got this same feeling and I tried to work out which relative, but it was a very dear friend who died while I was away. The dreams will start one day and continue until all of a sudden I can recognise who it is and then they stop. Although the dream stops, it doesn't mean I can change the outcome. I think they were warnings, because I was then able to handle the losses before they occurred.'

I wondered what Margaret's views on precognitive dreams in general were.

'I tend to think precognitive dreams come to awaken people to the fact that they can tap into all knowledge if they want to. They usually get a terrific

shock when the dream occurs. On the other hand, you get people who dream of an accident, particularly if it's for themselves, and then don't do anything about it, don't change anything in their life. They're being told, "This will occur unless you alter something," and it's like saying, "Hey, wake up here, wake up! You can actually do something about this!" Then they just say, "Oh I dreamed the other night I had an accident and today I walked out and had an accident." If I have a precognitive dream, I will immediately search and say, "Okay, is this definite, or what am I supposed to know about this to change it?" '

The last sentence underlines, once again, the nod in the direction of destiny that all precognitive dreamers, visionaries and psychics make, regardless of how much argument they place in favour of total free will and choice. This is not intended as criticism. It is an observation. The unconscious speaks loud and clear in acknowledging the paradox of an intertwining free will/destiny alongside an intertwining notion of linear time/no time. Confusion, yet clarity.

Many psychics report the presence of a spirit guide or deceased family member who stands by during the reading, seen or unseen, delivering messages or adding the extra insight the psychic needs. I asked Margaret her views.

'I used to believe in guides because I'd have very specific ones who came in. I'd go through a certain way of working and a guide would be there and then he'd hand me over to another guide and then I'd work in a slightly different way. The last guide I had sat there leaning on a stick, looking forward and never acknowledged anything. I'm not sure now. I've never had a female figure, they've always been male, so I wonder whether we present a guide because we feel better when there's an authority figure around.'

Whereas guides seem to be associated specifically with the clairvoyant, it seems the client often arrives with their own attendant spirits in tow. When it comes to spirits, in general, rather than specific guides, who seem to act in long-term partnership with their psychic, Margaret has more confidence.

'I do have spirits who come in and will tell me different things when I'm working with a client. Now again, is that a projection of my knowledge so that I'm able to project the person? Has the client projected the image of the person who's died, which I can then see or hear, or has the person who died come in as the spirit? I see them as holograms, so I assume they are their spirit.'

Apparently the spirit usually gives identifying information, often something that is known only to the client and is therefore believed to be a direct message from Spirit. Questions remain, of course, simply because the client *does* already know the information, and so could be projecting it for Margaret to tune into. The role of spirits, real or projectionary, in Margaret's readings seems to be that of healing the past, so the client can move forward into their future in a different way. In terms of the reading, the emotional release acts as a predictor of a future change.

I find this question of what the reader actually perceives interesting. My professional work with dreams has given me fluency with the symbolic language of the unconscious, or the right brain (for the purposes of this argument the language is similar, if not the same). Margaret states that she largely works with the subconscious and questions the validity of her visions of spirits as possibly being interpretations of her clients' perceptions. Do clairvoyants 'read' exactly what they pick up, in the direct language of symbolism, or do they interpret, much as I would interpret a dream into the language of the rational mind so that it is of more service to the dreamer in negotiating their waking world? To put it more simply let's turn to the folklore image of the gypsy woman gazing into her crystal ball.

The gypsy looks up and pronounces, 'You will travel over

water and meet a handsome, dark stranger.' A dream of travelling over water and meeting a handsome dark stranger would be interpreted in terms of the dreamer's psyche and personal or spiritual development. Water in dreams tends to reflect the dreamer's emotions, whereas the male figure generally represents the dreamer's male side (Jung's animus, the Chinese Yang, and the functions generally associated with the left brain). The union between the female dreamer and the dark stranger represents the union between her female side (anima, Yin, right brain qualities) and her male side. In dream terms, or in the language of the unconscious, the ultimate goal is recognition and union of the one integrated self: balance. So, looking back at the simplified dream, or reading, the unconscious is really expressing an understanding that integration with the woman's male side is best achieved by overcoming some emotional issues (travelling over water). The reason why the man is usually a dark stranger is that dark represents unknown, in the dark, and stranger is, of course, unknown aspects of the self. The question is, then, should the reader describe only what they 'see', or should they interpret what they see? How many psychics are capable of interpretation, and how many are ignorant of symbolism?

Another common expression of this, as I perceive it, is the death prediction. A person dreaming of death is usually dealing, at an unconscious level at least, with the symbolism of death of the old, birth of the new. The unconscious expresses the knowledge that the dreamer can transform his life by letting old beliefs and attitudes die to give way for the creation of new attitudes and a better life. Should the psychic, picking up the symbolic theme of death of the old, birth of the new from her client, or about her client, predict actual deaths or births, or should she interpret in terms of change for the better?

These arguments are based on Margaret's understanding that she is directly reading the subconscious. The case still exists that a psychic might preview an actual future death or birth, in the same way that precognitive dreams emerge occasionally among the symbolic ones, in which case the ethics change. I asked Margaret for her view.

'I pick up an awful lot of clients who've been told, "Oh, there's a terrible event coming towards you." They phone me and say, "Now I'm scared witless." I say, "Look, don't worry. All it is is you're letting go of the old and moving on to the new. You need to look beyond that transition, beyond that watershed and you'll see everything's going to be fine. You may lose your business or go through a divorce, but it's only going to happen if you want the changes. If you don't want them, it's showing you to make changes so you don't have to go through it." But some readers stop at the point where they see disaster and it frightens people.'

Margaret says she presents both views.

'When a person comes to me for a reading they get exactly what I see. If I see water, I'll say, "I see muddy, eddying water. Normally emotion shows up as water and muddy water means murky emotions you haven't sorted out, or you haven't got clear." Or if it's a waterfall: "There's some big change coming, some emotional or physical change. You have to interpret it according to what hits strongly for you. I can tell you what it may be and we can explore that." Or, with some people I can not only see the water but also clearly see what it represents.'

Taking a break from analysis and ethics, I asked Margaret which readings have given her the greatest joy.

'Seeing a retarded boy come right, seeing people who've got really horrible illnesses or deformities straighten through releasing blocks, seeing people who are going broke turning business around,' she listed. 'I had a guy who was on blood transfusions, dying of cancer. He wanted to see me. The doctor said, "You won't live twenty-four hours, so yes, you can go and see her." He reached an understanding of why he had the cancer and made

changes to release and forgive things that he'd done. This change gave him time, another four-and-a-half months to be exact, to put everything in order before he died.

'In another case I had one fourteen-year-old who couldn't read. I helped him to release one or two emotions and twenty minutes later he was on the phone to his mother, sobbing, "I can read!" All I'd done was release the emotions. I cry with them, it's just magic. I wouldn't swap this job for anything.'

Margaret summarises her understanding of life. 'We live, we choose for ourselves, we die, we go into spirit and we choose for ourselves whether we're going to remain in spirit or incarnate.' Alongside all this choice, she also says she occasionally tunes in to a person's life purpose.

'Very occasionally I have been able to stand up there on that time where you see all time and say to a client, "You're going through this, but this is what your life purpose is. If you go ahead with your plan, then in ten years time you're going to change jobs and then you're going to be sacked. It's out of your hands. It's a change that's going to force you back on the path of your life purpose. So if you want to fulfil your life purpose and avoid all that, let's make the changes now." '

Margaret's argument implies that it's not so much a matter of choosing whether or not to accept your life purpose, but of choosing *when* to accept it. The unseen forces, it appears, will ultimately put us on the right path one way or another. Choice? What choice? Is there really choice at the end of the day, or when viewed from the 'no time, one little ball' framework? The very essence of the word purpose implies an ultimate destiny: tick the right box, take the right action, fulfil your destiny and win the prize!

I drove away from Margaret's home pondering the subtleties

and uncertainties of human perception. Occam's Razor flashed again before my eyes as I wrote the final lines of this story in my mind.

Not only do we have the paradox of coexisting no time and linear time, but also the shadow of a paradox of choice coexisting with destiny. Perhaps the unifying solution, in philosophical terms, is that no time, linear time, choice and destiny are all but illusions of a greater phenomenon as yet unnamed by human intellect.

Margaret Stuart can be contacted through:

> Pinnacle of Life
> PO Box 2055
> Wellington Point
> QLD 4160
> Australia

Reverend Ruth Bennett, Dip Ed
Clairvoyant and Minister of Spiritualist Church

The Reverend Ruth Bennett seemed so fragile as she sat surrounded by her dogs and cats, contemplating me silently. I was experiencing one of those low-tech days when simple electronic machines such as tape recorders suddenly seem unfathomable. You know, those days when you feel a real idiot because your intellectual mind is racing ahead with questions, leaving the mechanical mind far behind. I stared alternately at the line of holes punched in the plastic casing and the wires in my hand and wondered how long it would be before I would remember where to stick what. I fumbled all the more when I noticed that Ruth kept watching a spot slightly to the left of my body, and I began to wonder what kind of entity might be looking over my shoulder. I pushed the wire into another hole to no avail, and hoped Ruth would deliver a message from Spirit to help. Instead, or perhaps in answer to my thoughts, her son entered the room and did the male mechanical thing for me. It was strange, though, because the whole tape recording was muffled and buzzy and very difficult to transcribe.

As minister of a Spiritualist Church in Queensland, Ruth, who has a diploma in education and used to be a primary school teacher, holds a religious celebrant's licence and conducts regular church services. Unlike the other clairvoyants I interviewed, Ruth is aware that it is still illegal for lay people to receive pay for doing readings in Queensland. Her situation, however, is different. 'As a minister of religion I am legally entitled to do counselling and to give advice, and I don't infringe the law by doing readings.' In careful consideration of the law as it now stands, Ruth also employs a number of psychic readers at her Tea Room. The long standing Tea Room tradition allows people to buy afternoon tea at a price which includes a 'free' reading. As long as the readers are not seen to accept money for their services, the whole operation is above board.

Between running the Tea Room, carrying out the duties of a minister of religion, and offering private readings at home, Ruth also teaches a Mind Dynamics course. One semester she shared the results of a dream experiment with her students.

'I started experimenting with seeing if I could dream the future, and I thought that horse races would be a good way to go because you get pretty quick proof of those. On a Tuesday night I used to put a programme in before I went to sleep that I would dream the winner of the race the following day which was Wednesday. I had, by this stage, a pretty well-developed sense of remembering my dreams and interpreting them, so I would work out which one had the horse race winner picture and then I'd look through the papers and see which horse fitted the dream. It

checked out every day for about seven or eight mornings. One night I was telling this to a group of students and one said, "Well, will you ring me up on Wednesday morning and give me the winner?", which defeated the purpose. If we were to use it just to make money it wouldn't work. What I was trying to prove was that you can dream the future by conscious desire.'

Ruth says everyone has the ability to look into the future but some people are better 'instruments' than others.

'I was aware of my clairvoyant, clairaudient and clairsentient abilities back in the early sixties, thirty-odd years ago. The other stuff, the body scanning with X-ray vision for example, I developed through practice on the Mind Dynamics course. As far as readings on a one-to-one basis went, the more I did, the better I became. So I guess it's like learning the piano, the more practice you get, the better you are at it.'

Ruth has been charging a very modest fee for her personal readings for the last five years or so, although she had been reading for Spiritualist churches for free since 1982. I asked her to define the basis of the Spiritualist movement.

'The Spiritualist Church has no set dogma or doctrine,' she replied. *'They have a set of seven principles and basically they encourage people to think and to reason and research and accept what seems right. One person's truth isn't another person's truth.'*

Despite her interest in the Spiritualist movement, Ruth usually rules spiritual guidance out of her readings.

'I feel you don't need to see a reader for that. The readings I do are sorting out everyday problems such as relationships, jobs, money and health. I look into future situations mainly to take action on them before they happen, advising the need to consult your doctor or have your car

checked out by a mechanic. I tend not to get into spiritual guidance unless I see a need. Most people who come for readings aren't looking for that anyway.'

Ruth described how she warned one woman to watch her purse and cancel her plastic cards.

'Later the woman left a considerable sum of money back at home when she took her kids on an access visit to her husband. While at his house her purse was taken. She thought he was responsible and that he was after the plastic cards because he knew all the PIN numbers. But it was too late. She had heeded the warning and changed banks!'

On another occasion during a reading Ruth insisted that a woman check herself in for a cancer smear test because she saw, through body scanning, the early stages of cancer.

'I said, "You get your butt down to a gynaecologist and get a smear test,"' Ruth recalled. *'She said, "Is it that bad?" and I said, "Yes, it's up to you, but my clairvoyance had got a good track record and this doctor of mine that comes through is saying it's urgent, so get your butt down, like yesterday." So she took my advice and went down the next day and the doctor put her into hospital, the smear test having confirmed the psychic diagnosis. A few days later her two daughters came back to thank me for saving their mum's life.'*

I understood body scanning was a Mind Dynamics technique enabling the reader to see or envision the body's physical organs, but I was intrigued by Ruth's description of 'this doctor of mine that comes through'. Which doctor? I asked.

'I feel I have a doctor there that's passed over, a spirit contact, helper, or whatever you want to call it, who is giving me the information, but who knows? I know I'm trained to pick up on medical problems through

telepathy, but I tend not to know some of the terms. If I start talking about endocrine glands or things like that, which I haven't had any training on, then I know I've got to be getting it from somewhere. Maybe I'm mentally scanning a medical textbook or just accessing it from universal knowledge. Or maybe I'm I getting it from a specific person who was a doctor. It's a million dollar question that I don't know that anyone can answer.'

While she was in philosophising mode, I asked Ruth how she saw time.

'The jury's still out on that one,' she laughed. 'I have a really active mind and I play with these concepts. I don't know if time's something we move through. I don't know if everything exists all at once and we merely move through experiences. I know time and space are connected and that we can't separate them, so I wonder whether somewhere Christopher Columbus is still sailing to America and I'm in a different place. Is time a case of action, you know, this action takes place then that action takes place and we call the sequence "time", or does everything exist all at once? I don't know. All I know is that I don't have any barriers to seeing something of the future, present or the past.'

She paused for a while and then summarised.

'At the clairvoyant level time doesn't exist. I just see things and if the client's good I can get a bit of guidance on whether it has *happened, it* is *happening or it's* going *to happen. I think time is what man has devised in order to cope with life.'*

In the linear time versus no time debate, it seemed Ruth leaned in favour of no time, with linear time as a false but necessary perceptual tool for negotiating life as it appears to be.

So how did she see the future: as a fixed destiny, as partially changeable, or totally at the mercy of individual free will?

'I liken it to watching kids playing cricket in the back yard. I'm looking out the window and I see a ball heading towards me. I've got three options: I can let the ball hit the window. I can open the window and let the ball come through or, if I'm downstairs, I could catch the ball or put the garbage bin lid up to intercept it.'

She answered, neatly illustrating all the variables I'd mentioned. Fragile in body she might be, but Ruth demonstrated a strong, quick-draw mind when it came to finding the right analogy. Perhaps, I thought, this is why she is drawn to tarot cards which are pictorial metaphors for archetypal situations in life. The theory is that the right cards come out in a reading in the right order according to what needs to be known.

'If I'm working on the church platform I don't use tarot cards, but when I read from the Tea Room or at home I use them to speed the reading up,' Ruth confirms. *'I can also involve the person I'm reading for, because you can point things out and the cards help them to memorise. If you want to come back to a point, or you want to refer back to something you've already said, the cards are there, so you've got instantaneous referral.'*

It's all too easy for anxious clients to believe in a fixed future, firmly sealed by a clairvoyant's spoken words and encoded onto audio tape for later reinforcement. Ruth advocates the need to educate people about their power to take action, and change their future.

'I tell everyone, "The future's never fixed. What you decide now, or what action you take now, what you do and what you think now, will set your future." If someone says, "You've brought a jinx on me," I say, "No, I'm only seeing something. You have free will. Your mind is supreme. So just because I see it, it doesn't mean it's got to happen. What I'm seeing will happen if you do nothing to change it." So I never leave myself open for somebody to come back and say, "After what you said, I decided there's

*nothing left in life for me," or anything like that. If they're writing it down,
or I'm taping it, I make sure I say very specifically that the future is never
fixed, and that they can do something about it before it happens.'*

What line does she take if she sees death? Does she see death in a
reading as a literal preview or warning of an actual death, or as
symbolic of her client's unconscious readiness for rebirth through
death of the old, birth of the new? Ruth's answer sidesteps the
question of symbolism for the moment.

*'I use my discretion. I tend to put it in such a way that I let them down
gently and then I always say, "Well, the future's never fixed," or "A clairvoyant could be wrong." Any death that I've seen is usually an older
person, where their body is so far gone that it's just a matter of time, and
I usually say something like, "Well, you realise your mum hasn't got that
much longer to go, you might not have her for Christmas, so send some
white light." If I feel that it's imminent, I'll say, "Well, just send her lots
of love and realise that she's chosen the time to go." I very rarely see an
accident or anything like that and I don't know that it's my privilege as a
reader to do so. If I pick up an illness I tell it like it is so they can go and
get treatment.'*

I returned to the question of symbolism and asked Ruth whether,
apart from the symbolism of the tarot, she noticed other symbols
coming into her readings.

*'I am of the opinion that each clairvoyant has his or her own symbols. If
I see shark's teeth, that's shorthand for saying, "Watch out—somebody's
out to get you." If I see an umbrella over somebody's head, that's "protec-
tion from Spirit". If I see an elephant I say, "You're going to be getting a
lot of help in a situation."'*

I wondered how Ruth could tell the difference between her own
symbolism and that of her client.

'It can be specific. I was reading for someone once and I saw champagne corks popping. I got someone from Spirit saying, "But be careful not to shake the champagne up: don't shake the bottle before you pop the cork!" I thought, "How am I going to interpret this?" I told her all this as I was going and I said, "If you shake the bottle up, when the cork comes off, some of the champagne's going to go onto the carpet, or onto whatever, and you're not going to have the whole full bottle of champagne. Why not have the whole bottle?" Then I went into the physical interpretation: you could sell your house now, but at the moment it's a buyers' market, so if you wait until it's a sellers' market, then you're going to have the whole bottle of champagne. Sometimes you've got to take a little bit of time to get that interpretation and that's where I feel a more intelligent person is just a little bit better at interpreting a symbol. Some clairvoyants just shoot their heads off, as if they're off with the fairies, saying, "Next year's going to be a good year because I can see champagne corks popping!" '

Plunging back into the more universal symbolism of the unconscious, as discussed in Margaret's story, I asked Ruth whether the popular old 'You'll travel across water and meet a handsome dark stranger' prediction was a case of delivering straight dreamlike symbolism without responsible interpretation.

'It could be, yes. I don't tend to get into that esoteric type of reading, I tend to get nuts and bolts. If I've seen milk being spilt, I don't say that straightaway. I'll say, "Watch that you don't shoot your mouth off" or "Watch what you say." Then I'll come back and say, "Because I'm seeing milk being spilt and you won't be able to take your words back." So I always give them the interpretation first, rather than come out straight with the symbol because that's very confusing. I always give them the symbolism as well, though, because I feel it's easier for them to retain the words. On the other hand, I might be shown a particular flower and I've got to interpret it, so I ask, "Can you tell me anything about a really dark,

red rose that's nearly black?" Often they'll say something like, "Yes, my husband used to grow them. That's his favourite rose." '

'Best clairvoyants in Brisbane: Best Tea Room' boasts Ruth's advert. With years of experience of hiring and firing readers, I wondered if she had identified any personality traits associated with being a good psychic.

'The best, especially those that are very good at channelling as well as telepathy, are typically earthy types, often uneducated. Some highly educated people with university degrees are good psychics, but generally the intellect is a barrier for many people because they focus on intellect at the expense of instinct or intuition. Musicians, painters, architects and inventors, who rely on inspiration for their creativity, often make good clairvoyants though.'

Since Ruth believes that psychic skills can be improved through practice, she offers advice and training for new readers starting out in her Tea Room.

'It's important to put your own desires or hobbyhorses aside and make sure that you're not reading your own wishes or pushing your own wheelbarrow. I have seen readers who are incurable romantics, saying, "Oh, you're going to get married soon, I can see this lovely man coming along, you're going to have this beautiful white wedding dress," to every unmarried woman. Other readers always seem to pick up on parental things, asking, "What sort of relationship did your parents have?" because their own parents had a problem they haven't come to grips with yet. Another one might have been a victim of incest and keep seeing the same issue coming up in her readings. I remind my students, "There are plenty of people coming for readings who are happily married and they're just coming for a little look-see into the future. Not everyone has tragic circumstances." '

Hands-on training comes in the shape of dummy runs or observation on the job.

'I do pretend readings for my new readers, so they get the idea of the type of circumstances I cover and how I phrase things. Alternatively I'll get them to sit near another Tea Room reader and listen in, to get an idea of what the primary focuses are, what's eating away at most people and what's driving them to book a consultation. Coming from a teaching background I'm used to training teachers with the philosophy: "You watch how I teach, then you get up and do that." '

I had just witnessed the pragmatic face of both Spiritualism and clairvoyancy and yet something was still missing. I switched off my tape recorder, took my farewells and walked to the car, focusing on the mechanical intricacies of a triple reverse turn. How often did my intellect get in the way, not only of mastering mechanical skills, but also of grasping the true nature of precognition?

Reverend Ruth Bennett can be contacted through:

> GPO Box 1945
> Brisbane
> QLD 4001
> Australia

Saanthi
Clairvoyant, Natural Therapist, Healer and Shaman

'I welcome this opportunity to give thanks today to saints and sages of all religions. May we humbly bow before you all, for lighting the lamp of freedom that we may now more clearly see our way to where we need to be. I ask that wherever you go in life, would you please continue to keep much

peace in your eyes and great love in your heart. Allow the spiritual healing essence of who you know yourself to be to overspill out, to enrich and uplift all others, including yourself, as you aspire upon your journey to divine prosperity. And with this I would like to bless you with the blessing "Sai Ram". I salute the highest divinity within you. May God bless you. Go forth.'

Saanthi sat back in her reading chair and smiled. Behind her hung a framed code of ethics, and on another shelf I could see a pile of feedback questionnaires. New blank audio tapes were stacked high beside them, as Saanthi insists that her readings are recorded for her clients to check through in the months to come. Outside her main street shop the sun was bright, but here, tucked away in her reading room, we were cosseted in surreal new age ambience. I had just asked Saanthi if she had a special routine to help her establish the right bonding for a reading and to mark the start and finish of her work. She had leaned across the table, held my hand and entranced me with the whole ritual: everything bar an actual reading. The opening paragraph is Saanthi's closing ritual, whereupon the reader–client transaction is complete.

Saanthi is a spiritual name acquired 'through Spirit' many years ago. It means River of Divine Peace. It's an apt name. Saanthi flows. She speaks quickly, using long sentences which tumble into each other, making transcription of our taped interview a nightmare. She uses flowery language, honeyed with phrases like 'I sought to discover', 'Do not go beyond where you haven't yet begun' and 'I determine and discern' that seem more fitting of ancient times. Well known as a reader who communicates with Spirit, I wondered who was really doing most of the speaking that day. 'If I say it quickly,' Saanthi explained, 'it's too clever for me, so it has to be channelled from a higher entity.' It's an indemnity based on Saanthi's trust in the world of Spirit after an agonising self-questioning period earlier in her career.

Saanthi's awakening to her psychic abilities occurred when she was sixteen years old. Raised to share the farm work on her parents' property, she would often sneak away from tracking cattle to spend time with her grandmother who lived across the creek. Saanthi would exchange a billy of milk for a boiled lolly and her grandmother's memories of the past or stories of the country folk. Years later, returning to visit her grandmother, she found the creek had risen to a raging river. The old lady stood and watched her safely negotiate the water.

'My last living memory of my grandmother was that she was standing beside this beautiful blooming cactus, waving a white gentleman's hankie to me as I went off. There was something very deep in my heart there and then that said, "You may not see your grandmother again."'

One morning a few months later, Saanthi awoke around five to prepare for a journey. She lay in bed for a while, waiting for her husband to finish his shower, savouring her last moments.

'I was very much awake when an apparition of my grandmother appeared to me with her arms outstretched. I was quite horrified because I knew she was still alive.'

At first Saanthi thought it was some kind of omen, warning them to take care on their long drive into Brisbane, but her anxiety grew and she phoned her sister and asked her to go over and check on her grandmother. She heard herself adding, 'Please go, because I feel there's only six weeks around her to live, or six weeks around me, and I don't understand this!'

Later that day they learned what had happened. Saanthi's grandmother had torn her skin in her rose garden weeks beforehand and the wound had become ulcerated. 'At some time between me seeing the apparition and eight o'clock that morning, she had collapsed. She died of pancreatic cancer six weeks later.'

This was Saanthi's first frightening experience of her abilities not only to tune into someone else through telepathy, but also to witness an apparition and to accurately predict a time of death. Today she is more comfortable in acknowledging her skills, defining herself as a 'sensitive'. She also practises as a healer and a shaman.

Nowadays many of Saanthi's readings include messages from Spirit or from her clients' deceased relatives or friends.

'Often when the client walks into the room I know on a vibrational level that someone [deceased] is there. I don't always mention it, but if there's a reason why they need to communicate, I'll share it with them.'

She often gives accurate descriptions of time and relevant phrases which identify the deceased, or reference to knowledge shared only between the deceased and the client. Saanthi is confident that she is indeed sensitive to the departed spirits, although it could equally be argued that she is sensitive to the memories of the deceased in her clients' minds, including turns of phrase or confidential knowledge.

Messages delivered in this way usually relate to past or present circumstances, or are advice about the future from the deceased, so this area of Saanthi's work is not directly relevant to the question of precognition. However, Saanthi is certain that she receives much of her information in readings, including future-specific information, directly from specialised guides, from Spirit. Once, when she felt the need to translate a message to make it clearer, she heard her guide 'state quite belligerently':

'Listen, Saanthi. We guides from the collective unconscious authorise you as courier to deliver the parcel but not to unwrap and rewrap it to how you interpret it should have been wrapped! Would you just present the parcel.'

Accepting responsibility as a reader is a key issue, as Saanthi sees it. 'I believe that everyone has the gift but I believe some people choose not to want to identify with it.' Two major experiences earlier in her career prompted her to re-evaluate her role as a reader and question the forces which determine an individual's future. Strangely, both experiences were of aborted readings: readings which, as far as Saanthi was concerned at the time, were not working.

'I had a lady come to me many years ago saying, "Oh hello, Saanthi, I've been told you do really lovely readings, and I'm all excited, I'm really looking forward to this. This is wonderful." She was outgoing, she was a joy. I thought, "What a treasure! This lady's going to be so easy, so happy with her reading." I did everything that was necessary, including the process to attune to guides to begin the reading. But in vain. There was no response. I looked at the cards. I couldn't remember or relate to them. They were just pieces of paper. I looked down and tapped my watch, and I said, "I do need to apologise. I just feel I'm not in tune today. They've pulled the plug." For all intents and purposes she probably thought, "This is a set up." I kept focusing on my watch and she said, "What's wrong with your watch?" I said, "It's stopped, it's got the wrong time." I went on like this for some minutes and nothing happened. I concluded this time to be unsuitable for a reading for anyone. She went away and two days later I found out she had suicided.'

Saanthi discovered that the woman had made suicide attempts before and told a close friend she was going to do it again. The friend, who had previously received a good and helpful reading with Saanthi, pleaded with her suicidal friend: 'Just do one thing. Go and see Saanthi and then make up your own mind because I can't feel responsible for what you do.'

After the suicide, the friend called Saanthi and revealed that the woman had gone to the reading looking for a sign. When the watch stopped she believed she had received her answer.

'I was very shook up about that. I just went into fear mode. I had gone out there to help people,' Saanthi explained. She spoke with a psychologist who regularly dealt with suicidal people and had come to terms with some of them succeeding in their quest, despite his counselling.

'He advised me to keep doing my work and suggested a more challenging approach if I found myself reading for someone with suicidal wishes in the future. His idea was to confront the person and challenge them to consider the feelings of loved ones who may find them in the event of their intentions being carried out.'

Not only had Saanthi been emotionally shaken by this event, but it also served to force her to face one of her most treasured beliefs. 'It was very difficult because I believe that energy follows thought and I wondered how much I created that situation.' A second experience, earlier in her reading life, had caused the same self-questioning.

A woman came to see Saanthi back in the days when she was working from home on a word-of-mouth basis. It was not an easy time. Saanthi had three small children and was recovering from an accident with a patch over her injured eye when the woman unexpectedly appeared for a consultation. 'I received the message that the woman was pregnant,' Saanthi said, 'but although I attempted the reading three times, nothing further was coming through.' Feeling the pain of her bruised eye and acknowledging her exhaustion, she thought, 'Right, they've taken my energy away because they want me to be on sabbatical. They want me to restore and regenerate before assisting anyone else.' But the woman was still insistent. After trying again, Saanthi placed her hand on the woman's shoulder to apologise when she heard a voice say, 'Tell her about how your son was born.'

Now, Saanthi's second child was born with lung disease and was retrieved after his lungs collapsed twice. Saanthi turned to the woman at the last moment and said, 'My guide has just told me to tell you a story about my son.' Saanthi's story led to an impromptu reading.

'I told the woman, "You're pregnant, did you know you're pregnant?" "No," she replied. "Well, listen," I continued, "I'm not prepared to put any of this on tape, so this is a sharing, not a reading, but I was given the impression that you're going to have a boy child who's going to be born in approximately six months. He's going to need to be retrieved and will be ushered to a neonatal centre. If you have any pain you must go to the doctor, because for some reason you will be eating chicken and around eight-thirty or nine I see you being admitted to the hospital. Your girlfriend will see that you get to hospital."'

The woman turned to her friend who had accompanied her to Saanthi's house.

'And she said, "Well, we live in Brisbane and my friends live in Bli Bli, so there's not much chance of that happening. We don't get together that much. But anyway, why not my husband? I've got a husband, you know." I said, "Because he'll be drunk. I'm sorry, you think I'm making it up as I go along, but I'm telling you that he's drunk."'

Many months later Saanthi received a bouquet of flowers with a message. 'Thank you very much for saving the life of my son.'

'It happened exactly as I had described,' Saanti continued. 'The girlfriend and her husband had been helping them to move house and by eight, eight-thirty that evening the men went out to buy some food and have a beer. They didn't normally drink, but on this occasion they had three or four. So the girlfriend ended up driving her into hospital that night.'

Although Saanthi had delivered accurate details of future

events to previous clients, it was the similarity of the two birth circumstances that raised a note of alarm. 'I wondered whether I created it because I sowed the seed of thought. I gave her the whole scenario.'

So now, many years later, what does Saanthi understand about the nature of the future?

'I'd say I predict probable futures. There are people who take responsibility for their actions and choose to do something about their life and there are others who choose to allow the Universal Will to lead and take them where it may. In some way I feel that there is a position of fate available to us, but as we sow so we shall reap, so we are creating our future based on association of previous memories, experiences, or the experiences of other people.'

Saanthi seems to be describing a mix of free will and fixed destiny which determines our individual futures: perhaps with different ratio mixes for different people. As a psychic reader she chooses the role of facilitator—someone who can highlight the probable options—leaving the decisions of active choice or passive unfolding to her clients. Using a metaphor to get her message across in her readings, she explains,

'You are in full control of your life. You are master of the reading. You are master of your own destiny. I'm purely in here as a navigator. I am in the passenger seat, darling, you're in the driver's seat. Let's see how fast and how far we can go.'

Saanthi's solution to the paradox of the nature of time is simple. The question is not so much one of linear time versus no time, but a melding of the two—and yet neither: 'Time is irrelevant. We have to live it now, in this moment. This is time. Time is now. This is the only moment.'

Saanthi can be contacted through:

> PO Box 36
> Montville
> QLD 4560
> Australia

Bruce Way
Clairvoyant, Author, Speaker and Business Consultant

'There's a psychic about to be interviewed on ABC radio, Jane,' Glen announced as he brought me a cup of coffee. 'He's just written a book and he's going to do talkback too.' I was sitting at my desk ploughing through the precognitive dreaming question-naire replies at the time. I had already drawn up a shortlist of clairvoyants to interview for this book and had heard radio psychics before, but I thought I'd listen in anyway. According to the radio promo, Bruce Way had a twenty-year background in business management and computers and had just had his second book, *How to Interpret a Psychic Reading*, published.

The talkback section was predictable, at least as far as the callers' questions were concerned. 'When will our house be sold?', 'Will I marry the man in my life?' and 'Will I get a promotion at work?' jostled alongside the inevitable cynicism, complete with disguised voice asking, 'What can you tell about me?' Somewhere between callers Bruce managed to squeeze in a few lines about his book, just enough to get me interested. Finally the radio presenter asked for a personal prediction. Cutbacks had been announced for the ABC and jobs were at stake, but at that time no one knew who would stay and who would go. The presenter brushed off Bruce's 'Do you really want me to tell you on air?' retort, and insisted. Bruce told him that he wouldn't lose his job in the first round and that a new opportunity would be presented to him mid 1997. The choice as to whether to stay with the ABC or to leave would then be his. At that point I decided to invite Bruce to be featured in my book whether the prediction turned out to be accurate or not. As far as I was concerned, anyone who had the guts to make a precise on-air prediction for a man in the public eye had to have the power of conviction behind him. It was that conviction that interested me. The presenter? He did survive the first round of cuts, unlike several of his peers, and mid 1998, is still there.

Bruce's radio interview and predictions were made over the phone from his Sydney home, distinguishing him as a distance reader, which added to my interest. I left a message with his publisher and Bruce was on the line before the day had ended. Resisting the urge to ask him about the future success of this book, I outlined the project and he agreed to be interviewed. I guess that was an endorsement in its own way!

'I read distantly ninety per cent of the time now because I am not as distracted and I believe it gives more evidence of proof.' Bruce's insistence on proof reflects his own journey of discovery, from his Seventh-Day Adventist origins to the establishment of his busy career as a clairvoyant and trance medium. 'Also I can put more information into thirty minutes distantly than in a sixty minute face to face,' Bruce Way the business management expert added!

'I am forty-five years old now. I realised I "had something" when I was about thirty-six. Before that, no idea. Most probably because anything psychic scared me.' Bruce's Adventist background had taught that psychics had a direct line to the Devil, but by the time a friend booked him a psychic reading for a birthday present, he was committed to following his curiosity rather than his religion. He endured a battle to begin with, tossing the taped reading into the bin, only to regret it later when several of the things the psychic had predicted came about. His early religious conditioning soon gave way to the testing sceptic. For several years Bruce consulted three psychics every six months, comparing every detail of their readings. In two cases Bruce would sit quietly and give no feedback until the end of each reading. His third psychic was a distance reader, which satisfied the sceptic in Bruce. He finally concluded that eighty per cent of each of the readings cross-matched. The sceptic shifted ground.

In the meantime Bruce had experimented.

'I used to give impromptu readings to friends, just telling them about themselves, with stunning accuracy. I would also get flashes of world events about to happen and seem to be able to get advice out of nowhere.'

On one occasion he was travelling in a car with friends, enjoying the general conversation, when he felt himself slip into a silence.

'The world stopped momentarily and I saw a city shaken by an earth-quake. The experience lasted for a few seconds and then normality returned. In shock I turned to my friends and said, "You're not going to believe this but Newcastle will be hit by an earthquake in two days." After that remark the ensuing silence was real. My friends looked at me as if I was crazy and, stunned by what I had just said, I was ready to believe them.'

Two days later, the Newcastle earthquake shocked Australians, who were unaccustomed to such damaging quakes.

Bruce has been working full-time as a clairvoyant for six years now and also teaches others how to develop their natural intuitive and psychic talents. With two books to his name and a strong media profile, he is considered an expert in his field. 'My healing ability came first, then clairsentience, then clairvoyance. The cap was trance mediumship which was studied for in earnest.' As a trance medium, Bruce delivers information directly from a spirit guide or spiritual source. He defines spirit guides as 'earth's graduating class', being, in his opinion, souls who have learned their earthly lessons and who take on the task of helping us to get through school too. Their ultimate goal is to reconnect us with the divine creative source or, as Bruce likes to express it, they 'act as the introduction agency to God'.

The following passage from his book, *How to Interpret a Psychic Reading*, is an example of one of Bruce's psychic deliverances on the purpose of life. It clearly states his position on the question of free will versus fixed destiny.

> *It is said by some that before we are born we plan out all the events, circumstances and people to meet that will give us the ideal environment for our learning. We then become human and in the process selectively forget about the plan. On this blueprint we arrange to meet certain people at certain times in our lives to experience certain things. Usually these times are conditional on us reaching specific stages of personal development. Psychics can predict the future because they can access the information source relating to the blueprint.*

In other words, Bruce sees a preplanned destiny which can be overridden by free will. We may, in Bruce's view, have fixed a date with destiny to experience an aspect of life we need to understand, but if we are not ready for the lesson, or if we have been an ace student and already got the message, we need not turn up. By accessing the blueprint, the psychic is therefore, according to Bruce, reading the original projected plan, which may or may not eventuate.

While the psychic has access to life's blueprint, he does not have to wade through the plans himself. Bruce's method is to be the intermediary, having a spirit or spirit guide consult the information and sift out what the client needs to know. The psychic tunes in to the spirit and simply passes on the messages.

'I don't read people. I communicate what Spirit wants me to give them.

Therefore my connection is with my guides not with the person. My most accurate skill is tuning in to my guides. They do the rest.'

The role of a spirit guide is to introduce the client to the 'destiny of your choosing, without interfering in the process of individual choice'.

As an example, Bruce tells the story in his book of a reading he did for a couple, Sue and Owen, in 1994. He opened the reading with the message, '"Well, I hope you like the United States of America because I can see you living there ..."' The couple were delighted, as this was one of their greatest wishes. Six months later, Sue rang Bruce.

She was very disgruntled! 'We are still in Australia. Have you ever been wrong before?!' Dumbfounded, I muttered something and she continued, 'My husband and I were so confident in your reading that we even cancelled the order for our new furniture.' The penny dropped. I explained to her that she and her husband were the missing ingredients. They had stopped living and were waiting for nirvana—two airline tickets to California.

The point was that Sue and Owen were on course for their 'date with destiny', but because they went home and changed things in readiness for the predicted move, they missed out on the chain of events which would otherwise have led them there. Bruce advised them to forget about the original prediction and get on with life for the next six months. This was the length of time they had steered off course so Bruce estimated it would also be the length of time needed to make up the distance. Naturally the story had a happy ending. Owen rang Bruce this time.

He rang to tell me they were at the airport waiting for their flight to Los Angeles. It transpired that his employer offered him the same promotion that he rejected after the reading because he thought he was going to

America. This time he took it. Within weeks, personnel advised him that this position was redundant and that a similar position was vacant in America. Did he want to go?!

It's important to point out here that Bruce's readings, in his estimation, are derived from two sources.

'About fifty per cent is from my guides, while the other fifty per cent is based on intuition, which is, when we think about it, both coming from the same source—God.'

In other words, guides bring outside information, such as blue-print details, while the reader's intuition brings inner knowledge from 'the perfect self within'. Bruce's experience of God is the all-encompassing whole that feeds both sources.

Now I was beginning to understand Bruce's air of conviction and confidence in his radio predictions. His messages are God-given, but it is up to the client to decide whether or not to act on the information or to allow the foreseen future to unfold. Consequently his predictions are possible or likely outcomes, but his faith in their source is one hundred per cent firm.

In his book Bruce describes his connection with God.

When I give a reading I know when some information is about to come through me because I am filled with the most beautiful sense of peace … This euphoric sensation I believe is evidence of God.

I asked Bruce where his responsibilities lay.

'I believe that what I am given must be transmitted, so I read on the understanding that Spirit will make its decision. I am just the vehicle not the evaluator of the information. I "give what I get" so I usually don't see the whole picture. It is none of my business anyway to know the nitty-gritty details. If I am having difficulty in interpreting the information, then

quite often I am given a much broader look at the situation so that I can put it into context for the client.'

His vision, then, is one of identifying, by God-given psychic or intuitive means, the future potential of his clients, and then encouraging them to take appropriate actions to fulfil that potential. The necessary action may be simply to stay on course or it may be to consider an alternative path. Either way, the client is the one who needs to make the choices and take responsibility for his or her future. Bruce sees 'inspiring people to find their own creative genius' as the most important part of his work. The down side rears its head 'every time a person will not accept responsibility for their lives and expect me to do it for them'.

Putting Bruce's view into my metaphor, he perceives a world where we each carry a road map, or blueprint, with a preselected route marked in invisible ink. Before birth we chose the ideal route to bring us our much needed lessons of life and nominated the co-voyagers we would meet along the way. Once born we carry the map around knowing we have the freedom to travel any path, but somehow sensing that life is a game, the object of which is to find the right path to bring us, via destiny, to a sense of God. We visit psychics searching for the magic eye that can see the inked route invisible to our own eyes. If only we could get on the right path, everything would be fine! Enter the paradox: the psychic may well possess the inner eye and may describe the right road and how to get on it, but you, the client, must take responsibility and make a choice based on free will before destiny becomes a reality. The ultimate lesson of life is taking responsibility for our thoughts and actions via choice.

Now, Bruce's theory requires certain aspects of our road map to be in place. We may choose whether or not to join a church, go to university or take part in a protest march, but if these are critical points in our individual life journey, then the church, the university and the protest march need to exist regardless of our choice to be on the same grid reference or not. On a simple level, this fits neatly with Bruce's observation that 'world or major events that are not personal always seem to be fixed. Otherwise any scenario is changeable if on a personal level'.

World disasters are a case in point. Bruce has predicted large scale events, such as the Newcastle earthquake earlier in this story. He believes the sole purpose of predicting a disaster is to warn people so that they can choose to avoid it or, where possible, take action to avoid the disaster happening. An air crash may be predicted, for example, but the forewarned can choose to take another plane or to warn the airline company to check the plane or cancel the flight. If Bruce's initial observation is correct, though, and impersonal events always seem to be fixed, the only real option would be to take another plane. This is where the theory gets murky! World events encompass people: a decision to declare war or launch a nuclear bomb is made by a person, or a collection of people, and it is the destruction of human lives that turns a natural event such as a volcanic eruption into a disaster. Where does the 'changeable personal level' end and where do the 'fixed world or major events' begin? On the blueprint map level, the church, the university and the protest march were envisioned, built or organised by people, so they are the outcome of the changeable personal level. Through such argument the borderline between the changeable and the fixed becomes blurred. Unless, of course, free will and choice is an illusion, and we were always destined to follow the original blueprint, always destined to make the choices which fulfil the grand fixed plan.

Perhaps Bruce's understanding of the nature of time would solve this paradox. I asked him how he saw time. 'I wish I knew. This one I have never been able to fathom for myself.' Once more I am struck by Bruce's faith and conviction. I realise he has no need to know the intellectual ins and outs because he has faith.

He has no need to analyse the overlapping pieces of the jigsaw puzzle to work out why they don't fit the theory. His theory is an approximation to the truth, but his truth is more relevant and important than the man-made puzzle pieces.

Bruce Way can be contacted through:

PO Box 5168
Chatswood West
NSW 2057
Australia

Summary Memo

The general consensus among the four clairvoyants was:

- 3/1 Some form of spirit (either Spirit, spirit guide or deceased person) helps with their readings. Two see themselves solely as couriers or vehicles delivering information from this source.

- 3/2 Free will is largely, if not wholly, the determinant of our individual futures.

- 3/3 Some degree of the future *may* be fixed.

- 3/4 Time is irrelevant to precognition: either there is 'no time' or 'the only time is now'.

- 3/5 Aspects of their readings are often received and delivered in symbolism.

- 3/6 They predict 'probable', 'possible' or 'likely' future outcomes.

- 3/7 Responsibility of the client for their own future is seen as paramount.

hypnotised into the future 4

I stumbled out of the house, blinking in the bright light of the afternoon. I had just had a reading with a clairvoyant as part of my research for this book and I felt disorientated and muzzy. How could I have lost track of so much time, I thought, especially when each tick of the clairvoyant's watch was clocking up the expensive bottom line for my consultation.

We're all familiar with that sense of timelessness, often experienced during periods of intense focused concentration, bliss, fun, meditation, daydreaming, dreaming or anaesthesia. Perhaps, during my clairvoyant reading, it was my focus and concentration on the psychic's words combined with the heady mix of receiving so much personal attention that lulled me into that timeless limbo. Or was it?

As I drove away I experienced a certain confusion. My attention to the road seemed perilously vague, and my physical body felt strangely without boundary. I felt floaty, ungrounded and imagined my body as a kind of blurred image seen through an unfocused lens. I pulled over and stopped to breathe fresh air, feel the grass beneath my feet, look at the distant horizon and the busy landscape and, most grounding of all, eat a bar of chocolate.

Had we shared a journey into a different dimension, a timeless place, the clairvoyant and I, leaving me with interdimensional travel sickness? Was I simply temporarily maladjusted to my return into the world of linear time? Had we moved together beyond the physical limits of our bodies and exchanged information at a dizzying rate in the ethereal, invisible realms of our fused subconscious or unconscious minds?

Were my physical and mental co-ordination confusions symptomatic of my brain trying to regain its previous perception of myself, including the boundaries of my physical body, while also trying to incorporate the clairvoyant's view of my past, present and future life? Or would a new image of myself be required to fit in with all this new information from the psychic reading, assuming I chose to consider it of course? Would I move forward to live the future that befitted a person like the new me?

Or had the psychic simply informed me about my predetermined future which would necessarily occur in spite of my confused state of mind?

In the long run, some of the things she mentioned did happen, but in the short-term I wondered whether my symptoms were the result of some kind of hypnosis or trance. Could a psychic reader, knowingly or (most probably) unknowingly, hypnotise a client in such a way that the client then unconsciously carried out steps to ensure that the 'predicted' future occurred? Although I had not, to my knowledge, been hypnotised before, my post-reading symptoms left me wondering about this possibility and I needed to investigate it.

I started by contacting John Suess, a well-known and successful hypnotherapist in Queensland, and asking him to describe how hypnosis can change a person's outlook and achievements.

Time Progression

'We call it "time progression",' explained John, describing the basic theory of therapy under hypnosis.

'The hypnotherapist helps the client to create a mental map by essentially taking a past situation into a similar future situation and discovering how it might be, given the changes we might have made.'

In the case of a smoker wishing to quit cigarettes, for example, hypnotherapy begins only after a discussion to determine why the smoker wants to kick the habit. This is to check that quitting smoking will not bring about an undesirable outcome, such as the emergence of an alternative habit, or the surfacing of emotional issues which the smoking had masked and the client will need to be ready to handle. John is alert to the dangers of hypnotism and uses techniques that ensure, to the best of his ability, that he obtains both the client's conscious and unconscious agreement to the therapy at each stage of the process.

Getting the smoker, for example, to undergo time progression during hypnosis and to project him- or herself into the future scenario of being offered a cigarette gives the hypnotised client the opportunity to experience the nonsmoking alternative self. John continues,

'Now certainly on one level that's imagination, but on another level it's highly predictable. That is to say, how people perceive that experience will be, probably ninety-five per cent of the time, how it is involuntarily.'

In other words, after making no-smoking choices during hypnotherapy and experiencing themselves as nonsmokers in a future situation, they almost invariably become nonsmokers. They powerfully envision and they become.

A caring professional hypnotherapist uses precise techniques to induce a hypnotic trance and chooses his or her words during the hypnotherapy process with integrity. The wrong words at the wrong moment could be disastrous. So could a psychic reader without training unknowingly induce a hypnotic state and invite the client to envision and experience a suggested future which then becomes a reality? Is a psychic, unaware perhaps of the power of hypnotherapy, capable of transforming the smoker into the nonsmoker, the single into the married, the married into the divorced, the underachiever into the achiever, the nonsinger into the singer, the financially struggling into the rich benefactor, the wealthy into bankruptcy, the sick into health and the healthy into sickness—the list is endless—albeit in innocence?

I was particularly mindful of the controversy over the use of hypnotism to uncover so-called repressed memories. Those who apparently recalled 'forgotten' or 'repressed' traumatic memories under hypnosis frequently absorbed these experiences into their conscious minds following the hypnosis session. In other words, they regained full sensual conscious awareness of the remembered event, together with an unshakeable insistence that it had really happened. Many hypnotists, however, argue that 'suggestions' about past traumas are easily implanted under hypnosis, and that the power of the hypnotic trance is such that the client, on resurfacing, then 'recalls' the suggestion as a 'real' remembered event, complete with associated emotional impact. The same arguments, of course, can be applied to the question of regressing people under hypnosis, not only to early childhood, but beyond into past lives.

Whether or not hypnosis restores genuine memories, implants a false past or transforms the smoker into a nonsmoker, one thing is for sure: the person who leaves the hypnotist's chair walks forward a changed person, a person with a new self-image and, presumably, a changed future. I asked John whether he believed hypnosis played a role in changing future outcomes during clairvoyant readings. He was of the opinion that genuine clairvoyants certainly exist, but that lesser scrupled hypnotists, or people with some degree of training in the subject, can and do earn public acclaim as psychics through applying simple hypnosis techniques. In between, however, he believes there are many clairvoyants working with genuine intent, blissfully unaware that they have not fully developed their psychic skills and that their success is, in fact, largely due to their unrecognised ability to induce suggestions.

'Some know it, some don't,' John ventures. *'They commonly won't look at you, but they're picking you up peripherally. They start by making some general statements and follow with some general questions, looking for feedback. This is what we call "pacing you" in hypnosis. Then they'll start making some general suggestions about the past, and before long they've induced you into thinking about your past and living that. Then they get dangerous: they start making suggestions about how the future will be and you may well make it come true if they are received as posthypnotic suggestions.'*

I thought back to my disorientated postreading feelings and asked John what, in his opinion, a tranced or hypnotised person would feel like at the end of such a reading.

'Most people in trances don't know they're there. The hardest thing to do in most people is to make them know or ratify trance experience. It is possible to chat to somebody and slip them in and out of trances without doing anything to ratify consciousness.'

So, if you were a client being hypnotically tranced during a psychic reading, it seems you probably wouldn't realise it. However, my experience was to feel disorientated after the reading, so I asked John what posthypnosis symptoms might present in such a case. Apparently the response varies enormously.

'The more the information someone receives mismatches their view of the world, or the more vague it is, the more their brain has to search to make sense of it. When you're creating conflicts in people, you can get all the typical signs of a conflict: posttraumatic stress disorder being an extreme example. Alternatively some people become totally compliant, feeling wonderfully at peace, or just not thinking.'

In the very least, it seems, the reaction, if it occurs, is after the event. My postreading confusion could have been the result of conflict induced through suggestion. Certainly in later months when I did experience hypnosis with John, I was always in a slightly different head space for a few hours after each session. I felt relaxed and light, but friends or colleagues sensed me as vague and spacey, apparently not my usual presentation! By contrast, under hypnosis I felt fully aware and conscious, although I was also aware that I was lolling around falling over the arm of the chair, strangely unable to sit back up properly: hardly fitting behaviour in front of a man I barely knew and in a professional situation! If I was at all hypnotised during my psychic reading, I was not aware of it at the time, maintaining my seated composure, as far as I recall. In general, though, John's descriptions fitted my experiences in the reading and he had confirmed that hypnosis may play a role in the successful outcome of some clairvoyant readings. Then he added another dimension:

NLP: controlling the future without hypnosis

Apparently you don't need to be under hypnosis to receive powerful suggestions directly into your unconscious. As an NLP (neurolinguistic programming) trainer, John is particularly aware of the use of nonverbal communication. Looking someone in the eye, for example, reinforces a word, while looking away reduces its impact. If you look someone in the eye and speak more firmly, this too increases its power. So does touching the person when speaking the key words. Now, take a simple sentence such as:

'I advise you to apply for the managerial position. Working as a building contractor could lead to bankruptcy and you don't want that to happen!'

A manipulator, wishing to be seen as supportive of his co-worker's desire to move into management but harbouring selfish reasons to keep him in the building contracting business, could use this sentence to deliver one message on the conscious level and an entirely different message on the unconscious level. This is how it works, according to John's theory.

The manipulator looks away from his co-worker for most of the sentence but turns to look him directly in the eye when he delivers the words 'managerial position', 'bankruptcy' and 'happen'. These three words are then given added impetus by saying them louder and tapping the co-worker's shoulder at the same time. The unconscious then receives the message: 'managerial position bankruptcy happen'. The co-worker has now, theoretically at least, been given two messages. The conscious message is to apply for the managerial position and the unconscious message is not to apply for the managerial position because of an implanted association with bankruptcy. In a battle between the conscious and the unconscious, it is the unconscious which usually wins! Our hypothetical co-worker is most likely to file the managerial job application in the bin.

The point of this example is to illustrate the theory that the unconscious can be programmed without obvious hypnotism and with no conscious knowledge of what is happening. This method could be used by anyone, psychic or otherwise, quite innocently, especially if that person usually speaks with emphasis and tends naturally to drive home important points through eye contact or touch. It would be easy to argue that an intense psychic reading with occasional strong eye contact, emphasised voice or touch, could deliver some powerful conditioning of the unconscious which then becomes a reality. It also satisfies my question, which is that a psychic, or any other person, need not be versed in the skills of hypnotherapy, or even happen upon the magical incantation to induce hypnosis, in order to affect the unconscious mind of another.

What I had learned from John until that point, then, was the possibility that some psychic readings may contain successful predictions because of a degree of hypnotic suggestion or direct communication with the client's unconscious which then acts out the predicted future under instruction. The argument here is not that there is no such thing as a genuine clairvoyant or that all psychic readings are really hypnosis sessions in disguise. Like John, I believe that genuinely skilled clairvoyants make accurate predictions which eventuate without the intervention of NLP or hypnosis. It is simply that, with no way of being able to guarantee the process being used, we need to be aware of the pitfalls. At the same time, I realised hypnosis could be a valuable tool for understanding the parameters which shape our future years.

The Real Adventure Begins!

Now, this is where the really exciting part of the story starts, a story which led me through both the elation of discovery and adventure and the fear that I might lose my sanity or find myself on the edge of something explosively powerful if I progressed any further. The Hypnosis Project results will stretch your credibility and require you to think laterally as well as deeply. As a scientist I dotted as many i's and crossed as many t's as I could when travelling in such open territory. Our hypnosis sessions were held in private and each was recorded onto audio cassette tapes. After each session I transcribed the tapes and sent John a typed word-for-word copy to keep on file. No specific details were discussed with others, except in general terms as reported in this story. Observations were similarly recorded and sent to John as replica copies.

The project was triggered when I was interviewing John about his views on past life regression. He responded that whatever you can do with regression into the past you can do with progression into the future, and that an experiment with progression had been published in the popular press by a dentist who hypnotised a television journalist two weeks into the future and had him read the news on the local television station. Three of the items actually occurred in that he had predicted an airline crash, the site of the crash, a school bus accident, and the name of the Russian general who was fired that day. All three became fact.

We began the project the week following the initial interview, with a simple hypnosis session to see if I was a good subject, as I hadn't consciously volunteered for hypnosis before. In typical scientist fashion I fought the induction suggestions, although I was also eager to get started on the adventure. If the results were to have meaning, I resolved, I would have to be as objective as possible. In retrospect this duality may have occasionally held back my willingness to progress into some areas. It can be difficult to be trusting and objective at the same time. On that first day, however, I consciously observed my upheld palm turn and fall into my lap despite my intention to the contrary, dropping the coin it had held, as the first battle was won. Unconscious mind: 1, Conscious mind: 0. Next week the real fun would begin!

FIRST PROGRESSION HYPNOSIS: 12 SEPTEMBER 1996
'I'm worried about describing something negative, like crashes, explosions or deaths,' I told John before we began. The story about the dentist and the newsreader haunted me because the

three predictions involved death or job loss, and many of the precognitive dreams and visions people had sent to me for my research were about disasters or deaths which later occurred. My own precognitive dreams and visions were generally either positive or apparently trivial. Even death previews, in my case, involved sharing the experience of the peace that would follow the particular death. It wasn't just a matter of wanting to enjoy only pleasant experiences under hypnosis. My deeper concern was ethical.

I was going into this whole thing as open-mindedly as I could, so I was starting with the assumption that all theories of precognition were feasible until proved otherwise. One theory was that the state of hypnotism was such that anything visualised strongly could happen, simply through the power of thought or word. If there was any truth in this theory, I wanted to take a responsible approach and look only for the positive.

Philosophically, of course, this was a naive statement. Enter the age-old question regarding any event objectively: was that a good event or a bad event in the long run? 'Good' events can lead to undesirable consequences just as frequently as 'bad' events can lead to good. For example, accident or loss of material possessions can lead a person to discover their caring or spiritual nature, while winning the lotto has been known to create havoc for the new millionaire. Scientific discoveries such as the use of atomic energy as a potential power source have been devastatingly abused. It's an ancient argument, but in the here and now of the hypnotist's chair, I wanted to stay with the positive, as I saw it.

John retorted that if I wanted to discover the true basis of precognition, I needed to open myself to finding that truth without restriction. People will use or abuse discoveries in any field, he argued, and it is they who take responsibility for their actions. I decided to place total trust in my quest and we went ahead with the project.

Under hypnosis I was asked to find myself somewhere in the future. As previously described, my conscious mind seemed totally aware. It was like being able to experience an event or vision while at the same time making dispassionate conscious observations. In this sense I was in two minds: the experiencer and the observer. It was the observer who communicated with John. It was the same observer who occasionally edited what I saw or changed to another scene or hesitated to give dates when asked. The transcript of that first session reveals much hesitancy and avoidance, at least on behalf of my observer self. I also took refuge in safety and proclaimed most events to be far in the future. That way, presumably, I wouldn't have to face the consequences just yet! Yes, my vulnerability is there in the black and white of that session's typed notes.

The essence of the first session was that I described three scenes. Briefly, the first one concerned being present at a meeting where new communications technology was being discussed and trialled, but I was as reticent about the technology as I was about the session. Pressed for a date, I came up with a Wednesday in May 1998. That felt right.

The second scene seemed to continue on in theme. No date was recorded but I perceived it as being several years later. I was investigating some kind of underground money deal involving an alternative society somewhere in America.

I dated the third vision as sixteen years into the future. I stood on a strangely silent beach watching a burning island. It had been a bird sanctuary but the birds had succumbed to an infection carried by wild pigs. Consequently it was being burned as a cleansing procedure.

My reaction on surfacing from this first session was to tell John that these three visions seemed to me to be dream material. For each I could see symbolism relevant to my life, reflecting especially my thoughts and concerns about the project. If I took each as a dream and interpreted it with respect to my thoughts at that time, they would have made perfect sense. I felt happy with that conclusion, but at the same time typed out the taped conversation we had had during hypnosis for future reference.

Since my dates were so far forward, of course, I cannot comment on the final outcome. However, around March 1997, a number of references from Scene One unfolded on one particular afternoon. I had travelled to Southport with others to edit some of my video tapes into a promo reel. I took a back seat from the technological–communications side which didn't really interest me. Around lunchtime I volunteered to go and buy lunch: a great excuse to escape the electronics. I ended up letting someone else drive my car while I sat in the passenger seat. On our return, when the car was stationary, I realised my windscreen had cracked. At that point I still had my purse on my lap, having spent a twenty-dollar note at the shops. The windscreen crack seemed strangely familiar, and I remembered the 'dream' I had reported under hypnosis.

Later, back at home, I checked the details with the transcript of the hypnosis session. They were not the same as the original script, but some details tallied. According to the transcript I saw a hairline crack in my windscreen while I was in the passenger seat of my car, which was stationary. I was attending a meeting using communications technology in a place I described as being 'not *Ports*mouth but Australia'. (We were in South*port*). I was wearing new brown sandals (which was true) and had a purse on my lap. I mentioned twenty-dollar notes and thought that I must have been shopping. I said that I wasn't taking the meeting, I was 'just there' and added that we were making plans for the future, setting something up. I also noted that a cat was present and that the pictures on the wall contrasted in period with the technology: both statements were accurate.

There were other similarities. At the same time there was plenty that did not fit the original scene. I was surprised, though, that many elements appeared, all on the same day, albeit that the given date was much further in the future. Final observations will need to be drawn when that date has been reached.

I can see hints of Scene Two emerging at the time of writing: tenuous but worthy of observing. Tantalising as it is, I will have to reserve judgement on that one at this stage.

So, in summary, I felt session one related well to my dreaming mind and carried pertinent symbolism at the time.

SECOND PROGRESSION HYPNOSIS: 3 OCTOBER 1996

The first scene witnessed during this session was very safe and domestic. 'Not again,' thought my conscious observer self. 'When will she get a bit more adventurous, take a few risks?' I started by watching sunlight warm a window seat and went on to describe the room which seemed very much like our lounge room, although I questioned whether it was. I gave the date as Monday 22 October. I thought we might have been to watch my fifteen-year-old son, Euan, playing his tenor sax in a band the day before and that there were about thirty people there and a bar. I noted, 'But he's young to play in a place with a bar.' I said the day before had had something to do with gold rings, though I added, in afterthought, that they might have been gold curtain rings. From there I was transferred to a plaza and was standing looking at a fountain, believing it now to be Friday. I said I was buying shoes.

I obviously thought I should get some adventure going for the second scene because I switched to 23 October of an undefined year and described a procession connected with Disney and metal chainlink, somewhere in America. President Clinton was there. At the end of the parade there seemed to be some kind of emergency or curfew, and I believed this was now Russia: 'Minsk'. By the time the political contract was signed I decided, while still hypnotised, that this was really just a dream.

Immediately after this session I felt dissatisfied. The second scene seemed very dreamlike and there was nothing I could do but put it on the 'we'll see' pile. The first scene was weak and particularly devoid of detail. My son was enjoying a good run of band gigs, so that part was foreseeable. We had just moved into the new house the week before so I had been observing decorating details, and I had no intention of buying new shoes. To top it all, when I looked at the calendar, Monday was 21 October, not the 22nd.

Back at home I transcribed the tapes and sent John his copy. Although my dates seemed slightly inaccurate, I decided to go along with the general theme of the second last weekend in October and wait to see if any of my mundane descriptions fitted. As far as the family (or anyone else) was concerned, they knew I was undertaking hypnosis experiments to try and predict the future, but they had no idea of content. They were, of course, suitably annoyed at being shut out of secret knowledge!

The first development took place the same afternoon as the session, when Glen announced that he had bought himself two new pairs of shoes that afternoon—a couple of hours after my session, as it turned out. It had been about twelve months since he last bought shoes. Well, it was a vague connection: after all, I was supposed to be the one with the new shoes. I somehow managed to engineer the totally offbeat question, 'Was anyone looking at a fountain today?' into the conversation, to which Glen replied, 'Yes, I spent the afternoon installing a papier mâché fountain into a show.' Curious, but perhaps not curious enough. I wrote it down anyway.

A few days later I was moving our furniture around, looking for the best layout for our new home. I put an antique wooden blanket box under the window, thinking it suited the room. Later I sat on the box with a cup of coffee and leaned on the windowsill, enjoying the view of the neighbour's garden. I realised then that I had unconsciously created the window seat of my session. I wondered whether I would have put the box there if I hadn't been hypnotised. Perhaps this is a very simple example of carrying out something previsioned by the unconscious mind. Alternatively I may have unconsciously solved the problem of what to do with the window while under hypnosis and then simply applied it later in the week.

Now, that mundane example brings up another possibility: that what we imagine or see as the future is a result of the unconscious working out a creative solution to a problem or advancing a likely outcome to a situation before the conscious mind is ready to address it. In other words, our precognitive insights could just be the result of the unconscious projecting ahead. The unconscious generally has much more creative and insightful solutions to offer than the conscious mind, so we might well react with surprise when a 'prediction' is seen to come true. All that has really happened is that the unconscious has delivered. Perhaps.

But let's move ahead to the anticipated weekend. Yes, Euan did play a public performance that had not been booked at the time of the hypnosis. It was on the Saturday, not the Sunday. It was at an outside venue which he had not played before and the stage was side on to a beer garden, so the 'he's young to play in a place with a bar' comment noted during my session was solved. We enjoyed a beer while we watched and, yes, I counted about thirty people in the audience.

Saturday was the day the mysterious gold rings were predicted to appear. In the early evening we went to the movies and saw *First Wives Club*. It was opening night and we were last in so we were in the front rows and the screen was up close and large. Somewhere near the beginning of the movie the camera zoomed in on a wine glass as the three women dropped their wedding rings into the wine. A whole screen of gold rings loomed large before me. Was I originally correct in the hypnosis in saying they were rings (meaning finger rings)? My lateral thinking started working over-time in the cinema to find a place for the curtain rings. The best

I came up with was that it was 'curtains' (divorce) for the three women in the movie, and that movie theatres have curtains in front of the screens. 'It's amazing what you can come up with if you want to,' I mused, and settled back to enjoy the film.

On the Sunday we kept an invitation to visit friends for lunch. Throughout this two-week period my scientific self had been working overtime to make sure I didn't wander into any shoe shops or stop and linger over fountains. If there was anything to prove here, I reasoned, it was going to have to happen with no conscious prompting from me. On the way to lunch Glen pulled the car over to visit some markets and I found myself reading the plaque on a fountain as we passed by, disappointed that I had come face to face with something from the session which I had been trying hard to avoid! We enjoyed our lunch. Our friends knew I was doing hypnosis experiments, but again had no idea of the content. During the afternoon the woman gave me two pairs of shoes she had bought for herself but which were too small for her. So my fountain and my shoes appeared two days later than mentioned in the hypnosis session, and the fact was that the shoes were a gift: I didn't buy them.

I was spooked, but the big question still remained: had I predicted, to varying degrees of accuracy, aspects of a fixed future, aspects of a possible future or ... had I somehow attracted these things into my life, or even created them, by undergoing the hypnosis? If I did attract them, how did I do it?

Stepping neatly away from these emotional and ethical questions, I scientifically summarised the situation so far. 'The following correlations with the hypnosis session were noted with varying degrees of certainty: shoes (twice); band gig; bar at band gig; gold rings; fountain (twice); window seat (tenuous). The predictions had been for a long weekend period two weeks after the hypnosis session. Give or take a few days, this timing was accurate for the majority of the correlations.'

THIRD PROGRESSION HYPNOSIS: 10 OCTOBER 1996

Let's go back in time a little now, because session three took place before the weekend of the shoes, and before we started getting more adventurous.

This time my wanderings took me to 8 December 1997, a day I believed to be a Wednesday. I saw myself in a room I described as containing 'movies, show reels on the shelves, storage space for cinema—not cinema, TV reels—films, people, man sitting, editing, green jumper, editing, editing film tape'. I went on to describe the film he was editing as 'a black and white film' showing 'female face, male face, looks like old movie, historical archives, these are archives'. I said I was involved in researching film archives because I was making a documentary film. I gave details, including some names and numbers, the title of the documentary and then added the name of the man editing the black and white film: 'Steven, the man in the green jumper is.'

The second scene was a flashback to childhood which concluded with the memory of going to a children's Christmas party where I entered a 'big black room' and, without warning, saw huge cartoon characters rushing all over the wall. It was, of course, my first movie, and I had no idea what was happening. I had not yet experienced television. This has always been a conscious memory, and I imagine the hypnosis session brought up the film link for a reason. Perhaps it was the first time my young developing rational mind was challenged by a radically different perception of reality. Whether or not that was personally meaningful, it was interesting to note that I went back in time when the focus was supposed to be on going forward.

In the last scene I was back in the role of researcher again, visiting an institute in Melbourne in March of an undefined year.

At the time of writing this book (April 1997), I have no idea what December 1997 will bring. The 8 December will be a Monday not a Wednesday. Back in October 1996, at the time of the hypnosis, I also had no idea that by February 1997 I would be recording four television programmes. As described earlier (pages 34–35), the television opportunity came out of the blue, at least as far as my conscious mind was aware. It was preceded by a dream which contained shades of precognition, however, so I wonder how much of a part this hypnosis session played either in keying into that future area of work or in creating it.

The thing is, the man who offered me the position and acted as executive producer of the show was named Steven, and he was Irish, which perhaps explains the green jumper. I didn't know of his existence or his name prior to our first meeting on set. One of the guests on my first show was a singer, chosen by Sue Manger, one of the producers. Sue suggested introducing the singer, Jenny Keyes, by playing a clip from a 1960s black and white film of one of her old television performances. Steven edited the film into the programme, and yes, she appeared singing with a male partner, thereby fulfilling the 'female face, male face, looks like old movie, historical archives, these are archives' observation, albeit ten months earlier than predicted. (I have to add here, that no-one had seen the content of the hypnosis session or heard mention of any details. Since nothing had transpired from the session at that stage, it hadn't become a topic of conversation. It was still in the wait and see basket.)

I've had some remarkable experiences with precognition in my life. The examples given in Chapter 1 were but a few of so many. Even so, as the full significance of Steve, the editing, the film and so on dawned on me, I felt numb and expansive. Each time I realise a connection between a precognition and the actual event, I have the strange sensation of losing the contours of my physical body, feeling light and formless rather than solid and confined. It is similar to the feeling described in the introduction to this chapter, the 'spaced-out, post psychic reading' feeling, yet, unlike the confusion generated by the reading experience, this is more of an enlightenment. If you ask me to describe that enlightenment, however, I just can't find the right words. Meanwhile, the Steven story did not stop there.

What is extraordinarily interesting, and maybe revealing at this point, is that Steven edited the wrong song. Sue had chosen a segment where Jenny sang alone, but Steven chose the duet. It was Steven's mistake that resulted in more adherence to the original prediction: 'female face, male face'. Had my prediction foreseen Steven's change of mind, or had Steven unwittingly been subject to my unconscious plan? Also, if all this was connected in some way to the hypnosis session, why was it happening so much earlier than predicted?

As a result of those February shows, I have extended my career in television and we are in the middle of negotiating a series as I write. I found myself surrounded by supportive friends and colleagues who virtually formed a production team around me and then invited me in! I don't feel the choice was consciously mine. Fait accompli! How much of this was due to the hypnosis? Would it have happened regardless: was I truly seeing the future under hypnosis, or has my unconscious been marching to orders received back on 10 October 1996? Now put yourself in the place of Steven, or in the shoes of Sue, the producer, who had the film clip idea and ask the same questions. It gets scaringly interesting, doesn't it?

But these developments are way ahead of our story. Back at home at the end of October, looking at my two new pairs of shoes, I felt it was time to be more precise about our hypnosis experiments.

The first stage, I believed, was to begin to investigate the question of the ability of the unconscious, under hypnosis, to create the future. I wanted to know if talk of the shoes, rings and other things under the powerful conditions of hypnosis had somehow created, or manifested, them into my future. It was a difficult question to design an experiment around. Indeed, proper scientific analysis would require more than a few sessions and a multitude of scientific controls to be set up. Remembering that a journey of a thousand miles begins with a single step, and that scientists fear to go where angels tread, I planned our next session. Not as an angel, I hasten to add, but as a scientist willing to enter the world of mystery with my analytical skills to the fore, regardless of whether or not that would satisfy another scientist. I had to start somewhere!

FOURTH PROGRESSION HYPNOSIS: 21 NOVEMBER 1996
To understand the experimental rationale I planned for this session, we need to review three possibilities here. I'm starting by assuming that the above stories demonstrate a correlation between the future described under hypnosis and some of the events which subsequently unfolded. The three main possibilities are:

1. The state of hypnosis is sufficiently intense that it amplifies any ability, proven or latent, that I might naturally have to predict the future with varying degrees of accuracy.

2. The state of hypnosis is sufficiently intense that the scene, vision or spoken description imprints on the unconscious in such a way that it acts on the suggestion and creates, to its best ability and by some mechanism, the best match in the future.

3. The state of hypnosis is one in which it is possible to transcend the present and experience either a predetermined or an already existing future. Descriptions of that future, and the predictions stemming from it, may differ slightly from the actual events for a number of reasons. For example, the future picture might be misunderstood or some of the substance lost in the interpretation. A second example is that such hypo- thetical 'time travelling' might access any number of alter- native parallel futures, so that the actual future which I later

experience in my own reality might differ from the alternative future I previewed.

There are other possibilities, but for the sake of argument, and for the sake of taking that first step of a thousand miles, I started with these.

I wanted to test number two: that the hypnotised unconscious plays a strong role in creating the future. It wasn't necessarily because I believed this to be the case, but I felt it was the easiest to test.

The difficulty in designing the experiment was to find some way of eliminating points one and three from the test conditions. The general idea was to select various subjects before I was hypnotised, tell John about these, and then ask him to discuss them with me once I was under hypnosis. The three subjects were each to represent a different category: a physical object, a number and a concept. By choosing the subjects prior to hypnosis, I successfully eliminated point three from the equation, that the state of hypnosis is one in which it is possible to transcend the present and experience either a predetermined or an already existing future (unless, of course, I had seen these subjects during a previous hypnotic time travel session and had, in the meantime, forgotten!).

I still needed to eliminate point one which allows for the possibility that I already have an ability to predict the future, an ability which hypnosis merely amplifies. If this is true, then I might unwittingly use these skills when choosing my subjects prior to being hypnotised. In other words, I could be using accurate prediction skills to select subjects which are very likely to make an appearance in my future, and then reinforcing this possibility under hypnosis.

Most psychics say that in order to give a reading or make a single prediction, they prepare themselves in some way. It might be a ritual, it might be prayer or meditation—any process which

effectively slows the psychic's brainwave pattern to a more receptive state. The general agreement is that they tune in before
making predictions.

Based on this 'tune in to predict' assumption, I decided the
best defence against point one was to think up my chosen three
subjects while focusing on being alertly rational, as far away
from tuned in as I could be. As a kind of control I also asked
John to pick three subjects too, to keep them to himself and
then to introduce them into our discussion once I was hypnotised.
The rationale here was that it was unlikely that we would both be
able to accurately predict subjects which might come into my
life. John and I had no contact outside his hypnotherapy clinic, so
he knew too little about my life to be able to make a good bet as
to what might be coming up for me—unless, of course, he was
psychic.

We chose a date of 4 December, two weeks after the hypnosis
session, as the due-by date for the manifestation of our chosen
subjects. The idea was to see which category, if any, came up, and
how. Future experiments, I thought, could be planned based on
these initial observations.

These were my subjects. The descriptions of how I specified
them are crucial to the story.

Subject 1: A Physical Object: 'A Bunch of Flowers: orange and maroon'

When I told John 'A bunch of flowers,' he replied, 'What colour?'
I looked down at the blouse I was wearing, a print fabric of large
petalled orange flowers set amongst maroon strips and borders
and said, 'Orange and maroon, like my blouse.'

Subject 2: A Number: '174—a cheque for $174'

I realised as I said this that my number had also become a physical
object by introducing the cheque, but I left it at that. At first I'd
said, '$174.80,' trying to make it such an odd number that I'd be

completely surprised if it turned up. Then I thought that was being overprecise, and we left it at $174.00.

Subject 3: A Concept: 'The Chinese Wall'
By this I did not really mean the physical Great Wall of China, but that someone would mention the Chinese Wall as a conceptual reference in a conversation. I have no idea why I did not name it properly as the Great Wall of China.

John wrote these down and then silently added his own list. The hypnosis session was carried out and we discussed these subjects under hypnosis. After the session, John summarised his three subjects for my records:

> **Subject 1: A Physical Object: A Bull**
> **Subject 2: A Number: John said he had chosen '2.5' but hadn't mentioned it verbally during the session.**
> **Subject 3: A Concept: A Poem**

John's subjects introduced a whole new angle, as I will reveal later. For the meantime, we'll start with mine: the bunch of orange flowers, the cheque for $174.00 and the concept of the Chinese Wall.

Firstly an important aside about the hypnosis session itself. After we had discussed my three subjects, John encouraged me to describe the surroundings I found myself in before he introduced his items into the conversation. I described finding a letter in our home mailbox addressed in French to 'Madame'. Then I thought I was in 'somewhere like Tibet' looking at a leather satchel on 27 November. Invited by John to look inside it, I replied that it seemed to be empty but smelled of goatskin.

First off the rank the next evening was the address to 'Madame', which was a very encouraging start. We have a post office box, so receive very little mail addressed to our home. We had no connections in France at that time. That evening, in a Mexican restaurant, the waitress came to our table to collect our drinks order. Glen referred to me as 'Madame', not in an attempt at grandeur but as part of an old joke: the 'Madame will have—sorry, I shouldn't call you Madame, I don't even know your profession' one. Not at all funny and we had heard it before, though not for a long time and never directed to me. It also seemed bizarre in a Mexican restaurant. It was, however, an 'address' to 'Madame' with a 'French' reference and was a 'home' joke. Naturally, as always, the family knew nothing about the hypnosis project other than the fact that I had chosen three things to see if they came up within the next two weeks.

On 27 November Glen bought himself a new mobile phone. Apart from the prefix the number was 081 774: the precise digits of the predicted '$174.80' (with an extra 7 left over). Now, I hadn't programmed the eighty cents into the hypnosis session, remember. It was discussed prior to the session and then dropped in favour of the simpler $174.00. I asked Glen if he chose his number or selected it from a given list, but he said it was the first one offered and he liked the look of it so he took it. As a bonus they added a leather pouch for the phone, although they were out of stock and it was a few weeks before it arrived. Notice that the date of Glen's purchase, 27 November, was the date I gave in my hypnosis for the episode with the goatskin satchel. I wondered how much the satchel I envisioned under hypnosis predicted the mobile phone pouch. When it finally arrived it carried no identifying label, so I have no idea of either its country or animal of origin. It was, however, soft leather, as in the vision.

So, the number didn't manifest as a cheque and emerged in jumbled order: 081 774. In discussion with John later, he explained that the right brain, under hypnosis, will often remember the numbers individually, as in this case; for example, '1', '7' and '4', rather than '174' (or even 174.80). The right brain also tends to sum the individual numbers together, as in 1 + 7 + 4 = 12. I have noticed the same predilection for number handling in dreams. This discussion took place at the end of the two-week period. During the fortnight I had noticed that the number 12 or references to a dozen kept coming up. I had been confused, and even wondered whether John's chosen number item 2.5 had actually been 12, and that he had tried to throw me off the scent by telling me, after the session, that it was 2.5. Looking back at the right brain addition idea, I could see an argument for having been hypnotised to create 12s during the test period. Applying the same addition principle to John's 2.5 (2 + 5) gives 7. Perhaps that was the source of the additional 7 in Glen's new phone number!

The Chinese Wall as a conversational concept did not manifest during the two-week period. At one point it seemed close when a chiropractor, standing in for my usual practitioner, told me a long story about his trip to China to study further techniques. He must have chatted on for about fifteen minutes and I was careful not to ask any leading questions because I didn't want to prompt mention of the Chinese Wall myself. He didn't anyway. Advancing a totally 'off the wall!' analysis, I could say he discussed some of the obstacles (walls?) encountered in working with the Chinese from an Australian perspective. The argument would be that I did indeed predict or manifest the *concept* of a Chinese wall, but perhaps that's stretching the limits a bit too far!

After the due date of 4 December, the Great Wall of China came up several times. On the 5 December I collected the free colour magazine from our mailbox and noticed a photograph of some people Glen knows through his business, so I started to read the accompanying article. It was a 'What's your favourite holiday destination?' type story. Halfway through it was revealed that they enjoyed business related dress-up parties held on the Great Wall of China. (Now that's a concept to consider, isn't it?!)

On 8 December my brother introduced the subject of the Berlin Wall, but the Chinese Wall didn't come into the picture.

That evening, however, he asked Glen which was the most impressive magic illusion stunt he had ever seen. Glen said, 'Walking through the Great Wall of China.' Now by this time, because our project due date had passed, Glen did know about my interest in the Chinese Wall, although I think he might have given that answer anyway. Because the experiment was over, I mentioned it to my brother, who then told me he was sure he had read a piece in the papers during the week about a second Wall of China having been uncovered.

A month later, in January, I received word completely out of the blue that a Chinese publisher had approached my agent with an offer to translate my second book, *Dream It: Do It!*, into Chinese. Was this another spin-off of the hypnosis experiment? Or had I tuned in to my then unknown Chinese publisher as he or she was reading my book, thereby choosing the concept for the hypnosis project? Or is China symbolically very deep and meaningful for me and therefore emerging on many levels in my life? Or was this 'just' coincidence, being several weeks beyond the chosen time frame for the Chinese Wall concept?

The bunch of orange and maroon flowers did not turn up during the test fortnight. About a week before Christmas, though, we were shopping at some markets and Glen bought me two outfits as a present. Pleased with his sale, the vendor tossed me a blouse off another rack and said, 'If that one fits, you can have it as an extra gift.' It did. The bright sunlight reflected gold colours against an orange background. It wasn't until a few days later, when the new blouse was in a pile of fresh laundry alongside the old blouse I had worn to the hypnosis session, that I saw the connection. Out of the sunlight the flower pattern, edged in gold, was actually maroon. Side by side, in indoor light, the two blouses were the same colour. The original hypnosis session had been carried out indoors, so these were the colours I had envisaged when I had looked down at my old blouse and said to John,

'Orange and maroon, like my blouse.' I didn't get a physical bunch of orange and maroon flowers during the test period, but in a way I received more precisely what I had asked for: flowers that are 'orange and maroon like my blouse'. It seems my unconscious had read 'like my blouse' literally, and manifested flowery fabric 'like my blouse'.

And how did John's chosen subjects go? Did they turn up during the test period?

His number 2.5 did not, unless it added to the extra 7 in Glen's phone number as previously described. However, he had said that he had chosen it in his mind but had omitted to discuss it during the hypnosis session.

John's concept was a poem. While I was hypnotised he asked me about the poem. I described the content of a poem, which did not eventuate. However, on 27 November I had a phone call from a friend to say he was bringing a couple of his friends to a talk I was giving two days later. One of these friends was a well-known poet, Bob. I had already met Bob once earlier that month when he attended a previous talk and spent the time writing several verses about dreams. Apparently he had been following my dream talkback radio programme for several years and had been inspired to create a poem. He needed to see me in the flesh and in action to complete it.

So, prior to our hypnosis session I knew about the poem, but not about its content. Had John, in picking the concept of a poem for our session, picked the subject out of my mind? That had been my reaction under hypnosis, to think, 'Oh, John's picked up on that poem!' After the session I thought it less likely, since a poem is a pretty broad concept. To return to the phone call from my friend on 27 November, I said, 'I'd love to see the poem Bob wrote,' thereby breaking my rule and introducing the forbidden topic myself. 'He's dying to read it to you,' my friend replied, so I invited him to perform it in public at the close of my talk. In the event, not only did Bob perform his excellent poem, but he brought along two other professional poets to parade their stuff too!

Poems and poetry therefore did surface during the test period, apparently initiated by an outsider, prompted a little by me, but then tripling in effect with the appearance of three poets instead of the anticipated one.

John's physical subject was a bull. He introduced it into the hypnosis session with one simple question: 'Can you notice the bull?' My muddled response illustrates my surprise. 'The bull? The bull—yesterday there was a—yeah—it's a long story about bulls from yesterday, in my life. So the bull would be connected in the same way. I have—interesting—the bull in my life at the moment is Chinese pictures.' We continued to have a very rational discussion under hypnosis in which, as far as I was aware, my conscious observer self was telling John about how often the symbol bull had come up in my life that week. Under hypnosis I was already asking myself, 'Is John reading my mind?' Suddenly the thought of him picking a poem earlier as a result of tuning into my mind didn't seem so unlikely after all.

Well, the bull discussion could go on forever. Suffice to say that the day before a woman had phoned me about a dream concerning a bull which led her to a place of needle pines and a sense of spiritual insight. I was sitting at Glen's desk at the time, looking directly at a picture on the wall of a bull walking on water, titled 'I never knew I could walk on water'. That night I opened the book I had been reading and turned to the next page. The first thing I read was a description of a series of twelfth century Chinese paintings known as the ten ox-herding pictures, a series illustrating the stages of spiritual enlightenment. The book described the penultimate scene as portraying pine trees. Maybe the dreamer who phoned me had seen the pictures and had forgotten them. It didn't matter because it was in my life that the bull was making its appearances now. Had John picked up on this, or was his mention of a bull just another in the line of examples which continued to come up for me for a while?

As far as the appearance of bulls in the test period as a possible result of my hypnosis, I must report that no physical bull appeared in my waking life, but I did have a very powerful dream featuring two huge and wonderful bulls on 2 December. Were my dreams applying themselves to the symbolism as a matter of course? Was the symbolism of bulls, begun prior to hypnosis, simply working its way through my system towards resolution of the deeper issue they represented? Or were the dreams manifestations of the hypnotism project?

Head and body reeling with the enormity of it all once more, it was time to slip into dispassionate scientist mode to type up my conclusion.

'In summary, sufficient correlations to the original hypnosis experiment emerged to give weight to point two, i.e. that the state of hypnosis is sufficiently intense that the scene, vision or spoken description imprints on the unconscious in such a way that it acts on the suggestion and creates, to its best ability and by some mechanism, the best match in the future.'

Staggering though, hey?!

FIFTH PROGRESSION HYPNOSIS: 5 DECEMBER 1996
By this time I was beginning to feel rather ambivalent about continuing with the hypnosis project. I had discovered some extremely deep and convoluted connections between my dreams and events occurring for several other people in my life, and I was feeling the fear of uncertainty. I was trying not to analyse too much, just to roll with the project and record my observations, but my dreams were reflecting both a fear of progressing and a confusion with comprehending precognition and time. I felt I needed to take time out and rethink the whole situation. We

decided to make session five the last one, at least in principle. John wanted to test my reactions if he used concept questions aimed at elucidating more concept based answers. This session was John's project and the transcript suggests that I gave the kind of responses he was looking for.

Under hypnosis I believed I was in 1857 where I described a geometrical analysis of astronomy; from this point we roved towards present time and I ambled on about models of 'holographic geometry' before I took refuge in a Slavonic carrot garden! My conscious observer self was thinking, 'Yes, Jane. The edge of madness! Need for time off confirmed!' Towards the end, walking down a narrow road towards a church believed to be 'ten years in the future' I saw 'a bee or a wasp. I don't know what that's got to do with the church'. I finished off with some reference to that famous line, 'Death, where is thy sting', noticed a numbness in my ankles and mumbled something about the trinity: 'three, trinity, body, mind and soul, coming together of things. There's the bee again. The bee collects the nectar from a flower which blossoms. A bee is in a poem about death. The sting is painful. New beginnings, pain endings—all in the same creature, the bee.' I was beginning to sound like a rambling psychiatric case.

I was glad to finish that session, type up the transcripts and take a break.

That same day, while sweeping the front verandah, I knocked a wasp's nest and was immediately stung on my right palm. It was my first sting, that I could recall, since being a young child. It wasn't a bee, and although the little wasp's nest had been there for months, I did ask for trouble by knocking it. A week later I received a Christmas present of a book from someone who knew that I had been stung by a wasp following a hypnosis session about a bee. I don't think I'd told any further details. The first page featured a piece about the symbolism of the bee in the Rosicrucian order. A stained-glass church window design of a beehive was illustrated on the following page. According to the old Rosi-crucian order, the bee symbolised the soul and the beehive the place where the soul could grow. Had I known or read about this before and forgotten about it, or was I accessing information previously unknown to me? If so, where was I getting it from: the collective unconscious, the mind of another person, a past life, a parallel life, a spirit? Life was getting complicated, and this stung soul needed time out.

I didn't think we'd do a sixth progression hypnosis, but eventually I realised I had to go back and try one last thing, and that turned out to be the most challenging of all.

SIXTH PROGRESSION HYPNOSIS: 19 DECEMBER 1996

I rarely have headaches but I experienced some painful ones at this time and wondered if they had been brought on by the hypnosis or by the intellectual confusion. My experiments so far had indicated that, under hypnosis at least, the unconscious was capable of shaping, creating or manifesting some aspects of my future, occasionally doing so, apparently, by involving other people as actors in my created scenes.

Some of those created scenes were so complex (for example, Steven, Sue and the editing of the wrong piece of black and white film, see page 120) that they seemed beyond the scope of one person's creation. After all, wouldn't everyone else have also been busy unconsciously creating their own futures, even without the accelerated help of hypnosis? Shouldn't we have been battling it all out somewhere in some kind of universal unconscious precreation committee? A battle of unconscious wills perhaps?

It all began to take on the proportions of the 'predicting the ripples created by the pebble in the pond filled with jumping fish ...' analogy which I described in Chapter 3's story on Margaret Stuart (see page 68). In her case I was arguing that it seemed against the odds to be able to predict accurately a detailed future event by projecting present conscious and unconscious forces into the future. Surely, I argued, it is easier to explain detailed clairvoyant accuracy by saying Margaret simply saw a predetermined future. Although our hypnosis experiments strongly suggested that I was creating or manifesting aspects of my own future, exactly how much was I responsible for? I'd have felt much more comfortable, both ethically and scientifically, if I believed I was merely bringing some extra things into the framework of either a predetermined or a chance future, rather than creating it in its entirety. Where, after all, would such creation stop? On the other hand, if we *are* totally responsible for the creation of our futures to the delicate degree of bringing other people into our lives, then we can't react to these experimental results by ignoring the issue. On the contrary, awareness of and responsibility for ourselves and for others would be of paramount importance.

The problem was that I had tested the possibility that I could create aspects of my future and proved to my own satisfaction that I could. However, I still needed to test for aspects of a predetermined, fixed or pre-existing future. After all, several of the clairvoyants in Chapter 3 had indicated the possibility that free will and fixed destiny may, paradoxically, intertwine. This was, I have to admit, my own gut reaction too, but so far I had not sought any evidence for this. For my own mental stability, and hopefully to release the headaches, I needed to have one last hypnosis session to attempt to address the question.

The simplest solution, I decided, was to ask John to hypnotise me and then direct me to look for a predetermined, unalterable event on a specific future date and describe it. Then all we'd have to do would be to wait for the date to come round and see what happened. There were plenty of holes in the experimental design which was based on the supposition that my unconscious self would recognise truth and respond with integrity. I had no guarantee, but I did have headache pain to shift, so we did it.

I asked John to choose the date. He chose 2 January 1997. The transcript of the entire session is included here. All our sessions were of a similar length. It is important for you, the reader, to realise that we were not fitting future events to screeds of tape transcripts, wallowing through ten pages per session looking for two or three sentences which matched events. I'd also like you to experience the sixth session, and its outcome, in the same way that I did.

John always switched my tape recorder on just after he had finished the hypnosis procedure and as he was about to ask the first question.

JS: Good, I'd like you to go ahead and tell me about this predetermined event.

JA: I keep seeing a mountain and a camera—a mountain and a camera is Japan, isn't it?

JS: I don't know. Is it Japan?

JA: And water, crystal coloured water. A holiday resort and plains—plains as well as mountains.

JS: And what's happening?

JA: The emphasis is on the plains now.

JS: And what event is this referring to that's of significance to our interests?

JA: Something to do with horses ...

JS: You can find that data. Tell me about it now.

JA:: Famous horse race ...

JS: Famous horse race ...

JA: But not modern horses—not modern race ...

JS: And what's significant about this horse race?

JA: I don't know. I keep seeing a wire with dots along it, like barbed wire, so ...

JS: And is there a deeper level in the unconscious that can give us more detail?

JA: I've already been going down—down under the ground ...

JS: To what?

JA: I keep seeing just like rooms under the ground, but I'm seeing bells as well ... bells ... so it's confusing. Japanese writing, characters, scripts, bells ringing again, so it could be a ceremony. The horses might not be real horses; they might be made of wire, like frames. Yes, frames.

JS: That's right ...

JA: I'm not seeing anything there any more.

JS: Fine. And is there any information with respect to what may be a predetermined event that this information refers to on the second of January 1997?

JA: I don't know the answer to that but I'm seeing bright blue —as if bright blue is coming up from under the ground now ... breaking through to the surface.

JS: Okay. I want you to let that imagery fade completely. On the very same day, *I'd like you to be interested in discovering some event that has been influenced by the thought of man or men or human beings* [my emphasis]—something that has been caused to occur for comparison as an influence of human thought, projections, ideas, wishes or even dreams. Now tell me, what's coming to mind now?

JA: A car like a jeep, a bicycle ...

JS: And?

JA: Must be a parade. Streamers.

JS: Are there people in the parade?

JA: Can't see the people.

JS: Okay, what can you see?

JA: The car. Inside the car, the seats, the upholstery.

JS: What colour is the upholstery? Is it noticeable?

JA: Red—leather.

JS: And if you look around and you see the edge of the car and the road in which it is moving ...

JA: Black car. Asphalt road.

JS: What else do you notice?

JA: Cornfields, something yellow, like I don't know, it would be France or America. And my body's moving.

JS: To where, to what?

JA: I don't know. I see parachutes coming down in the fields. And the road is bumpy.

JS: And what significance can you put to these events and details, if anything?

JA: Celebration, flags, political celebration.

JS: Which country—do you know?

JA: France or America …

JS: Is there anything else you can notice now?

JA: Birds in a cage.

JS: Which birds are these?

JA: Blue parrots in a cage.

JS: Where is the cage?

JA: In the mountains.

JS: Oh, which mountains?

JA: Back in Japan again. Yellow road. Yellow line. Cartoon characters, characters and outlined in yellow … It's going bizarre now. Big lake.

The next part, very short, revealed a confusing instruction from John. He asked me to discover an event 'absolutely unpredetermined, absolutely happened without the influence of thought'. I described a silver necklace, but dismissed this section of the transcription once I realised the mistake. Then we continued.

JA: It has a silver hand attached to it as if it's being given numbers, numbers like the face of a clock in the background. Clock with no hands. It was very beautiful. It's something for me, so that's strange.

JS: Intriguingly so?

JA: Yes.

JS: And when you've got enough of that, I want you to find again some event that has been influenced and shaped by the thought and actions of man—tell me what that is.

JA: Carved wood, a grandfather clock … grandfather clock … and a watch glass, like a little watch glass with water in the bottom—(What do you want a watch for?)—no … I'm just getting different symbols of time—sundial.

JS: Is there some significance you can place on it? Some meaning that would help?

JA: Well, yes, these are all things that measure linear time, aren't they? So there's two phases of time—yes, this is it—yes, this makes sense. Two types of time … you know, one we influence which is linear time, the one which we don't influence which is no time … and a little red bird like an embroidery …

JS: Gather all you can now, and all you need to gather to understand, and let me know when you've done that gathering … Is that all?

JA: A little red light so that must be stop!

JS: Okay—END.

I took the second half of the transcription to represent my unconscious solution to the paradox of predeterminism and creative manifestation. Then I waited for two weeks to see what 2 January would bring.

It turned out to be an uneventful day. We took an overnight guest to the station and spent the rest of the day at home. We were tired from the New Year celebrations, and I was also aware that 'delivery date' was upon me and I was determined to make it work hard to prove itself, if at all! 'So much for my 2 January predictions!' I thought as we sat down to watch television, settling on an interesting documentary on the Wright Brothers. Vaguely I thought there were slim connections between the programme and the hypnosis session, but saw no further correlations at the time, even though I did go and glance at the transcript. I was aware of still being fearful of what I might discover.

On 9 January I was discussing the hypnosis project in general with Kerry, a good friend, over lunch. When Glen came home the discussion turned to family businesses and by way of example Glen started to tell Kerry about the Wright Brothers documentary. When he used the word plane for the umpteenth time I suddenly had a blinding flash. How stupid! I couldn't believe I was so silly to miss it! I was sure the session started with me describing PLAINS (not planes), but it is the shape and sound of the word the unconscious often prefers over the concept. I went off to get the transcript and brought it back into the kitchen saying, 'Sorry for being rude, but I've just discovered something. Keep on with your conversation and don't mind me. I'll explain later.' They chatted on and I underlined the word bicycle at the exact moment Glen said, 'They were bicycle mechanics actually.' I continued to underline words as follows:

JS: Good, I'd like you to go ahead and tell me about this **predetermined event**.

JA: I keep seeing a mountain and a **camera**—a mountain and a camera is Japan, isn't it?

JS: I don't know. Is it Japan?

JA: And water, crystal coloured water. A holiday resort and **plains—plains** as well as mountains.

JS: And what's happening?

JA: **The emphasis is on the plains now**.

JS: And what event is this referring to that's of significance to our interests?

JA: Something to do with **horses** …

JS: You can find that data. Tell me about it now.

JA: <u>Famous</u> horse <u>race</u> …

JS: Famous horse race …

JA: But <u>not modern horses—not modern race …</u>

JS: And what's significant about this horse race?

JA: I don't know. I keep seeing a **wire with dots along it**, like barbed wire, so …

JS: And is there a deeper level in the unconscious that can give us more detail?

JA: I've already been going down—down under the ground …

JS: To what?

JA: I keep seeing just like rooms under the ground, but I'm seeing bells as well … bells … it's so confusing. Japanese writing, characters, scripts, bells ringing again, so it could be a ceremony. **The horses might not be real horses they might be made of wire, like frames. Yes, frames**.

JS: That's right …

JA: I'm not seeing anything there any more.

JS: Fine. And is there any information with respect to what may be a **predetermined event that this information refers to on the second of January 1997**?

JA: I don't know the answer to that but I'm seeing **bright blue** —as if **bright blue is coming up from under the ground now … breaking through** to the surface.

JS: Okay. I want you to let that imagery fade completely. On the very same day, I'd like you to be interested in discovering **some event that has been influenced by the thought of man** or men or human beings—something that has been caused to occur for comparison as an influence of human thought, projections, ideas, wishes or even dreams. Now tell me, what's coming to mind now?

JA: **A car like a jeep, a bicycle …**

JS: And?

JA: Must be a **parade. Streamers**.

JS: Are there people in the parade?

JA: Can't see the people.

JS: Okay, what can you see?

JA: The car. Inside the car, the seats, the upholstery.

JS: What colour is the upholstery? Is it noticeable?

JA: Red—leather.

JS: And if you look around and you see the edge of the car and the road in which it is moving …

JA: Black car. Asphalt road.

JS: What else do you notice?

JA: **Cornfields**, something yellow, like I don't know, it would be **France or America**. And **my body's moving**.

JS: To where, to what?

JA: I don't know. I see **parachutes coming down in the fields**. And the **road is bumpy**.

JS: And what significance can you put to these events and details, if anything?

JA: **Celebration, flags, political celebration**.

JS: Which country—do you know?

JA: **France or America …**

JS: Is there anything else you can notice now?

JA: **Birds in a cage**.

JS: Which birds are these?

JA: Blue **parrots** in a **cage**.

JS: Where is the cage?

JA: In the mountains.

JS: Oh, which mountains?

JA: Back in Japan again. Yellow road. Yellow line. Cartoon characters, characters and outlined in yellow … It's going bizarre now. Big Lake.

The words I underlined constitute thirty-five per cent of the total number of words spoken by myself in the transcript excerpt above. Some are literal correlations with the documentary, while many are expressed using the more symbolic language of the unconscious (dream symbolism, or right brain language: for the sake of the argument, assume these are equivalent).

These were the connections with the documentary on the Wright Brothers, as I saw it.

JS: **<u>predetermined event</u>**

JA: **camera**
We saw documentary (film) including many photos and lots of original film. A cameraman was taken on one of the earliest flights to film the event. The plane crashed and he was killed—the film survived. Significant to the history of photography, these would have been the first photos taken from a plane.

JA: **plains—plains**
Planes. Glen added that they chose the Kitty Hawk plains in USA for all their test flights (I didn't remember this from the documentary).

JA: **The emphasis is on the plains now**.
Whole emphasis of programme was on planes—and some plains too.

JA: **horses**
Old-fashioned transport?

JA: **Famous** horse **race**
Famous race to build a flying machine.

JA: **not modern horses—not modern race**
Not modern planes—old-fashioned planes.

JA: **wire with dots along it**
Metal struts of planes? Also some of earlier flying machines in documentary.

JA: **The horses might not be real horses they might be made of <u>wire</u>, like <u>frames</u>. Yes. frames**.
Wire frames of biplane wings.

JS: **predetermined event that this information refers to on the second of January 1997**?

JA: **bright blue—as if bright blue is coming up from under the ground now … breaking through**
Bright blue like skies? Strange perception of sky and ground from the air (e.g. in turning flight sky can look like it's coming up from under the ground). The invention and building of the first successful planes was indeed a 'breakthrough'.

JS: <u>**some event that has been influenced by the thought of man**</u>

JA: **A car like a jeep, a bicycle …**
Interesting that I'm still on same topic. The Wright Brothers were bicycle mechanics. On demonstrating the flying planes in France the Wright Brothers were declared winners of the Race to Fly and Glen recalls the documentary showing a parade complete with ticker tape streamers.

JA: **parade. Streamers**.
As above.

JA: **Cornfields, France or America … my body's moving**.
I remember seeing acres and acres of what I thought were cornfields in the USA where they carried out the secret test flights and kept the plane in a secret hangar. The Wright Brothers' first trip overseas was to France where the French and others were demonstrating what they believed were the first flying machines. The Wright Brothers won. A third of the documentary was centred in France and the rest in America. Moving body? Flying??

JA: **parachutes coming down in the fields … road is bumpy**.
French competitors focused on hot-air balloons, not winged machines. Glen thought parachutes were balloons. I wondered if they referred to some of the more bizarre and less successful 'flying' machines in the documentary. Roads there as well as flights would have been incredibly bumpy.

JA: **Celebration, flags, political celebration**.
The celebrations in France to declare the race won. The political component was that the Wright Brothers had hoped the USA government would buy the plans, but (as far as I can recall) it was the French who bought them.

JA: **France or America**
As above.

JA: **Birds in a cage**
They studied birds and bird wings. It was the realisation of the structure of birds' wings and how they moved the wing tips that led the Wright Brothers to design the bits on the plane wings that move to control lift (the engineer speaks!). Cage: could be as in 'caged' (ground bound), or cage could refer to metal strut structure of biplane wings. When one or two men laid flat in the biplane (like flying a hang-glider, as shown in the documentary), the 'bird in a cage' image could be correct.

JA: **parrots … cage**.
Parrots are talking birds? Flying men as talking birds?

Our earlier hypnosis experiments with manifestation had shown that it was my unconscious/right brain picture which manifested over my left brain ideas. (The 'orange and maroon flowers like my blouse', see pages 122, 126–128, and the $174.00, see pages 122, 124–125, for example.) Also our initial hypnosis sessions had seen me describe what I believed to be meaningful dream material, only to be surprised later when some of the symbols from these dreams manifested in my future.

The question was, then, under hypnosis did I use the language of the unconscious to *describe* the documentary (the predetermined event on 2 January)? Or was the process still operating in the original direction, with my symbolic language *creating* the future event which, in this case, was the screening of the documentary film on the chosen date?

My initial conclusion had been that I must have seen a preview of the documentary on television or watched the film before and noticed it advertised again in the print media. It would be easy to register the fact, even unconsciously, and then trot it out for John on demand, in native tongue. I phoned SBS, the television company. It hadn't been screened in Australia before and I hadn't travelled overseas since it was made. It was not advertised in any form until *after* my hypnosis session.

Another possibility was that I had unconsciously accessed, through telepathy, the mind of one of SBS's documentary commissioning editors who had previewed the film.

However, the original purpose of this particular experiment was for me to agree, under hypnosis, to find and experience a 'predetermined, unalterable' event on 2 January. If I responded with integrity and did, in fact, do this, then do the results mean that the screening of that documentary on SBS had been a predetermined, unalterable event since the beginning of time? Did it mean, alternatively, that the screening at the time of the hypnosis was predetermined and unalterable as far as the television programme planners were concerned? Or did it mean that the *subject* of the documentary, that is, the invention of the bi-plane, was the predetermined, unalterable event which was drawn to my attention on the agreed date? If so, then the invention, as indicated by the hypnosis transcript, falls into two fields. One was the aspects of the invention which were predetermined (e.g. the planes flying), while the second was the variables (e.g. France and America as locations).

I may have failed in my integrity and 'simply' found a future probable event, most likely by reading the mind of an SBS employee. If that was 'all' I did, then I still demonstrated an ability, under hypnosis, to access a future event and describe it in detail using the language of the unconscious, or the right brain. I have to draw that conclusion because I find the alternative—the idea that the whole documentary and its screening on that evening was manifested by my unconscious hypnotised mind—just too confronting to believe. Unless, of course, this world and my perception of it is all an illusion after all.

We will return to the mystery of the Wright Brothers' prediction later in this book, but the immediate sequel to this story was that my headaches disappeared. I think I responded to John's closing command under hypnosis on that last session: 'Gather all you can now, and all you need to gather to understand and let me know when you've done that gathering.' I took time out before proceeding with writing this book, by which time the gathering was complete and the conscious understanding had emerged. I suggest you do the same. Take time for this chapter to sink in, to blend with what you may already know. Let it gather momentum and meaning at the deep unconscious level where all is understood.

Summary Memo

i) *General*

- 4/1 An individual's future can apparently be changed through hypnosis. (The assumption is that the individual did not have a fixed future which included the fact that he would be hypnotised on a certain date and emerge a 'changed' person. The assumption may be wrong.) *E.g. pages 104–5.*

- 4/2 Other processes, such as NLP (neurolinguistic programming), can be used effectively to programme a person's unconscious in a way that changes their belief system and therefore changes the way they approach their future life. *E.g. pages 106–8.*

- 4/3 Either of the above processes, hypnotism or NLP, may be used wittingly or, more probably, unwittingly in the course of some psychic readings, so that the client's unconscious then creates the future 'predicted' or programmed by the psychic. *E.g. John Suess, page 109.*

ii) *From the Hypnosis Experiments*

- 4/4 Most visions under hypnosis seemed little different from dreams in content, symbolism, continuity/discontinuity or application in terms of meaning to my personal life and thoughts. The difference was that I was also conscious and therefore not totally immersed in the 'reality' of the dream (*pages 113–14*).

- 4/5 Aspects of these visions (or dreams) surfaced in my waking life days, weeks or months afterwards, either as events or as physical manifestations. Frequently other people became the actors in the waking life versions of my meaningful visions or dreams. *E.g. Steven and Sue, pages 118–19.*

- 4/6 Specific dates given under hypnosis were sometimes inaccurate, especially in relation to days of the week not matching dates (*E.g. Monday 22 October page 114*), and sometimes accurate (*E.g. 27 November page 124*).

- 4/7 There was some suggestion of unconscious problem solving under hypnosis resulting in automatic application of a solution at a future time. Prediction of future events could therefore be due to observation of aspects of the unconscious problem solving process. *E.g. window seat, page 114.*

- 4/8 I was able, using hypnosis, to manifest physical items, numbers and concepts into my life without any conscious follow-through process. Some appeared within the fixed time frame (two weeks) and some appeared a week or two later. These manifestations were not exactly as previewed in my conscious mind but were very strongly related. *E.g. Fourth progression hypnosis, pages 120–29*. Within the parameters of the experiment I was probably creating these aspects of my future under the powerful conditions of hypnosis.

- 4/9 The hypnotist, John Suess, unknowingly demonstrated an ability to link telepathically with me (*E.g. bull, poem, pages 127–29*), suggesting that our relationship during hypnosis may have been synergistic (mutually enhancing our results). This may not be the case in all hypnotist–subject transactions and may have been a contributor towards the success of our experiments.

- 4/10 The manifestations I apparently created came about in ways which involved other people, although this was not intentionally programmed into the hypnosis session. *E.g. Fourth progression hypnosis, pages 120–29*.

- 4/11 The mismatch between the *intention* of my attempts at creating specific manifestations into my future and the *actual* manifestations which resulted can all be explained in terms of the difference between left and right brain language. *E.g. Fourth progression hypnosis, pages 120–29*.

- 4/12 The right brain, largely responsible for dream symbolism and which may also be the agent (or intermediary) of visions, appeared to receive or generate visions or dreams under hypnosis while also shaping or creating aspects of my future. *E.g. First progression hypnosis, pages 109–13*.

- 4/13 Aspects of some long-term predictions which emerged much earlier than the time frame stated under hypnosis tended to arrive grouped together, on the same day. *E.g. crack in windscreen, etc, page 112.*

- 4/14 It may be possible to access a 'predetermined, unalterable' future event. *E.g. Sixth progression hypnosis, pages 131–44.*

5 and the big questions are ...

The evidence for precognition is overwhelming and complex! Before launching into the hows and whys of the rest of this book, you might like to review the summary memos at the end of each of the last four chapters. As in any court of law, the body of evidence may appear contradictory in parts, and in the final analysis all may turn out to be not quite as it seems on the surface!

Assume you are a member of a jury, assessing this summing-up. Review the clues, ask yourself more questions and take a sideways look at the whole subject. Is there another angle, another view? How much of this evidence can you tie together? What picture is emerging for you so far?

I have reserved the evidence according to science for the next chapter because it seemed to belong more with the hows than the whats. How is the focus for Part Two and why for Part Three.

How can the evidence be explained? Is there a satisfactory theory which covers it all and, if so, can we put it to work and use it to advantage in our everyday lives?

More importantly, is precognition solely a biological, physical or mathematical phenomenon, or does it carry meaning and purpose on a spiritual level? Can we see beyond the hows and be uplifted by the whys?

Following your review of the summary memos, you might like to add your own questions to the list below, which covers some of the main themes raised by the evidence so far.

Telepathy

When previewing a future event can be explained by telepathy (a connection to a present thought or event occurring for someone else):

- *How* does the person receive the telepathic information?
- *Why* does the person receive information about a *specific* person, thought or event?
- *Why* are so many of the previewed events connected with death, illness, accident, travel and change?
- *Why* is the information sometimes received in literal detail and sometimes in symbolism?

Precognition

When previewing a future event cannot be traced back to telepathy:

- Is the previewed future event still explicable in terms of links to the present, such as:
  * projection of present probabilities?
  * unconscious problem solving?
  * unconscious manifestation?

- Is the previewed future event absolutely untraceable to the present, because:
  * it is a predetermined, fixed event?
  * the future already exists in a timeless dimension?
  * an outside agency such as God, Spirit, spirit guide or deceased person is communicating information from a level of understanding which is beyond human intellect?
- *Why* does the precognitive information refer to a *specific* person, thought or event, and not to any other person, thought or event? (Is there meaning in the future glimpsed, or is the future seen a chance effect?)
- *Why* are so many of the previewed events connected with death, illness, accident, travel and change?
- *Why* is the information sometimes previewed in literal detail and sometimes in symbolism?
- *Why* are only some dreams seen to be precognitive?

The free will/fixed destiny paradox

The paradox
The precognitive experience generally inspires an increased sense of awe for the power of free will in determining the future, while also leaving room for a distinct faith in some degree, however small, of a predetermined destiny. The Hypnosis Project suggests the paradox may be valid.

- *How* can free will reside alongside fixed destiny, or is the paradox a reflection of human misperception?
- *How* much of our individual future is shaped by our individual free will?
- *How* much of our individual future is shaped by predetermined destiny?
- *How* much of our individual future is shaped by the free will

of others: the family, society, politics, geography, world events and so on?

- *How* much are we the sculptors of the shape of things to come?
- Can science explain *how* free will or predetermination shape our individual futures?
- *Why?* Is there purpose in possessing free will, or purpose in predetermination?

The linear time/no time paradox

The paradox

The precognitive experience generally leads people to feel that there exists, beyond our everyday perception of linear time, a dimension of timelessness where past, present and future are combined in one all-existing 'now' moment.

- Are there two co-existing time dimensions, or is the paradox a reflection of human misperception?

part two

the mind
questions
'how?'

the mind questions 'how?'

where is 6 tomorrow?

Looking up into the night sky we may gaze upon a star and contemplate its existence as a huge ball of hydrogen gas atoms getting so compressed and so hot that they coalesce to become helium and emit huge amounts of incandescent heat energy: or starshine. Suspended in space at distances we can barely comprehend, stars reach a fairly balanced state of being and burning until the scales are tipped and the fuel runs out, leaving the dying star to collapse in on itself. At death its most probable fate is transformation into a black hole.

What do we, here on earth, see when the star light is extinguished? We still see the star, at least for years afterwards.

Our nearest star, Proxima Centauri, is four light-years away, this being the time it takes for the starshine light to travel across space and arrive within our range of sight. We look up and see, not Proxima Centauri, but the light emitted by the star four years previously. We see, not Proxima Centauri as it is today, but as it was four years ago. If it were to burn out tomorrow, we would still see it, burning brightly, for another four years.

Four light years away is twenty-three million million miles. Most of the stars we can see as we casually glance up at the skies are, or at least were, within a few hundred light-years distance. Our night sky is therefore a snapshot of a variety of different star states, all past. One star, as you see it, is actually as it was four years ago, while another is a glimpse of starlife a hundred years ago, and yet another the starshine of a light long extinguished, all depending on how far away they are. Should we say, as we look skyward, that this starscape is now, the present, as far as our earthly perception is concerned? Or should we say it is a mosaic of past years, past events, brought into our present time? Where does the past end and the present begin? Is the future similarly entwined within our perception of the present? Which time is it now? How does science see time and how can its insights be used to develop an understanding of precognition?

The sun is eight light-minutes away, so even as we watch the setting sun we are deceived by eight minutes. We experience sunlight in delay. We are warmed by the sun that was, not by the sun that is. But just as much as the presence of the setting sun is an illusion (doubly so, for it does not 'set' at all!), so is the precision of eight minutes. Being earthbound, grounded, we all agree eight minutes is eight minutes. We set our watches by the pips when we phone for the time, and by such agreement we meet at the right places at the right times. Sir Isaac Newton described time as absolute, passing in same-sized chunks, minute following minute, hour following hour, laid out in a long chain of flowing linear time. Sir Isaac, though, didn't have the benefit of observing time from above, where the view changes dramatically.

In 1971 two scientists (Hafele and Keating) borrowed four precision atomic clocks from the US Naval Observatory and took them aboard commercial aeroplanes travelling east from the United States around the world and back to America again. They repeated the trip flying westward. Each time they landed they

compared the time according to the clocks which had circum-
navigated the world with the time on the same kind of clocks
which had been kept firmly grounded. They discovered that,
basically, the clocks were an average of fifty-nine nanoseconds
(billionths of a second) slower than the grounded clocks on their
return to America. Time, according to the clocks, had been
stretched, albeit only by a few billionths of a second, by travel. The
clocks had measured the timewarp experienced by the planes and
their passengers. Eight minutes on the ground is not the same as
eight minutes spent whizzing around the earth. Time does not
come in linear, premeasured chunks. It can be stretched and
warped, so that different people, in different situations, may
experience time differently (if minutely) relative to each other.

If you went up into space and travelled in a rocket for a few
years, everything would appear normal in a time sense. You would
age normally, in keeping with your perception of time. It would
only be on your return to earth that you would discover the timewarp, because your earth-bound friends would have aged more
than you. They would have experienced more years than you did
because their time was fast relative to yours, and your time was
slow relative to theirs. You would be able to agree that you shared
the same moment of take-off and the same moment of landing,
but there would be no agreed now moment between those two
times.

Timewarps have a real and observable effect in many high
technology applications. Satellite navigation systems, for example,
are affected by relativity. At a subatomic level some devastatingly
exciting examples of timewarp reveal the reality of the relativity of
time. Space radiation bombards the earth in the form of cosmic
rays which travel at such high speed that their timewarp, relative
to earth time, is one hundred billion. If it were possible for you to
climb aboard that cosmic ray, three thousand earth years would
pass in what would seem to you to be just one second.

Real life and laboratory observations have measured the reality of timewarps and relativity to the point that Newton's concept of absolute time is no longer accepted by science. It was Einstein who, at the beginning of this century, realised that time is relative rather than absolute. It is warped by motion and by gravity because time is physically linked to space. Time is not a separate 'thing' from space. Instead there is 'space-time'.

Imagine space-time like a huge three dimensional patchwork blanket spread throughout the universe. (Space-time is really a four dimensional concept since space already exists in three dimensions, so the addition of an extra dimension—time—makes four dimensions in total. However, since the four dimensions are difficult to envisage, a 3-D imaginary blanket will suffice to get the picture!) The patchwork squares may stretch and curve when pulled by the gravity of a nearby planet, or elongate under the tension of localised motion. The lines forming the edges of the squares (curved or otherwise) are chunks of time, some long, some short, each sharing corners with intersecting lines (points of agreed now moments), but each experiencing different time values relative to each other. Apart from the intersecting corners, there is no common agreement on now, just as there can be no agreement between the rocket traveller and her ground-based friend on any shared now moments other than the beginning and end of the rocket's journey.

On this space-time patchwork blanket, where is the present moment if no now points of time can be agreed? Take one now point. Do all the other now points fall into either past, future, or (maybe) present moments relative to this chosen now point? If so, the future already exists, just as much as the past does. No longer does it become a matter of when is tomorrow, but a weird mixture of where and when.

This is the timescape view of time understood by many modern physicists to be the best model for the reality of time. Just as we can stand back and view a landscape, they argue, so we can perceive a timescape, where past, present and future all exist together. This model, also known as block time, not only suits their theories, but also suits their scientific observations.

Our personal experience as human star-gazers tells us that our perception of now is not necessarily accurate. That star we see is not now as far as the dead star is concerned, and the sun slipped over the horizon (or the earth flipped backwards—it's all relative!) some eight minutes before we perceived it to do so. Even the horizon itself is merely a perception. There is no actual horizon, although the illusion of its existence led generations of people to perceive a flat earth. Indeed our human experience is entirely illusory. The very images received by our brains are upside down because our eyes are like cameras. Light rays from an image, perhaps a tree for example, are focused by the eye's lens onto the retina at the back of the eye. The eye lens is convex, like a camera lens, and the retina is like the film in the back of the camera. The tree image is turned upside down by the lens, appearing inverted on both retina and camera film alike. The 'upside down tree' message arrives at our brain via the optic nerve. Since the brain learned in very early infancy that the upside down images did not relate to what the baby hears and touches, it turns all visual images up the right way again. So we see the tree the right way up. Life works better for us that way, but it is, nevertheless, a life built on a perceptual adjustment: an illusion. How much of our life do we reinterpret to make it fit in with what we 'know' to be 'true'? Perhaps we can never be sure, even with our scientific observations.

In 1905 when Einstein first put forward his theory of time and relativity he also advanced some new ideas on atomic theory. In the history of science, Einstein is regarded as the father of modern physics because he initiated these two branches: relativity and quantum physics (atomic theory). These two fields represent the points of departure from the old classical mechanistic physics as developed by Galileo, Newton and others, which had been accepted as fact for the preceding three hundred years.

Even though Einstein opened up the world of quantum physics, he remained unsold on some of the ideas and theories it later generated. In many ways Einstein became 'stuck' on the relativity-inspired view of a world where all time is set out as a timescape and where time does not flow, yet he also found it difficult to assimilate this into his picture of everyday reality. I find it interesting, from a metaphorical point of view, that in his last seven years of life Einstein suffered an aneurism of the aorta which caused him severe abdominal pain. In other words, his aorta was swollen and dilated, interfering with the normal blood circulation or 'flow' and threatening rupture or clotting. Finally the aorta did rupture and Einstein died from the haemorrhage which resulted. I wonder how much Einstein grappled with assimilating, in those last years, the paradox presented by his work on relativity with its 'no flow, block time' and the quite different picture of an indeterminate, all responding world painted by quantum physics. Could he really not 'stomach' the idea of a nondetermined, flowing-time world? This is, indeed, his recorded view. Or did he, as he lay on his deathbed, finally succumb, in keeping with the metaphor of his rupture, to the pressure of evidence supporting the 'flow' he so resisted?

Yes. That's right. While science prefers a model of fixed block time, with past, present and future all laid out, it has also discovered a world of constant indeterminate change. Welcome to the world of scientific paradox.

Quantum physics is the study of the physical world at the atomic and subatomic level. Its hallmark is arguably a mathematical equation known as Heisenberg's Uncertainty Principle established in 1927, which basically describes subatomic particles as difficult to pin down, measure and predict. Take electrons, for example. Electrons whiz around the general arena of their atom environments, absorbing and releasing energy as they go. Science likes to measure, observe and categorise, but electrons have uncertain lifestyles which are difficult, if not impossible, to examine precisely. According to Heisenberg's Uncertainty Principle, you can measure either an electron's speed or its position, but not both, and this uncertainty applies to many facets of electron behaviour. The classical laws of physics, with their emphasis on prediction based on precise measurement, no longer apply at the subatomic level.

In fact, scientists cannot even be certain about the very existence of a specific particle from one moment to the next. Instead they describe a particle as having a 'tendency to exist' or a 'tendency to behave' in one way rather than another. Probability replaces certainty. Since the entire universe, as we understand it, is composed of atomic particles and space, the notion of the fixed, determined timescape painted by relativity is undermined by a universal basis of uncertainty.

Uncertainty even pervades the concept of a dotlike particle. When a particle is tending not to be dotlike it acts more like a wave: not a particle tracing out a wave shape, but a total wave form. This duality of matter and energy is known as the Principle of Complementarity and the 'chosen' form, from one moment to the next, seems to be more a product of probability than of cause and effect.

One of the most interesting observations to emerge from quantum physics, in my opinion, is that if you split a photon particle (light in particle form) through a crystal and watch the paths taken by each half of the original photon, they may take off in opposite directions, but they move in related ways. If one spins, so does the other. If one changes direction, or has its direction changed by manipulation, its partner's direction is seen to match. These changes are simultaneous. It is as if the partners are in instantaneous communication, having precise knowledge of the whereabouts and behaviour of each other. Newton would be at an absolute loss to explain a world functioning beyond the laws of cause and effect.

The world of matter and energy seen at the subatomic level is an interconnected, indeterminate one, which may operate, at least occasionally, on simultaneity and 'knowingness' rather than on cause and effect. Perhaps it is a world best viewed as one whole system, comprised of a web of intercommunicating, interchanging matter and energy. The old ideal of classical science that scientists should stand back and observe the results of their experiments objectively is lost at the quantum level because the scientist observer is also a part of the whole system she is watching. Not only does she interpret her observations according to her human perceptions, but she is also a part of the subject. Her view, her perceptions, her actions in measuring or observing are part of the whole outcome. Total objectivity, that old cornerstone of classical science, is not possible.

What have we learned in this chapter about the when or where of tomorrow according to science?

- Since time is relative there is no such thing as an agreed now. There is my now and your now, but we are not necessarily sharing the same now.
- Science strongly supports the relativity timescape model where the past and future already exist 'over there' somewhere.
- The laws of cause and effect do not describe all events at a subatomic level.
- Some subatomic events occur simultaneously with similar subatomic events, without apparent cause.
- Subatomic particles exist and behave with uncertainty, often apparently without cause.

- Quantum physics supports uncertainty and indeterminacy as the underlying basis of the universe.
- Quantum physics supports an interconnected holistic system view of the universe, impossible to measure scientifically with total objectivity.
- Quantum physics reveals a world of duality, where matter and energy are complementary forms of the same phenomenon.
- As human beings we perceive our world according to our beliefs; each to his own illusion.

In short, science presents us with proven paradoxes about the nature of time. The future already exists and yet it is uncertain and indeterminate. Now or at least our individual experience of now, is a fairly safe bet, but then the human experience itself is illusionary because it is based on perception. Paradox itself is acceptable to science because science has observed the duality of matter and energy, and yet science is unable to observe and measure with total objectivity.

In summary perhaps three main points emerge in considering what science can offer towards an understanding of precognition. Firstly, an already existing future is a valid scientific model according to which 'tomorrow' is out there 'somewhere', in some kind of 'now'. Secondly, not all events are the result of cause and effect. Thirdly, it is acceptable to live with paradox.

How exactly these points contribute to my understanding of how precognition occurs will become clear as the following chapters unfold.

When I sat down to write this chapter I decided then and there to open with the idea of seeing a star long after it had collapsed and extinguished. I wrote the first paragraph, then sat back to contemplate developing the idea of a night sky as a mirror of a multitude of times past, depending on the individual distances of all the stars. Midcontemplation my mail arrived. One letter was from Rebekah confirming that my chosen extracts of her precognitive experiences were to her satisfaction and giving me formal permission to publish them as they appear earlier in this book. In a short covering letter she told me about a book she was enjoying and quoted just one line: 'A star is as near as it is far.'

Rebekah would have had no conscious knowledge that I intended to write about the distances of stars and I had no conscious knowledge that her letter was already winging its way towards me. Who had the precognition? Rebekah, me or neither of us? The quote arrived at the moment of my contemplation and was an event apparently beyond the influence of cause and effect. Above all, the saying itself presents a paradox in the same fashion as the koan riddles of Zen Buddhism. These were offered to disciples to illustrate the inadequacy of logical reasoning and lead them towards enlightenment through more holistic, intuitive insight. One of the best known koans is, of course, 'What is the sound of one hand clapping?' Another is, 'We are facing each other all day long, yet we have never met.'

Through its acceptance of paradox, science is one step away from the mystical approach of synthesising, through contemplation of a specific paradox or koan, an enlightened, whole understanding of the universe, unreachable through reasoning alone. The findings of science as stated in this chapter, despite paradox, are all-encompassing of the ultimate truth. 'A star is as near as it is far.'

safe
science   7

Back in the late sixties when I was a high school student in Hampshire, England, we were faced with the question of our academic destiny at the age of thirteen or fourteen. It was time to specialise, to choose between science and the arts. It seemed a momentous decision, one that would set us on a path of no return —for life. I recall the advice clearly. We were to choose eight subjects unless we intended to be scientists or historians, in which case we should add Latin because it would help us puzzle out the meaning of technical or ancient words. Students wishing to become 'real' scientists, we were advised, should choose chemistry, physics and maths, leaving biology to the arts students. Although my arts marks were probably better than my science scores, I was born with the surname Newton and spent much of my school life rebutting jokes about falling apples. Some revenge was required. I also impressed one science teacher sufficiently with my apparently innate understanding of why you need to punch two holes in a can of soft drink before you can pour yourself a glass. That was it: my label of scientist was complete.

I found science to be an exciting and challenging subject which seemed, despite playing with test tubes, largely historical. Maybe that explained the Latin rationale after all. I studied drawings of atoms ringed with orbits, each orbit carefully strung with exactly the right number of electrons, like beads on an abacus. The electrons got excited, jumping around between orbits and occasionally popping off to join in the orbital delights of neighbouring atoms, but all was strictly according to mathematical formulae. No flights of fancy or uncertainty were permitted here. Order, order and more order.

I learned that there were three subatomic particles: the excitable but predictable electrons and two extremely boring sleepy particles, protons and neutrons, snuggled together as the little dot drawn at the centre of each atom. Life and the universe was, quite simply, entirely constructed from energetic balls, sleepy balls, invisible orbits and enormous spaces filled with the magnetic tension which held all the balls together. All we had to do was learn the geometry and mathematics of the structures, predict chemical reactions with certainty and explain the physics of electricity, light, heat, mechanics and magnetism strictly in terms of cause and effect. It was all incredibly neat, tidy, predictable and as classical and dead as the Latin grammar I laboured with between times. Every exciting discovery we made in the lab had already been discovered by someone else, usually centuries earlier.

In the big outside world people were timewarping in rockets decades after Einstein had formulated his theories on relativity. Heisenberg had confidently announced uncertainty forty years before I entered the school science lab, before even my parents were born. Schoolboys interested in big mechanical machines and explosions were excited by the new Concorde and mumbled about supersonic sound and the breaking of the sound barrier, but the speed of light had more to do with science fiction, in our school world, than reality.

I learned the methods of good science: control experiments, objective observation and quantifiable, measurable outcomes. If I was indeed a descendant of Sir Isaac, I hoped I did him proud. No one told me, at the time, that he had room in his life for his passion with magic and the occult and was closely associated with key Druids of his time. School science, was narrow, focused, classical, rational, mechanistic, reductionist and very useful for explaining how things generally worked in the everyday world of mechanical things. It was also totally blinkered to the realities of modern physics and to the observations and theories born some sixty years before and established as common currency in higher scientific circles for two generations.

At university my scientific world widened when I discovered that I could study biology as well as chemistry and physics. I remember Heisenberg's Uncertainty Principle making a fleeting appearance in the shape of a long mathematical formula, peppered with Greek algebraic symbols chalked on the physics blackboard. Greeted by our consternation it was hastily erased by the lecturer and remained only as an ink squiggle in my lecture notes, alongside a facetious comment of mine that perhaps Greek would have been a more appropriate school subject than Latin. By contrast I was wooed by the fascinations of biology with its menu of genetics, ecology, animal behaviour, neurophysiology and embryonic development which seemed somehow more relevant to life and more open to debate and conjecture. I made the full transition to biology at the end of my first year.

The older professors in the zoology department were suspicious of the younger staff who enthusiastically researched ecology and animal behaviour, observing whole interconnecting systems like 'desert ecosystems' or 'population behaviour' and drawing holistic conclusions rather than analysing constituent parts. These systems, the older professors noted, had a distinct tendency to add up to something larger than the sums of their parts. Biology was being described from a top down perspective and, worse still, they argued, some of those descriptions were qualitative.

As we were funnelled into our final year, academic specialism required us to select our final choices and I chose neurodevelopmental biology because it seemed challenging, open to extraordinary new developments and, above all, speculative. It was an okay subject to muse about, to throw around concepts and to be totally awestruck by the process of formation from a fertilised egg to a whole animal or human: an entity which was surely more than the sum of its parts.

I graduated from university with little if any understanding of the implications of the previous sixty or seventy years of modern science. I had heard of Heisenberg's Uncertainty Principle yet I was conditioned by a classical science education which gave me a personal uncertainty about the scientific worthiness of the holistic systems I was intellectually and intuitively attracted to. Maybe the old school was right, I pondered. Maybe, as a biologist I could never be a 'real' scientist after all. I was overjoyed later to finally encounter nonclassical modern physics and its liberating ideas, such as those described in the previous chapter.

My own teenage children now study science at school as an adjunct to their greater passions within the arts. While biology has been transformed and updated, the physics and chemistry curricula have not changed much since the sixties. The basics are still the same. Why?

Modern physics is difficult, but no more difficult than some of the more classical areas of science or mathematics. Classical science has been keenly taught via analogy for decades, and modern physics is surely exciting territory to describe with imagery. School students today have imaginations well stretched and exercised through their exposure to high technology and a pervasive media. The concepts and findings of modern science, taught with analogy, should be exciting and inspirational material well within the grasp of such fertile minds. Infinitely more so, I would suggest, than the sleepy and sometimes inappropriate laws of classical science.

Classical science has its place and all school students need to be grounded in its basics. It provides the knowledge we need to deal with important aspects of everyday life, such as technology, electricity, plumbing, medicine, mechanical machines, chemicals, engineering and so on. But it is only half the story, and until we undertake to teach our children the findings, implications and paradoxes of modern physics, they stand to lose a more balanced perspective of the way the universe really works.

stunned
8 by
synchronicity

'A star is as near as it is far.' How can a star be both near and far?
The star in the night sky is but a pattern of light emitted from a
gaseous ball which may or may not still exist. The night sky is but
the void of space. The star in the sky is as illusory as the star image
in our eye or the star message delivered to our brain. We perceive
outer distance, but the consciousness of the star is first registered
deep within our minds, within our being. The star, if it exists at all,
exists equally as much within as without. It is both near and far in
the same moment: now.

The future, tomorrow, may be just as illusory. Our learning
and the greater part of our experience tells us that tomorrow
follows today and that what we do today causes tomorrow's effects.
When we encounter an event in our future which we have already
seen, we are amazed and label it precognition. Yet science shows
us that tomorrow is already out there somewhere on a timescape,
already existing in a kind of now. Science tells us that things do
not always happen through cause and effect, but that events can

occur simultaneously, as if invisibly joined together in a mutual state of being in a shared now.

Most people have experienced that simultaneous now. It is the experience of deeply meaningful coincidence known as synchronicity. Sometimes the strange coincidence seems to carry a message and the meaningfulness is understood. More often synchronicity leaves you with a feeling that you have touched some sense of meaningful but indefinable mystery.

Receiving Rebekah's letter with its gift of 'A star is as near as it is far' at the exact moment that I was composing the paragraph about stars and distances is an example of synchronicity. In its purest form, it is an outer world event (the letter and its contents) which coincides in a meaningful way with an inner world event (my thoughts).

The famous psychiatrist Carl Jung frequently experienced this phenomenon and it was he who labelled it synchronicity in the 1920s. His best-known example concerns a woman who booked in to see him after reaching the end of her tether with her two previous psychiatrists. Jung realised that she was a very rigid thinker who needed a rational explanation for everything. He asked her about her dreams and listened as she described her dream of an Egyptian Golden Scarab beetle. While she was talking there was a tapping sound at the window and Jung walked over to open it. As he did so, a beetle flew in: it was the nearest equivalent to the Egyptian scarab beetle that Austrian insect life could provide. The woman was so stunned by the coincidence of the arrival of the beetle at the exact moment she was describing the beetle of her dreams, that she broke through her rigidity and became more open and willing to change through therapy. For his part, Jung saw the scarab beetle as a universal dream symbol of transformation, so its arrival at the exact moment the woman was describing, through her dream, her unconscious readiness for transformation was deeply meaningful in its endorsement.

One night I had a long and bizarre dream which seemed heavily significant. The next day I sat at my desk working through the meaning of the dream, but I was stuck with one part about someone administering LSD up someone else's nose! Luckily, at the moment I woke up I had the feeling that LSD really meant pounds, shillings and pence, but I couldn't work out the connection between old currency and this person's nose. I closed my eyes and concentrated: I really wanted to understand this one. My thinking was interrupted by the sound of the phone ringing. It was someone wanting to send a fax of a newspaper article he had enjoyed. I switched the fax on and watched the headline roll through first: CREDIT RATING GETS RIGHT UP YOUR NOSE. I hadn't seen the article before, so it hadn't inspired my dream. It was exactly the clue I needed to complete my interpretation.

The dream episode with the nose was a beautiful example of a visual cliché: at the time of the dream there was an old money situation that was really getting right up mine! The fax was the outer world event that coincided with my inner world thoughts in a meaningful way. I had already had the dream, and no doubt the man had already cut out the article, but the important point was the exact coincidence of both events as experienced by me. The outer world mirrored my inner world at that exact moment and the resultant synchronicity enlightened me.

These synchronicities are simple examples of an outer world event coinciding, at the exact moment in time, with an inner world thought. Furthermore, in each case the person was aware of the subject matter of their inner contemplation. However, the more common situation experienced in our busy, outer world oriented culture is a convergence of people or events *without* consciousness of the state of the inner world at the moment of synchronicity. The situation registers as meaningful because it seems ridiculously beyond the odds, or even heaven sent.

Common Synchronicity Themes

Synchronicities often occur at times of change or transformation, when new ideas, thoughts, insights or understandings are breaking through from the unconscious mind. The scarab beetle, the star and the fax all arrived at breakthrough moments: indeed they may have been the midwives present at the births rather than heralders announcing the events.

The full meaning of a synchronicity may not always be obvious to the person who experiences it, largely because it is often wrapped in symbolism, much like a dream. The inner world process is often unconscious or dreamlike, so its outer world partner frequently reflects the same language. A very common synchronicity, for example, is to encounter repeated incidents of broken glass at times of personal breakthrough. In dreams glass often appears as a symbol of an invisible barrier or limitation. Once you break through the glass, you break through the illusion of a personal limitation. Without an appreciation of this symbolism, breaking glass synchronicities remain puzzling, seemingly having no link with your inner world.

Travelling tends to facilitate personal change and transformation as we encounter different cultures and alternative views and ways of life. Moving away from our usual routines encourages us to see our lives from a different perspective, and journeying with a partner or friend often challenges relationship issues. It is for all these reasons that synchronicities tend to occur while travelling. What comes up for us during our journey and challenges us to extend ourselves beyond our previous mental limitations meets us in the outer world through the mirror of synchronicity.

The following are two typical travel synchronicity stories. (These experiences were related to me during radio talkback and I am reporting them from programme transcripts. From here on these will be indicated with an asterisk*.)

Leda was travelling with friends from San Jose to Lake Tahoe in the States when they stopped at a town named Auburn to have a Big Mac. Who should then walk into the restaurant but three young men from their home town back in Australia, all friends of her daughter. Later they realised their car was parked right next to theirs too!

Meanwhile another traveller, Julie, was in Pompeii visiting the ruins. Just as she was about to leave, she started talking to a couple of English people and they ended up having a drink together. The English couple knew only one person in Australia and that turned out to be a good friend of Julie's.

I have no idea what was going on in their inner thinking when these synchronicities occurred to Leda and Julie, but I have no doubt that if I sat down and talked with them I would discover the personal limitations their travelling was challenging and which these meetings had mirrored.

Another common synchronicity theme is reunion, which often mirrors inner personal breakthrough such as integration, harmony or healing of the past. Someone or something from the past will present in the most unexpected circumstances just as the person is on the verge of readiness to handle or heal that area of their life. Mandy's story reflects this.

Mandy's father in Australia had traced his family history to Cornwall in England. While she was living in the UK, Mandy and her husband decided to drive down to Cornwall one weekend to have a look at the records in an old church. A service was in progress by the time they arrived, so they searched the headstones in the cemetery looking for signs of the family name, but without luck. Eventually they spoke to the vicar who told them that no records had been kept during the years that interested them, but he invited them into the vicarage for a cup of tea anyway. 'There's another chap here from Australia,' he said. 'You might as well meet him.'

As they were introduced they realised they shared the same surname. The man had come all the way from Australia specifically to trace his history, arriving at the church on the exact same day. It turned out that they were related and Mandy discovered a whole branch of the family she didn't know existed. Back in his home city in Australia, the man became great friends with Mandy's parents.*

Although I didn't have the opportunity to discuss her experience more deeply, I'm sure that both Mandy and her new-found relative had each reached an inner readiness for some kind of integration and self-discovery and this was mirrored in their finding each other.

The last group of common synchronicity themes is accident, death and birth. Death and birth tend to greet unconscious surfacing of the need for death of the old and birth of the new, while synchronicities around accidents generally signal the unconscious recognition of 'wrong way' and the need for a change in personal direction or attitude.

One night Peter was driving home from the movies with his wife when he saw a car accident. He stopped, gave his name as a witness, then continued on his journey. Two days later he had to go down to the police station to report his father's car as stolen. While he was sitting waiting, a young couple were talking at the counter. He heard them mention a car accident and the fact that there had been a witness. He looked out the window to see the car which had been at fault two nights earlier. Some time later he was told that his father's stolen car had turned up and he went to the car yard to identify it. As he was standing in the office, the same young couple turned up to enquire about having their car fixed.*

Again, I don't know what Peter's synchronicities were mirroring within his inner world, but I would guess that he was beginning to realise (witness) 'wrong turnings' he had taken in his personal direction which could be 'fixed' by identifying something about his father's attitudes.

Notice that the main synchronicity themes are the same as those associated with most precognitive dreams and visions, as discussed in earlier chapters. An understanding of synchronicity will help elucidate the phenomenon of precognition, since they are, in effect, closely related.

Not all synchronicities fall within these main themes, though, and some can seem quite trivial at first.

Steven's story, for example, concerns his broken toilet lid. His wife really wanted it to be replaced, but he wasn't that bothered and kept putting it off. He also knew that you can't buy toilet lids on their own because they come in sets with the matching toilet seat. It seemed a waste of money. Several months passed before Steven noticed a plumbing store as he was driving and decided it was time to take action. He parked the car and entered the shop three paces in front of another man. 'You better go first because my problem's going to take a while,' Steven told the man, hoping to be able to talk the plumber into selling the lid without the expense of the seat. The man approached the counter and asked for an ivory toilet seat. 'Yes, that's the one but I don't want this,' he said, tearing off the lid and giving it back to the plumber. Steven stepped in and offered him some money for the lid, but he was given it for free.*

After months of doing nothing, and after driving past any number of plumbing stores, it was only at the exact moment Steven decided to take action that the second man also appeared on the scene and the synchronicity occurred. Despite the apparent triviality, I know from experience that there would have been inner world changes within Steven which were surfacing at that particular time and which his outer world simply mirrored. How much more might Steven have gained from his synchronicity than a bargain deal on a toilet lid and a funny story to add to his repertoire if we had been able to discuss the inner world side of the picture?

The Detective Work

When you first start experiencing synchronicities the usual reaction is to be, quite simply, awed. The experience inspires a sense of interconnectedness or oneness with the world and a feeling that there is a deeper meaning and purpose behind the everyday facade of life, although what exactly that meaning is may seem quite elusive. It is tempting to look for cause and effect explanations, but they are difficult to endorse. Telepathy is often given as a cause, as in, for example, 'I was thinking about him (cause) so he phoned (effect).' Most synchronicities, however, do not stand up to this kind of analysis.

When Rebekah sat down to write to me about the star, I was not thinking about her and I had not thought about opening the chapter with any discussion on stars. By the next day, as I sat at my computer and composed my astronomical paragraph, it could be argued that I had read Rebekah's mind or letter unknowingly through telepathy and that I was taking my cue from her theme. However, the letter did not arrive before or after I had written the paragraph, but tantalisingly right in the middle of it, in true synchronicity fashion. It simply fits the definition of synchronicity with its tell-tale tingling sensation of meaningfulness better than it fits the alternatives.

For the person experiencing it for the first time, synchronicity brings a sense of the mystical which, even without any analysis of inner meaning, is sufficiently rewarding in itself. A finger beckons to explore a wider world, an existence beyond cause and effect, a world of 'now' which promises, perhaps, enlightenment itself. Once you enter that now possibility, synchronicity events seem to multiply. It's as though you start with a little hole into the now world which keeps getting bigger as your perception of reality expands.

If you can acknowledge, at this point, that synchronicities symbolically mirror your inner personal development, you can read these outer world signs as indicators of inner changes on the way. Inner processes are expressed by the unconscious, the right brain, the stuff of dreams: universal symbols, associations, visual cliches, archetypes, word puns, emotions and so on. A thorough versing in dream language acquired from a professional source, such as *Sleep On It and Change Your Life*, is important for the serious synchronicity buster. For the sake of simplicity I have chosen examples which are easy to follow.

I was sorting through some papers and got sidetracked into a box of mementos when I found a card from a Carol I knew many years ago, which set me thinking. Later that morning I received a fax from another Carol and a phone call from yet another Carol, a woman I hadn't talked with for many months. I thought I must be in the middle of a synchronicity, but I didn't understand it. I couldn't immediately match it to any inner thoughts I was aware of. The last Carol told me her name meant song of joy. Like a Christmas carol, I thought to myself. There had been no other phone or fax calls so far: no other names had flown into my day. Later, after having the answering machine on for a while, I replayed the tape to find just one message had been left, by a friend whose surname is Manger. 'Like a Christmas carol,' I laughed to myself, still ignorant of the deeper meaning. Her message began, 'Oh, it's ...' and that was all, just two words, but I recognised her voice. There followed a minute and a half of classical music, a click, the rest of her message, another click and then a further two minutes of music. What had happened, of course, was that she had received an incoming call at the moment she started to leave her message and she had put our phone line on hold. Still unsure about all these joyful Carols, I let the day continue to unfold.

The afternoon brought three letters: one business letter and two personal ones. The two personal ones each informed me of address changes. Only the day before we had received a letter from some friends to tell us they had moved house and, I realised, one of the Carols had phoned me specifically to give me her new address. What's more, the person who sent me the business letter had inadvertently enclosed three letters from her desk which she must have picked up when she put the sheaf of papers for me into the envelope. Since two of the letters did relate to me and were not private, I read them. One recommended a woman by the name of Carol as a possible collaborator on some work.

Now, you have to really love detective work when you make the commitment to understand the synchronicities in your life! These were my clues so far:

Over the space of less than a day, I had three Carols I knew, one Carol I didn't know, one tenuous Christmas carol and four notices of address changes. One of the Carols overlapped with the address-change theme and the unknown Carol could represent a new address in my professional diary. I also had a fleeting clue that Carol meant joy or music. At this point I turned to pen and paper. What did all these people have in common?

The known Carols, I realised, all felt that they had been inspired by my work, but at the same time they had each provided me with inspiration and opportunity for career advancement. Each Carol was associated with a different phase of my career. The Carols as a group therefore symbolised mutual exchange at a time of moving forward.

The common link between the four people who had moved

house was freedom. One gained freedom from a controlling landlord; one exchanged a city terrace house for acres of freedom for her growing sons; one moved to gain freedom through access to medical care, and the fourth moved to be rid of stairs which were becoming too painful to climb.

Putting all that together, I had an outer world which was mirroring, 'I am moving ahead to a freer phase of life through joyful mutual exchange.' Once I had done the basic detective work, it made perfect sense. After more than three years researching the material for this book I am beginning to taste freedom as I write my way towards the final full stop to send this book on its own journey. Self-funded research and writing are highly disciplined, solo, self-motivational tasks which can, at times, feel restrictive and lonely. Precognition has been a difficult area to research but it was also a necessary labour of love. I needed to fully understand why bits of tomorrow kept invading my todays. The hypnotism project added headaches to the consternation, and towards the end I realised that I needed to close the Dream Research Bank and cease other related work to allow me to nurse the book baby through its final months of gestation. As I write now, the big picture has clearly fallen into place and I am enjoying the last stages of the creative process which always brings joy.

This research period has been exciting, difficult, expanding, restrictive, emotionally exhausting, insightfully uplifting, an immense labour and an exhilarating sense of achievement. Some of my past has been written into these chapters and much more has been examined and let go. Leading up to the 'Carol Synchronicities' I was beginning to realise that I was ready for change: for more teamwork, more mutual exchange, more reward received for effort given and the extra freedom that all these things bestow. Before the synchronicities these seemed vague notions, ideas toyed with in my sleeping dreams. By analysing the synchronicities, the thoughts gained impetus and solidified into an attainable goal. The synchronicities underlined the emerging feelings and, deciding I liked their reflection in the mirror of life, I chose to fully empower them.

(*Postscript*: The Carol synchronicities did indeed herald the shape of things to come. Today is 17 December 1997 and I have been given the task of reviewing my manuscript before it goes to print. Two days ago we moved into a beautiful new house. We had wanted to move a month earlier, but this is the way it has turned out. A superficial review of the Carol synchronicities reveals a hindsight prediction: 'You will have an address change by Christmas.' At a deeper level, the other changes discussed in this chapter have broken through to become my new way of life, one of collaboration and teamwork concerning the documentary (which is also a career advancement), and a freer, more joyous phase of being.)

All too often people read synchronicities as green lights which need to be followed. Sometimes this may not be appropriate. Imagine, for example, a man working a house renovation business. He's just finished a big renovation project but didn't make the amount of money he had expected. He also worked too much overtime. He's exhausted, but he needs just one more property to renovate, a real gem: the one that will really bring in the kind of dollars he's set his mind on. He looks around to see what's available, and he's amazed because every real estate agent he visits tells him about a fire-damaged house that would make a big return for the right renovator. Is this a sign from God? Is it a synchronicity to follow?

Our imaginary investor is experiencing synchronicity. His outer world is reflecting his inner world, only he's probably too exhausted to be in touch with the reality of that inner world. He is, of course, 'burned out', as are the properties being drawn to his attention. Rather than invest in a burned-out house and go round the same cycle of renovation and exhaustion, which obviously hasn't worked to his personal satisfaction so far, he would be better to examine his patterns of work, or his expectations of financial returns, and approach work from a different angle.

Synchronicity, then, is a mirror of what is emerging from the unconscious mind, what is soon to break through into consciousness. It tends to occur at a stage before full conscious-ness (while, by definition, it is still 'inner', still 'breaking through') and its outer world image is as symbolic as its inner world counterpart. In its purest form it is an instantaneous reflection, a phenomenon occurring in a world of now, not relating to notions of cause and effect. It is frequently misinterpreted as a signpost towards a better future. It may well herald a sign of the shape of things to come, but whether the signs have to be endorsed by action is a question of free will.

thoughts in a coffee cup

9

Synchronicity happens. My personal experience and research leads me to believe that Jung's model of an outer world reflecting emerging inner psychological processes is an accurate one. What can science contribute towards understanding the mechanism of synchronicity: how might an inner thought be met by a matching outer world event?

What is a thought? What is an emerging inner psychological process? Does it have any identifiable shape or form? Can it be measured? As thinking, feeling, developing human beings we know the reality of thought regardless of the question of its measurement. Electrodes placed on specific areas of the brain pick up electronic pulses or frequencies, the 'brainwaves' associated with different brain activities. At the very least, thoughts, as we experience them, are encoded nerve impulses resulting from the movement of ions and various biochemical reactions in the brain. At the very least, as electronic or magnetic impressions of chemical reactions, they have some overlap with the subatomic world of matter and energy occupied by solids, liquids and gases. They exist, therefore they are a part of the universe.

Modern physics tells us that particles are sometimes waves and waves are sometimes particles, that there is duality, that matter is energy and energy is matter. They are one and the same thing. Electronic equipment portrays brain nerve impulses as waves. These brainwaves, as a whole, can be measured in terms of different frequencies which characterise different brain states. One wave pattern characterises deep sleep; another, dreaming sleep; another, wakeful alertness, and so on. They are distinctive patterns of brain energy measured and displayed as waves. Are thoughts also particles? From this point there is controversy and disagreement. No one has pinned down the nature of a thought or isolated consciousness in a test tube.

Modern physics has taught us that all things are interconnected, at least at the subatomic level. Since all matter, big, middle sized, small and microscopic is made up from subatomic particles, these observations must hold true in general, even though we see distinctly separate objects in our everyday reality. We trust that big things like tables and chairs generally hold their shape, even though we know from Heisenberg's Uncertainty Principle that we can't be certain of the reality of the comings and goings at the subatomic level of existence of the table or chair. Matter is energy and energy is matter, but how much is energy and how much is matter at any one moment is not absolutely predictable. Perception of separateness rules, but reality is continuous interconnectedness. We're just too big to notice.

Yet human experience, for all its apparent delusion, cannot be discounted from the big picture. Quantum physics shows that the observer is a part of the whole and that her perception of what is happening affects the overall picture. We can't isolate science and we can't isolate human experience from the true nature of the universe, because they are both a part of the same world. All we can do is blend the two in search of the most satisfying picture of reality—or live somewhere between the paradoxes presented by both camps.

And so we come to my blended concoction, the model of synchronicity that best fits the results of my research and contemplation of the paradoxes, but which, above all, works for me in the practical everyday reality that I experience.

Life on an Ocean Wave

Pressed to describe our world of coexisting, interchangeable matter and energy, most people go for a picture of material forms such as people, objects, liquids and gases caught up in a life cycle of death and rebirth, sharing and recycling atoms and particles throughout time. Invisibly threading the whole lot together, the story goes, are energy forms such as light, magnetism, sound and thought along with, perhaps, memories, spirits, guides and angels, depending on your spiritual outlook.

The world makes much more sense in my view, however, if this general picture is reversed. I see energy as the main 'stuff' of the universe, with the material world as condensations of energy at points in space-time where it resonates at matter-forming pitch. Imagine a coffee cup half filled with smooth, black coffee, so still that you can see light and shade reflecting on its surface. Now imagine shaking the cup at a regular vibration so that ripples begin to form. What happens next? If you experiment, you will find a rate of vibration at which the ripples going out from the centre of the cup strike the walls of the cup and rebound to meet the on-coming waves in such a way that they form 'standing waves'. This is where the coffee surface appears to become a pattern of stationary ripples. In my world view, you and I, along with all other physical forms, are material condensations of resonating energy in a sea of thought. In our apparently fixed, matter-oriented world, we are deluded. Our greater reality is a flowing existence as waves of thought energy on the ocean of the collective unconscious of the universe. Life as a physical form on the ocean wave suddenly seems transiently precarious.

In such a picture, the human form seems secondary to the greater size and depth of the ocean, the mere flotsam and jetsam perhaps of resonating thought forms. Until, that is, we remember that matter is energy, and energy is matter, that they are both one and the same. As humans we have physical bodies that mostly exist in the material world, according to the vagaries of modern physics and biology, but we also have thoughts and perhaps other energies which meld with the ocean and intermingle with all other life, matter and energy. We are from thought yet we are thought. We are paradox itself. We are interconnected and our influence is huge. Our thoughts are out there vibrating and if they meet thoughts of similar vibration at the right angle and resonate, they might form standing waves: matter. This is the theory of material-isation or manifestation of thoughts into form.

The biggest hurdle in this model, but the one worth persever-ing with, is the understanding of yourself as thought materialised, at least in part, into physical matter, rather than as physical matter generating thought. We are not what we eat, but what we think, consciously and unconsciously. We are our own manifestations. Since we are also, according to science, inseparable from every-thing else, the outer world as we each perceive it is also a product of our conscious and unconscious thoughts or, at least, of those strong enough to resonate in a matter-forming way.

In my world, then, thought, conscious or unconscious, comes first. Matter may or may not follow thought, depending on factors such as intensity, resonance and so on. Just as standing waves in a coffee cup are of the moment (they cease when you stop jiggling the cup), so the material world, as we individually perceive it, is of the moment: it is a now reflection of the most resonant thoughts. Enter synchronicity.

I see the everyday reality each of us perceives as being entirely reflective of our individual thoughts, conscious or unconscious. One of the properties of the unconscious is that it occasionally

solves conflicts and delivers the solutions as 'insights' to the conscious brain. This is why you often wake up, having 'slept on it',
with the answer that was so elusive the night before. The unconscious solution becomes conscious. At certain times in our lives, as
I see it, the unconscious, in the process of bringing up a big
solution, carries such a huge amount of transformative energy
that it materialises in the outer world, just like the standing waves
in the coffee cup. Suddenly we find ourselves surrounded by the
stuff of what we are only just in the process of absorbing consciously. This is, of course, synchronicity. It occurs instantaneously
with the 'coming up' of the insight. It feels so meaningful because
it carries the symbolism of the unconscious: deep down you
understand the change of perception this burst of insight will
bring, but at the same time it feels elusive because the conscious
mind is taking time to integrate the insight with its previous
perception of self and the world. Conscious knowledge of the
symbolic language of the unconscious, together with an open-
minded readiness to change, helps this integration process.

Checking in with many of the observations of quantum physics
as already described in this book, this theory also, to some extent,
fits in with relativity's picture of a world of now. While in simple
language relativity sees the future as already out there, in reality it
states that the future is illusory. There is no future, no past, no
present, just a now as each individual experiences it; and personal
experience, according to quantum physics, is a valid part of the
whole picture, despite the paradox of our differing perceptions of
the same world. As science has again shown us earlier in this book,
it lives with paradox, so we can too. A star is as near as it is far.
Which is the ultimate reality: the illusory star in the illusory sky or
the illusory star image in the illusion fuelled brain?

Recently life delivered to me a beautifully simple example
of how our individual realities are reflective of our individual
conscious and unconscious thoughts. Glen and I were driving

along the road and Glen saw a man who had collapsed on the footpath. He was being attended to so we drove on. I missed the whole scene. I must have been looking across to the other side of the road at the time. Further along, Glen saw a hearse with a family gathered around it down a side street. Again, I saw nothing, my attention being drawn at that moment to something else. Glen experienced two outer world signs of death of the old, which was obviously more relevant to his personal journey at that time than to mine. We can walk the same world and experience different things according to our individual realities. We can live with paradox.

But wait. We have been so immersed in synchronicity and the experience of now that we have perhaps forgotten the greater part of our human experience which tells us that, according to our perception at least, there also exists a world where linear time, cause and effect seem reasonable. Are there two realities, a now reality and a cause and effect linear reality? What of the future our human experience tells us is ahead of us, changeable and yet to come? Furthermore, where did our discussion of precognition slip away to?

time as a red herring

Bev was visiting a friend and they were discussing the forthcoming seventy-fifth anniversary of the high school they had all attended forty or fifty years ago. The name of one of the prefects came up and Bev said, 'Oh, I remember her, she gave me some lines to learn for not wearing my black gloves.' Anyway, a couple of weeks later Bev went to visit her son who showed her an old tin trunk he had bought at a swap meet six weeks earlier. Bev's husband decided to take it home and do it up. When they looked inside they found it was lined with two sheets of newspaper dated 11 November 1933. One sheet carried four birth notices: one announcing the birth of the baby girl who later became the prefect who gave Bev her lines!*

Although we are not privy to Bev's inner thoughts at this time, all the talk of the school reunion must have sparked much reflection. No doubt in reminiscing old times and old school friends, some deaths were noted, but Bev's synchronicity revolved around reunion, birth and renewal ('doing up' the trunk). Reunion and birth, as noted earlier, are two of the most common synchronicity

* Radio talkback transcript.

themes. I would guess that reminiscing over old times triggered, for Bev, a time of inner rebirth and renewal which was being reflected in her outer world.

What is most interesting here, though, is the way past and future are drawn into the one synchronicity. At the time of reminiscing about the prefect, Bev's son had already bought the trunk containing the birth notices, yet this did not come to Bev's attention until several weeks later. Although no precognition was involved, shades of future events pervade this synchronicity story.

It is similar to the Mike and Elizabeth story told in Chapter 1 (pages 37–42), where my dreams overlapped with their encounter with murder and the aftermath of the traumatic event, as well as possibly with the pain and thoughts experienced by the murdered man on that Central American hillside. The intriguing factor was, again, the timing. Sometimes my dreams seemed precognitive because the dream details matched future events in Mike and Elizabeth's lives. Sometimes they seemed retrospective, matching events which had occurred a day or so earlier in Central America, although I knew nothing about it, consciously, at the time.

Overlapping Worlds

The whole episode made best sense when I viewed the time factor as a red herring. If you take any analysis of past, present and future out of the picture, you are left with an overlapping of my inner world, as viewed through my dreams, with Mike and Elizabeth's outer world experiences.

I interpreted my dreams as they arose and was satisfied that I understood their relevance to my life, acting on them accordingly. The dreams dealt with my inner feelings about the risks of mentally travelling beyond previous limitations, particularly in exploring new territory with the hypnosis project. I knew that risks went with adventure but I wondered about the dangers of knowing too much, of discovering knowledge that could be considered dangerous in the wrong hands. I knew I had to surrender to my quest, but I was finding the results, as I understood them at the time, hard to stomach. I was feeling ill and considered quitting. Maybe I didn't need to go the full distance. Ultimately I considered killing the project before it killed me, but above all my dreams showed me it was fear alone that I feared. So I resolved to face the fear and do it anyway. If I hadn't interpreted the dreams, I might have called the whole hypnosis project quits.

By acting on such dreams you align with the unconscious to resolve a conflict at an early stage. According to my understanding of synchronicity, if I had not resolved these issues, I would have expected to see them mirrored back to me in my outer world. By dealing with them through dream interpretation, my outer world reflected resolution instead. In actuality, I eventually went back and finished the hypnosis project and ultimately discovered that my fears were unfounded.

What seemed to happen instead was that Mike and Elizabeth experienced the type of outer world events my unresolved dream conflicts might have met. Why?

I am close to Mike and Elizabeth. Mike and I are both writers and I have lived in South America where they were heading for a six-month stay. Before they left on their travels Mike and I experienced some synchronicities: one night, for example, I dreamed he went up in a space rocket, dressed in 'spaceman' gear. I told him about it a couple of days later and he showed me an old black and white photo which had arrived around the time of the dream. It was a childhood photo from his father, showing the young Mike dressed as a spaceman with the inscription 'Space cadet' on the back of the photo. We could have labelled this incidence precognition or telepathy but it was, in my opinion, a shared synchronicity. The stuff of my dreams was reflecting in my outer world in the shape of Mike. From his point of view, I was reflecting the stuff of his thoughts as he pondered memories evoked by the arrival of the photo. After a number of such synchronicities it became obvious to me that we were similar people going through similar things and reflecting it all back to each other: perfect mirrors.

The main difference was that I was adventuring within as a source for my writing while he was heading for overseas adventure as a source for his. In reality, our separate journeys were likely to teach us similar stuff, as I believe they probably have. I have travelled across borders, seen different perspectives and met joys and conflicts within, while Mike has done the same on his outer world travels.

My feeling is that handling conflict at the inner level, through interpreting and acting on dreams, empowers you to resolve issues before the inner shit hits the outer fan. The inner level is unconscious thought and all thought is potential matter, but it has to be at the right resonating strength to form those standing waves which are the outer world. My dream thoughts went out there, but they never did build sufficient strength to materialise in my outer world. Mike, on the other hand, less adept at catching and interpreting his dreams, saw his less resolved conflicts played out in his outer world. In essence, he saw what I nipped in the bud. Yet undeniably our worlds collided.

A similar experience with Beth reveals how. I have met Beth only a handful of times, but we exchange letters, dreams and phone calls from time to time and discover that our lives frequently overlap. Beth's understanding of dreams is very close to my own and she carefully records and acts on them. She is also a writer. She has come to see, as I do, that the outer world is a reflection of the inner world, and she has learned the comforting art of interpreting her outer world in times of trauma so that she can come to terms with the experience or act on her understanding to control the outcome. She says that just as understanding a nightmare transforms a frightening experience into a beautiful enlightening dream, so the same applies to conscious reality.

'Even in traumatic situations there is now a most profound inner calm,' Beth reflected in a letter following an event which she described as a living nightmare of the first degree.

'I was returning home from the hairdresser when I saw great billows of smoke emanating from a region which would roughly approximate to my home. I put my foot down and got home fast, but I couldn't enter my driveway because of a raging bushfire. The children were at school, luckily, but my pets are my babies. I parked my car on the main road and ran down my long driveway lined with searing hot, eighty foot high flames and got my pets out the house, back up to the car and away from danger. It was a huge drama all round. At one stage Mum and I thought we'd lost both our husbands and our homes to the fire. I thought Mum was going to have a heart attack.

'Our husbands survived with minor burns and all our pets survived. The house was saved except for a tiny bit of scorching and I keep a back-up copy of my book in my handbag at all times, so I only lost three pages of my story. It's a miracle really. At one stage our homes were completely encircled by fire.

'But even though I experienced this fully there was a solid centre of inner calm. I knew that, whatever happened, I would be left with what I need.'

In her calmness Beth was able to interpret the living nightmare while also experiencing it. Instead of the shock and trauma of it all, she said, it became a revelation.

'I processed the trauma while it was happening, there were no residual anxieties left after the fire was over. I didn't do any processing in my dreams. While other family members are still dealing with the fire damage in their dreams I am free, completely untouched by the incident apart from a most helpful insight.'

The revelation concerned Beth's feelings about the land which she and her husband were subdividing.

'The surveyors had been walking around the properties. I saw them from the verandah, chopping down a tree for the surveyor's line and I must admit I felt as if I was being violated. Strangers on this virgin land! I wondered how I would cope when they selectively cleared some of the forest. How would I feel when it was all changed? Maybe we had made the wrong decision. Maybe it wasn't our right to change nature by chopping her trees. Then the fire came to take the decision right out of our hands. The fire burned all of our six acres and changed it completely. And I realised the lesson is: change is the nature of life.'

The outer world gives perfect feedback, through reflection, on what you need to understand about your life—if you can interpret the event. Faced with the same reality, Beth has coped with the fire in a different way from the rest of her family, because she could extract meaningfulness from the event rather than fear. Seeing our thoughts manifest, as in synchronicity, can be an incredibly powerful lesson, more powerful perhaps than the processing of a dream.

Was Beth's experience a synchronicity, a 'death of the old, birth of the new' insight that the whole family was struggling with? Certainly Beth describes her inner conflict, prior to the fire, as resistance to change. As her unconscious worked on the problem and got close to delivering the 'change is good' message, her outer life reinforced, through mirroring, the same picture. Lastly, it exhibited several of the common synchronicity themes again: death, renewal, change. In Beth's mind the whole episode was a beautiful example of a deeply meaningful synchronicity, an outer world reflection of an emerging inner world thought.

Now take another look at the situation from my point of view. As I read Beth's letter which was dated 3 December, a thought crossed my mind. Although I could see the relevance of burnout and change in my own life at the time (Beth being an outer world symbol for me too), I vaguely remembered dreaming about a fire engine and I had a niggling feeling that it might have been a precognitive dream. Beth's letter had given me no indication of when the fire had been, so with all the excitement of a detective at work on a case, I consulted my dream journal.

My dream entitled 'Fire Engine' was recorded as, 'Can't recall, just know I dreamed of a fire engine.' A little disappointed with myself for the distinct lack of detail, at least I had a date. My dream had occurred during the night of 13/14 November. I had interpreted the dream as 'beware burnout'. I checked back through my diaries and my memory and estimated that I'd probably only remembered around three or four dreams of fire engines in my life, so it wasn't as if they were regular features in my dreams. I wrote back to Beth confidently predicting that the date of her fire was around the date of my dream. I was right. The fire had occurred on 14 November, only hours after I awoke from sleep.

Now we seem to have a labelling dilemma. Although my dream recall lacked detail, my level of confidence in replying to Beth indicates a strong connection between my dream and her reality. My dream could have sat snugly in Chapter 1 as a simple example of a precognitive dream, albeit a tiny one. Yet from Beth's perspective, the fire was a synchronicity in the now. Precognition and synchronicity begin to intertwine, the definition dependent only on the point of view of the observer. The timescape model of a timeless, futureless, pastless world of now springs to mind. What appears to be the future already out there on a different grid reference on the timescape map is, in reality, an illusion, since there is only now. Time is in the mind of the beholder. We overlapped and shared the same moment, one in dream reality, one in waking reality, because our similar inner thoughts coincided. We are thought. Where thoughts coincide, we do too. The moment was the same, but our individual perceptions of the time differed.

Where thoughts coincide, we do too

I believe this is indeed the point. Perceptually we are, as human beings, a pretty deluded lot. Illusion is our daily bread. We believe we distinguish a difference between precognition and synchronicity, whereas in fact the difference is an illusion based on our inability to rid ourselves of the concept of linear time.

In this one ever reflecting now moment that I believe life is, my own inner observation of potential burnout and change was a thought form captured in a dream yet also out there in the ocean of thought. My thought, partially resolved through attention to my dream, was not strong enough to create the material fire in my own life but it coincided with Beth's thoughts which were sufficiently resonant to materialise as a bushfire in her own back yard. Imagine a set of crystal glasses shattering in unison as a perfect high-pitched note is played, resonating the crystal to breaking point. So it is, I believe, that similar thoughts, like crystal glasses, resonate at a similar pitch. The purest crystals, the strongest thoughts, may materialise. For example, burnout thoughts may materialise as fire. The less pure thoughts, burnout tinged with survival perhaps, are violently shaken but do not eventuate. The concept of tuning in to someone else's thoughts when you are going through similar circumstances may be an extremely accurate metaphor!

You are thought, indeed myriad thoughts, each with its signature frequency, each pitched to resonate in unison with similar frequencies, be they conscious or unconscious, another person's thoughts or your own. Where resonance reaches a critical threshold level, thought energy becomes matter. Your thoughts materialise. Your physical body together with the outer world that you perceive in this now moment is the material flip side of your strongest thoughts. What is coming up from your unconscious, especially at times of change, emerges with sufficient energy that it frequently and multiply materialises in your outer world as synchronicity. The upcoming energy is often expressed first as a dream, so understanding the dream empowers you to accelerate the blossoming of the thought and its materialisation in your outer world, or to defuse it by making appropriate changes in your conscious world.

In the same moment we are all interconnected, and prematerialised thought knows no geographical bounds. We share one ocean of thought, hanging our individual hats on the different waves we call our bodies and daily reality, but really, underneath it all, we communicate on the one collective unconscious net. Where similar thoughts are shared, we resonate at the same frequency and tune in to each other's mirrored reflections of ourselves. Our lives overlap in the one everchanging now, be they dream worlds or waking worlds, be they labelled as precognition or synchronicity. We are thought and where thoughts coincide, we do too, with or without the physical body, with or without the illusion of time.

hocus pocus
11 or just
plain focus?

Is everyday life really so deep and reverberatingly meaningful? The last chapters have painted a picture of only our strongest thoughts materialising, mostly those connected with the emergence from the unconscious of the big heavies such as transcendence of limitation, change, death, rebirth, accident and reunion. Yet we know that our lives are also filled with seeming trivialities and the results of simple, conscious decision making. How powerful are our conscious thoughts in creating daily reality? Are they generally overruled by the big unknowns, our unconscious conditioning and the unconscious emergents, the 'emergencies' in our lives, which determine the major shape of things to come?

Through my experience and dream research I have observed that the bestlaid plans of mice and men are frequently thwarted by the greater conditioning of the unconscious. Where there's a will there's a way, as long as the unconscious doesn't get there first. Tongue in cheek I've used these clichés for a reason. We are creatures of habit who unthinkingly opt for the verbal cliché, the well-worn path, the tried and trusted; in short, we are easily driven by the conditioned response.

Daily reality, for most of us, is a familiar backdrop against which changes, some subtle, some momentous, act out on front stage. The familiar backdrop includes our conscious expectations (thoughts), such as the daily rising of the sun, the falling of leaves in autumn, the regular arrival of bills to be paid, ageing, predictable responses of our family and friends and the exchange of work for pay. It is also fabricated by our unconscious thoughts ingrained through conditioning. The child consistently told that life's a struggle may grow to experience life as a struggle. He may hold many conscious thoughts to the contrary, but if he is unconsciously conditioned to expect struggle, he will meet struggle, because unconscious thoughts are powerful. Alternatively a child may learn, through experience, that the only way to get loving attention is to be sick. In later life she will generally fall sick whenever she feels unloved. Her conscious thoughts about sickness and love may be quite different, but unconscious conditioning is weighty, until it is drawn into the light of consciousness and released. We are thought, and our daily life is a reflection of our strongest conscious and unconscious thoughts. Daily reinforcement sets our individual view of the reality of life in concrete. How could my life be any different?

Out on front stage are the changeables. Fleeting conscious thoughts which occasionally gain sufficient strength to materialise may drift through a few scenes, bringing small daily changes. Whenever crumbling unconscious conditioning rises towards the surface, huge momentous emergencies may play havoc on centre stage. Mid-crisis the comfortable stability of the whole stage set is threatened through synchronicity until the breakthrough insight smoothes the transition into life's next scene. Meanwhile, out in the wings, the greater, untouched unconscious ocean awaits its call. Life is indeed a stage we each design and upon which we play out our own self-scripted dramas, according to the materialisation of our thoughts. But how easy is it to change our scripts once the ink has dried? Can we edit and rewrite every unfolding moment of our lives, or are some chapters irrevocably carved in stone?

Do we progressively seal our destiny through repeated conscious and unconscious thoughts, restricting our life to one predictable outcome? Or can we change our scripts and the shape of things to come by influencing which thoughts manifest?

Dreams are often the battleground between our conscious and unconscious thoughts. At the very least, if we can interpret the dreams, we can understand the dilemmas in our lives. We may see why our conscious efforts are undermined by our unconscious conditioning and then take steps to undo that conditioning. Frequently the dream resolves the issue, the conditioning is broken and the insight emerges, heralded by synchronicity. Life shifts, reflecting the shift in consciousness.

Recently I designed an experiment to see what would happen if a conscious thought was deliberately implanted into a dream. I wondered whether it would meet its unconscious counterpart and stir things up a bit. The idea was to increase my understanding of how conscious and unconscious thoughts interact and to see if there was therapeutic value in this.

Challenging the Unconscious

Through the Dream Research Bank I asked people to think of an insignificant object and to follow my instructions to induce it to appear in their dreams. The method involved intense focus on the object prior to sleep and was based on the principle that whatever is unresolved as you fall asleep tends to be considered in your dreams. By choosing an insignificant object I was really asking each dreamer to pick something relatively free from meaning or conflict. By the time they had thought about the experiment and focused on the task at hand, the object was no longer insignificant: it now symbolised the dream task itself.

Tara chose a white glass marble as her object. It appeared in her dream variously as a small white ball, a plastic ball instead of a glass one, four balls, a billiard ball and an egg. At one point in her dream she explained to someone,

'You see, I've been trying to find my white marble. The plastic balls, the billiard ball and now this egg show me that the universal powers are getting my message, but somehow I'm not conveying it quite clearly enough.' Finally her dream presented her with a gold neck chain threaded with a white ball before she flew up to the heavens where 'the stars shone brighter than ever and were the size of ... my marble!'

Tara interpreted her dream and concluded that she had a tendency to be indecisive and unclear of her goals at times, as well as a bit of a perfectionist, searching for the ultimate perfect white glass marble rather than the near-fit alternatives she had cleverly produced in her dream.

So far, so good. The marble was an introduced conscious thought symbolising 'dream task' which had entered the battleground of Tara's dreams to stir up questions of perfectionism and indecision. A conscious thought, it seemed, had been successfully used to elucidate her unconscious response to task performance.

What I hadn't anticipated was what followed next. Tara noticed her marble appearing in her outer world as well as in her dreams. Firstly her son chose six story books at the local library.

'I hadn't noticed what they were until I began reading them to him that night. The first book was called Roger Loses His Marbles, *and it told of a pig who spent all day searching for his yellow marbles. Eventually his aunt found them during the night (dream time!) in Roger's bedroom on the windowsill. On the last page there was a picture of a jar containing*

over fifty marbles of many colours, with only one white marble among them! The next two stories that I chose randomly from the six also referred to marbles, but only fleetingly: a monster with 'greedy eyes rolling like marbles' in one book, and a boy playing marbles with a monster in another book.

'A couple of days later I turned my calendar page to February and there was a picture of two marbles above the word February. The picture for that month was of a teddy bear at school surrounded by marbles. Then the next day my husband told me he had an elaborate dream about diving down into water and retrieving my marble from the bottom!'

Tara was experiencing synchronicity because, I assume, focusing her conscious thoughts on the 'dream task' had challenged her unconscious thoughts on 'tasks, goals and measures of success'. These unconscious thoughts were challenged to emerge into consciousness heralded by the classic breakthrough sign of synchronicity. Tara's life became temporarily flooded with marbles because these were the outer world reflections of her inner world symbol for 'tasks, goals and measures of success'. Significantly they first surfaced as a search for something lost, then progressed through confrontation (monsters) and finally emerged associated with learning and a comforting teddy bear. Her husband's dream delivered the final symbolism of the marble's 'outing'.

Beth's experience of the dream task was a little different, since she was unable to induce her chosen object, a 'garden shovel' into her dreams, at least as far as she could recall them. However, as in Tara's case, synchronicities followed.

'On the second day I went out to greet my husband as he arrived home and stubbed my toe on a garden shovel which was on the driveway, a most unusual place for our shovel. On the fourth day I took my children down to the beach and was sitting in the shade chatting with my mother when she said, "Goodness, would you look at the size of the shovel your son has

brought to the beach!" There he was, digging a hole in the sand with a huge garden shovel. He had stowed it away in the boot of the car without asking me.

'The sixth day saw my father arrive at our house asking me if I had borrowed his shovel because he couldn't find it anywhere. Then, when I visited my sister-in-law on the eighth day, she produced two tiny plastic spades her ex-husband had given the children and said, "Look at these. Aren't they ridiculous? They might as well be teaspoons. It would take all day to fill a bucket!"

'While the shovel saga continues, my dreams have been digging down deep into my subconscious, presenting to me things that were well and truly buried. So it seems the reverse has happened so far: that my subconscious has taken the symbol in and dug down deep with that old shovel. I find it most interesting, though, that the shovels should be manifesting in my waking life instead of in my dreams. "Wow! This has potential—now what else would I like to manifest?" But what then would happen to my dream life? If I choose to focus on an open door every night before going to sleep, would new doors open in my waking life?'

Well, would new doors open in her waking life? The answer, Beth, according to my experience, is that they probably would, but not in the way that you mean.

Years ago we lived in a beautiful townhouse with a little back garden that led down to a harbour. I used to enjoy having water at the back door. When we needed to move, I sat the family down and asked everyone to think about what they wanted in our next house and we compiled a grand list of all our wishful thinking. I added 'water at the back door'. Well, you can probably anticipate the end of the story. The first house we looked at the very next day had everything on our list except it was inland, away from the sea. It was built in a U-shape, enclosing an unfinished courtyard. I looked through the glass of the back door, and there it was: the whole courtyard was flooded to a few inches of water. I had got my 'water at the back door', but not the kind of water I had really meant!

We did move into the house because it checked with our other requirements but it turned out to be a difficult year. I look back on that time as an emotional watershed, symbolised by the 'water at the back door' (water symbolises emotions in dreams). Ultimately it was cleansing, as water always is, since we were able to use the challenges that year presented in a positive way and move forward to a more fulfilling lifestyle. What I had done, I now realise, was focus my conscious thought of 'water at the back door' which challenged my unconscious thoughts on water (symbol of emotions) and back door (symbol of private self or what you put behind you). Synchronicity heralded the stirring up of old emotional conditioning which bubbled up for recognition and resolution.

The old adage 'be careful what you ask for because you might well get it' is true. Each of these three examples involved a focused conscious thought challenging an unconscious reaction. The unconscious delivered literally, yet the manifestations, the marble, the shovel and the water were symbolically meaningful in the contexts in which they arose.

The obvious link here is to the manifestations encountered during the hypnosis project described earlier in the book.

The Hypnosis Project Revisited 1

Let's revisit the fourth hypnosis session (pages 121–30) where I took three conscious thoughts (a bunch of orange and maroon flowers, a cheque for $174 and the concept of the Chinese Wall) into hypnosis to present them to my unconscious self. John, the hypnotist, was my prompt, writing down the three thoughts, hypnotising me and then discussing these with my unconscious once I was in a trance. The point of the experiment at the time was to test to see whether I was creating, through hypnosis, the shape of things to come rather than simply seeing the future.

As discussed earlier, the three ideas all manifested in forms varying slightly from the original *intention*. The flowers came in the shape of a gift of a flowery orange and maroon blouse following the exact description I had originally but unintentionally given John when I said 'orange and maroon, like my blouse'. The cheque came in the shape of Glen's new mobile phone number, with the numbers rearranged and including the original '80 cents' which I had dropped from the experiment at the last minute. The Chinese Wall, as a concept, manifested more fleetingly to begin with, but finally resonated in a series of Chinese references including the 'out the blue' offer from a publisher to translate one of my books into Chinese.

Tara's marble, Beth's garden shovel and my 'water at the back door' were all examples of focused conscious thoughts which challenged our unconscious thoughts, at a symbolic level, to emerge and declare themselves through synchronicity. The key-words are *focus* and *symbolic*. Under hypnosis I was always aware of 'two Janes': the one experiencing the hypnotism and the one objectively taking notes. It was as if I stood at the borderline between my conscious and unconscious worlds, one foot firmly planted either side of the line. In the manifestation experiment John kept me focused on my previously chosen conscious thoughts while also in direct communication with my unconscious through hypnosis. I *focused* and the thoughts manifested *symbolically*. I can look at the final manifestations and understand my old uncon-scious programming more clearly through the way it handled the symbolic challenges, just as I might look at a synchronicity in my life and learn from it accordingly.

In short, I created, through conscious focus, what I needed to know about myself. I manipulated aspects of my 'future' by challenging my unconscious to unfold in response to the stimulus of a focused thought. The question now becomes: how much is our future determined unconsciously, how much can it be changed through focused conscious thought and how much directional control do we have over that focus?

gathering
threads 12

Five or six centuries ago the world was flat and the sun voyaged daily through the heavens. Later generations lived on a round planet which circled a stationary sun. Yesterday our round earth still orbited the sun at a measurable speed of thirty kilometres a second, but old father sun no longer stood still. Instead he travelled much faster than our medieval ancestors believed when they pictured his daily arc across the sky. Yesterday the sun orbited our galaxy at 220 kilometres a second, while the galaxy, being only one of many, itself orbited another centre which orbited another and perhaps another. Yesterday our earth spun around the sun which spun around the galaxy which ever outward spun while we, with relative breathtaking speed here on our tiny planet, each felt oh so steadily unbreathtakingly still.

And what of today? And tomorrow? Will the incredulous remain numb to the implications of modern physics simply because they do not open their minds? Intellectually we understand the earth spins, but perceptually it stands still. Intellectually we know we human beings are largely composed of space and energy, but perceptually we are solid. Intellectually we may know time is relative and linked to space, but perceptually time ticks by, it flows, it passes and we all drift at the same rate in its steady, measurable stream. Intellectually we may know that time is not linear, that the future is already out there and is therefore a part of now, but perceptually it is untouchable, yet to come.

Intellectual knowledge is not the same as the 'thought' referred to throughout this book. Intellectual knowledge is information acquired through reasoning. We can reason without belief. Thought, which we are, is an energy form beyond mere information: it carries the emotional charge of belief. The more conditioned we are, consciously or unconsciously, to believe in the world we are taught to see, the stronger these thoughts become. With each strengthening we reinforce our concrete view of the world. As we think, so we are and so our world is.

We find it so difficult to align our perception of the world with the insights discovered by modern science because, at root, our conditioning is so heavily to the contrary. Our conditioned beliefs are so at odds with the reality of our being that we cannot shift the way we see the world to match. We cannot see a world where we are all interconnected as a pulsating ocean of thought existing in a timeless now because we cannot rid ourselves of our conditioned belief in a world driven by cause and effect and the unfolding of linear time. The moment we are successful in undoing that conditioning we see a different world: one which makes much more sense. Are you ready to break your conditioned thoughts of cause and effect, of past and future, of flowing time? Are you ready to move beyond a perception of time, beyond the question of precognition and into the light of a world ever mirroring the shape of your own thoughts? Look at today: it is yourself.

So what do we now see? Part One presented the evidence for precognition through precognitive dreams and visions, through the eyes of clairvoyants and through the experimental work of the hypnosis project. In terms of our everyday language, we proved that, as human beings, we frequently experience the 'future' before it happens—often in great detail.

Precognition: The Big Picture
A Summary So Far

Through Part Two we have taken the fact of precognition and allied it, via science and observation, to synchronicity. Discovering that the future was illusory, we realised that thinking about time was throwing us off course. Time, we saw, was a red herring in a world where scientific reality is an everlasting now. Instead we realised that precognition was a special case of synchronicity.

We considered ourselves primarily as thought energy which materialises into the physical matter of our bodies and our personal outer worlds, rather than as physical bodies producing thought. We saw ourselves and our worlds as being the material reflection of our strongest conscious and unconscious thoughts, and we acknowledged that our unconscious thoughts generally win the day. This process was compared to the formation of standing waves in a vibrating coffee cup: where the (thought) waves are strongest they resonate and materialise.

We observed synchronicity as an indicator of personal change and psychological development. We saw that under pressure of change our unconscious conditioning rumbles, shakes and shatters, releasing old patterning as new insight breaks through. We noted that these changed thoughts emerge with such strength that they materialise in the outer world, usually in symbolic form. These outer world synchronicities, we saw, usually involve change, travel, accident, death, birth and reunion, underlining their inner counterparts of transformation. Each person experiencing synchronicity, we understood, was witnessing a fragmenting and restructuring of their personal world view based on their changed perception. These, we realised, were also the main categories of precognition.

We saw ourselves as thought, interconnected as one ocean, each hanging our individual hats on the different waves we call our bodies. Yet, we argued, unmaterialised thought knows no geographical bounds and where similar thoughts are shared, we resonate at the same frequency and tune in to each other's mirrored reflections of ourselves, like crystal glasses resonating at the same pitch. So it is that we can tune in to another person's thoughts, feelings and intentions: a phenomenon we usually define as telepathy. What we call precognition is exactly the same, since time is a red herring. In an everlasting now where time does not exist, we tune in to similar thoughts and, since we are thought, where thoughts coincide, we do too. We share thoughts, events, processes and information because we coincide.

Precognition involving another person is where, for a moment, our worlds overlap and one of us is conscious of it, whether through experiencing a vision or recalling a dream which recorded the shared resonating thought. It is therefore a kind of synchronicity as well as a kind of telepathy. Where we cross paths in resonating thought we sometimes remember. Since precognition is resonating thought we can only experience precognition of people and events that reflect our own strongest thoughts, conscious or unconscious. We considered the story of the car journey where Glen and I travelled together but each saw different things. Each person's outer world is a reflection of themselves. Each synchronicity, each precognition, is an outer world reflection of an inner world shared by two people: a world experienced where two inner paths cross.

We saw also saw that focusing our conscious thoughts under the right conditions (hypnosis, dream incubation or intense concentration) challenges our unconscious thoughts on the subject to resonate and produce synchronicity: to form material representations of the unconscious counterpart of our focused thought. The synchronicity, we saw, may appear in symbolic form rather than as anticipated by the reasoning conscious self. We can carry out simple conscious thought processes, such as buying a bunch of orange and maroon flowers, or we can manifest the flowers through focused thought via unconscious delivery; however, these manifestations are more likely to reflect the unconscious version of the thought than the conscious intention. The more synchronicity matches our original conscious thought, the more accurate we believe our precognition to have been. If we were more adept at translating the language of our unconscious, we would discover our truly vast potential to predict our future manifestations.

This, then, is the Big Picture which explains how precognition occurs, but there are still some loose threads to gather together and draw into the final tapestry.

The Hypnosis Project Revisited 2
When Dreams Come True

Rather than viewing the visions of the earlier hypnosis sessions as glimpses of the future, let's consider them as manifestations of synchronicity. Following the sessions there appeared physical objects such as new shoes, images such as gold rings, concepts such as curtains meaning endings, events such as the band gig and location details such as the bar at the gig. Other people became involved as the actors in my unfolding visions, including Steve, the film editor, and Sue who introduced the black and white film. Some things appeared in literal fashion, such as the shoes, while others were more symbolic, such as Steve's green jumper in the vision manifesting as his Irish accent in the outer world. Later sessions brought a wasp sting, a book, revelations, a French address, a leather satchel and, finally, the Wright Brothers television documentary: all can be seen as near-fit symbolic versions of my original visions under hypnosis.

The scenes I saw while hypnotised had seemed dreamlike both in storyline and in symbolism. When I treated the visions as dreams and analysed them, they related to my life. I believed I was simply viewing some of my unconscious processing, much as I might in a dream, with the added benefit of alert conscious observation. This is the point, I think. Dreams are usually highly symbolic and we are rarely conscious of the fact that we are dreaming. Our dreams generally feel totally real and we have no idea that we have another life which seems to be 'the real one' too. Under hypnosis, however, I was focusing my conscious self on my unconscious dream process, so I had the magical intensive mix of conscious *focus* and *symbolism* which produces synchronicity in the shape of symbolic manifestation. The only difference between this process and the deliberate experiments aimed at manifesting items was that I was starting with the unconscious dream process and then focusing on its symbols through conscious observation and comment. In other words, the manifestation experiments used a focused conscious thought to resonate with and 'out' its unconscious counterpart, whereas the 'natural' hypnosis progressions involved consciously focusing on symbols already under consideration and reconstruction (dream processing) by my unconscious.

Now all the manifestations, all the precognitive visions seen under hypnosis, can be understood as synchronicities delivered by my unconscious mind which had been challenged (manifestation experiments) or reinforced (natural dream-processing sessions) by focused conscious thought. All these futures were cloaked in the language of the unconscious, just as synchronicities always are. We need to take great responsibility for our conscious thoughts because they can evoke resounding unconscious responses which take shape in our outer worlds.

And what of the Stevens, the Sues, the mobile phone company employees, the wasp, the market vendor who gave me the blouse and all the other people who played their parts in manifesting my future through synchronicity? Was I responsible for the roles they played in my life? The answer is simple. I was in their outer worlds too, so I was a reflection of their thoughts and synchronicities, just as much as they were a reflection of mine. They were a part of my world because we resonated to the same thought, like crystal glasses. All interactions are balanced unconsciously, even though they don't always appear to be so on the surface.

Why do so few dreams come true?

Dreams are snapshots of our conscious and unconscious thoughts on various issues usually pictured in symbolic form. As we are primarily thought, dreams really represent our true self, although this idea is a difficult one for people who identify themselves by their conscious thoughts and their physical forms alone. For those unacquainted with the language of the unconscious, the idea of really being a bundle of bizarre dreams seems outrageous!

Through symbolism our dreams work on integrating conflicting thoughts and experiences. They may reflect various stages of unresolved conflict before finally synthesising new insights. All the while the strongest thoughts, conscious or unconscious, manifest in our outer worlds. The weaker thoughts, or those 'under construction', form a blueprint of the possible shape of things to come. If they acquire the right degree of strength, they will materialise, perhaps heralded through synchronicity.

The question is, if dreams and visions seen under hypnosis 'come true' so easily, why are so few 'normal' dreams precognitive?

The two key factors observed in the hypnosis project mani-festations were, remember, conscious *focus* and *symbolism*. The manifestations, although symbolic, were obviously related to the consciously observed dreams and visions.

Normal dreams are not associated with the same degree of intense conscious focus and do not usually seem to manifest so obviously. However, a closer look, through the eyes of the language of dreams, reveals a different story. A common experience is to dream of the death of a child, and I am frequently contacted by people worried that such a dream is precognitive. Dreams of death generally symbolise aspects of our thoughts or our lives that are 'dying', or things we need to put an end to, depending on the nature of the dream. These 'deaths' may play out in our outer worlds as job loss, leaving a city, finally quitting an outdated atti-tude, overcoming an illness and so on. In these ways our strongest thoughts may be showing up in our dreams and manifesting in our lives, but because we don't understand the symbolism, we don't realise the dreams are precognitive.

Another common example is the tidal wave dream. Many people make predictions of turn of the century tidal waves because they have seen them in their dreams and believe their dreams to be literally precognitive. Instead they should be looking at their own lives where they have usually repressed huge emotions (water symbolises emotions) which will overwhelm them when they break through, heralding great turning points. The tidal wave dreams are potentially precognitive if the dreamer takes no preventative action, but because most people do not understand symbolism, they do not realise this fact. They await the world's doomsday instead of paying attention to defusing their own.

Our dreams can be seen, therefore, as symbolic blueprints of the shape of things to come, reflecting our inner worlds, our true selves. What we see in the mirror of life are our strongest thoughts manifested, while what we see in our dreams are the possibilities. Some will gather strength and materialise and some will fade out of the blueprint, depending on how our dreams eventually resolve the various issues.

I am often asked why we need to interpret our dreams if dreams are a natural process of integration anyway. Most people have at least one recurring dream or recurring dream-theme. These are dreams which are 'stuck' in trying to resolve an issue, so they endlessly repeat, going round and round the same old scenes, getting nowhere. A good dream interpreter can take a more objective view of a recurring dream and interpret it to reveal the unconscious conflict the dreamer is stuck in. With the benefit of this insight the dreamer can usually consciously apply herself to resolving the conflict once and for all. Usually the recurring dream stops, along with its outer world reflection, as soon as the issue is addressed. Here we see again the importance of adding conscious focus to an unconscious process to 'out' it and become enlightened. This is the power of dream interpretation.

Most of your dreams will naturally resolve your inner conflicts in time, but if you learn to interpret your dreams immediately and act upon them by applying conscious focus, you will accelerate resolution and all the good things that come with it. Dream interpretation helps you to know your true self more fully and to work towards your best expression.

Interpreting your dreams and acting upon them speeds up your personal development and the expression of your best blueprints, so more of your best dreams will 'come true' while your warning dreams will be defused. Learning symbolism will also help you realise just how many of your dreams are precognitive in a symbolic way. You can also play the game backwards and interpret the symbolism in the mirror of your daily life to understand the inner conflicts you need to attend to.

The dreams which seem to be more literally precognitive are

mostly those resulting from tuning in to others. These also seem to be the most obvious precognitive dreams and the easier ones to discuss since they need little understanding of symbolism. The important point is not to get so carried away with the excitement of having tuned in to someone else's life (with real proof!) that you overlook the fact that the tuning in says something about your own inner world. You were only there because you resonated in thought, so you need to take the time to identify those thoughts and *still* interpret the dream! Imagine, for example, the excitement I felt with my Lotto dream (pages 23–24). I had my dream journal in one hand and the lotto results in the other: the proof of precognitive dreaming! When I later interpreted the dream and the event I realised that I was conditioned, at that time, to believe that 'I always get so near, but never near enough'. Learn from your precognitive dreams and move on.

Clairvoyants

There are plenty of well-meaning but incompetent clairvoyants advertising their services alongside the charlatans that inevitably are out to make a buck out of people's gullibility in times of despair, but there are also those whose skills seem to be genuine. This section discusses precognition in relation to genuine clairvoyants.

The four clairvoyants interviewed in this book generally agreed that time is irrelevant: either there is 'no time' or 'the only time is now', which fits with the notion of the ever-reflecting now presented in this book. They also agreed that they predict probable, possible or likely future outcomes, which is in alignment with the blueprint shape of possible things to come. They all saw the necessity for their clients to take responsibility for their own futures, which accords with the perception of our outer worlds as the material form of our strongest thoughts.

Their additional contribution towards the study of precognition was that they all believed some form of spirit (either Spirit, spirit guide or deceased person) helps with their readings. This is a dimension which has not entered our discussion so far.

The picture I have painted until now portrays us all as interconnected thought energy materialising in parts into physical form. Each person that exists in physical form was shown as the manifestation of their true self's strongest thoughts. No doubt you therefore imagined that each true self materialises into a body. But need this be the case? If we choose not to materialise, do we still perceive of ourselves as individual people without form, or do we diffuse more into the flow of the ocean of oneness? I do not intend to give answers here, but merely wish to make sure you give yourself a perception check. Reality, remember, is thought energy manifesting as matter, not the other way around!

My personal feeling sways towards a notion that since all thought is accessible through the interconnected ocean, and since time is a red herring, *all* thought, 'past, present or future', exists now. People whose physical form has faded and passed from view remain, as impregnated thought, within the ocean. We can play all sorts of labelling games from this point. We can talk spirits, ghosts, guides, angels, fairies, divas, dissociated parts of the self, aliens from outer space or pink elephants—but if all thought is interconnected, the labelling truly becomes redundant. In tuning in to invisible help, we are tuning in to all that is, of which we are both a part and the whole.

To this extent I believe genuine clairvoyants have a better developed system of access to the ocean of thought, Jung's collective unconscious, our dream images, our blueprints. Non-professional seers in this book explained that their visions tended to occur unbidden and that they could not control them or summon them up at will, yet clairvoyants seem to be able to do this. Some say, 'I can only tell you what I see,' but even this indicates they don't have to sit around waiting for the unbidden moment: they can perform within the time frame of the reading.

I have described precognition as an experience related to tuning in to another person because their inner thoughts resonate with ours, or as synchronicity due to emerging insights which manifest in our lives, or as an extension of our dream process gathering strength and reflecting our strongest thoughts into outer world materialisation. In summary, precognition for the nonprofessional has been portrayed as inescapably bound up with their own inner personal development and thoughts. Yet a professional clairvoyant is expected to read for anyone, regardless of whether the client's inner thoughts have any overlap with the clairvoyant's own personal world. How can they do this?

Perhaps they are incredibly evolved beings whose inner world experience is so vast that they can find resonance with anyone. I don't think so. My suggestion is that they have learned how to connect through the ocean of thought with the reservoir of *all* inner experience and use this, without necessarily understanding how, as a tuning fork which vibrates with their clients' strongest or emerging thoughts. This leaves the clairvoyant as the intermediary, relaying and interpreting the points of resonance to identify their clients' blueprints. This also fits in with two of our clairvoyants' description of the process as being the 'courier' or the 'messenger' only. As human beings I guess they perceive a sensation of tuning in through a 'person', a spirit rather than a giant tuning fork! As they home in on areas of their clients' blueprints which resonate with family, friends and spouses, they find it easy to paint the physical, bodily expression of the thought forms. Hence they genuinely 'see' and can describe people, alive or dead, who are important to us.

By alerting us to our blueprints and our emerging thoughts, clairvoyants can predict the possibilities ahead. It is then up to us whether we go with the flow or take actions to accelerate or diffuse what the psychic sees. Free will remains ours.

Clairvoyants may also, I believe, influence the way we deal with our life through unwitting hypnosis or neurolinguistic programming (pages 108–9). We have already seen how, under certain conditions, focused conscious thought frequently challenges the unconscious to manifest itself through synchronicity, for example, pages 200–06. I firmly believe that along with their natural talents of reading our blueprints and predicting the chain of events to come, clairvoyants also create the ideal conditions, through a reading, for the client's focused conscious thoughts to stir the unconscious to manifest in material form according to a changed agenda.

Yet throughout this discussion of possible futures and personal responsibility, the clairvoyants interviewed here still had a suspicion that some form of predetermined destiny operates. How can we account for this? Are some thoughts irreversible and therefore destined to materialise? This leads us to the final thread to be gathered into our picture: the Wright Brothers documentary!

The Hypnosis Project Revisited 3
Are some things predetermined?

Under hypnosis I was asked to describe a predetermined event which would take place on 2 January 1997. I saw several scenes which turned out to be an accurate symbolic version of a televised documentary on the Wright Brothers on the prescribed day. (See full details and discussion, Sixth Progression Hypnosis pages 131–44.) In summary I was confused: did I indeed foresee a predetermined event, and if I did, was it the screening of the documentary or the Wright Brothers' invention of the plane that was predetermined? Did I tune in to find a resonating thought which matched my interest on 2 January (the television programmer perhaps)? Did I find the documentary on the big tuning fork of the collective ocean of thought, like a real professional? Or did I, in accordance with all the other hypnosis project results, focus my conscious thoughts on the dream material of my unconscious, stirring it up and producing the outer world synchronicity, the manifestation in the shape of the television documentary? Just think about it: if I apply the results of the rest of the hypnosis project, then I created the screening of the television programme that you might have watched on that same night too. To test this out, I took a closer look at the symbolism of the television documentary to see if it matched my inner personal development at the time. Hold your hat, believe in the paradox fairy, as science does, and read on!

The documentary concerned mankind's breakthrough into mastery of the air through the invention of the plane. On a personal level I was experiencing my final hypnosis experiment and I was on the verge of making my own personal breakthrough into mastery of the mind (air symbolises the mind). Until that point in history, mankind had conquered the land (physical self), the water (emotional self) but not the air (the mind). Now that I have put the final touches to the last chapters in this book, I can clearly see the reflections of my own inner mastery of the mind. I take confidence from the fact that it was the Wright (right) Brothers who achieved this in the outer world television show that reflected my inner progress back to me!

I saw sufficient symbolic connections (too complex to relate) between the documentary and my inner thoughts and progress to satisfy me that I may easily have manifested the event of sitting on the sofa and switching on the television, perhaps even of creating the screening of the show on that date. This is the result of reasoning according to theory and experience, but I realise it may seem incredible.

Or was it, after all, a predetermined event? Under hypnosis I reported both predetermined and nonpredetermined aspects. Only the following elements were seen as being predetermined: camera, planes, famous race, metal frame construction and bright blue breaking through from under the ground (thought to be the vision of sky from the flying position). In other words, translating the symbolism, the predetermined elements were seen as the use of the camera, a race (i.e. several groups involved in competition), the development of metal-framed planes and a breakthrough in the form of an idea.

On my inner level my breakthrough was from the unconscious (underground) into the conscious mind (blue sky: air) to achieve mastery of the mental 'plane'. On my outer level I saw a television documentary reflecting my own breakthrough. In accordance with the laws of synchronicity, the outer world frequently reflects what is *still breaking through*, which explains why it took me another week to recognise the fact consciously.

In historical terms I can only assume the Wright Brothers were going through their own processes of mental breakthrough which their outer world achievements mirrored.

Of much greater significance than the Wright Brothers or myself, however, was the evolution of mankind's mental processes. Man's evolution, according to biology and geology, progressed from a soup of wayward chemicals floating in the primordial sea, through to creatures with basic brains capable of maintaining the physical side of life, through to animals with emotional centres in their brains, through to the evolution of our brains today, complete with their capacity for higher mental processing and reasoning. According to my theory, of course, these are progressive manifestations of our strongest thoughts: mere reflections of our true being. Perhaps these stages represent the materialisation of our mass conditioned perception of life. It may take just as many millennia to undo the perception, but perhaps we have to evolve to a point of conscious understanding before we can see the folly of our beliefs, of our fabricated illusion of a world.

Mankind's evolution can therefore be seen as an evolution of consciousness, an enlightenment which, as a process, will finally reveal the ultimate reality of our being. While each of us in our own individual way is personally evolving, we also, as part of the whole human race, contribute to the overall evolution of our mass consciousness. Since synchronicity heralds what is about to break through, perhaps the fact that several countries were simultaneously working on developing a flying machine symbolised a forthcoming mass insight into the nature of mind and how to master it to gain mastery of mind. Compared to the time span of mankind's evolution, this mental mastery may well be imminent. In evolutionary terms, I am suggesting that this process has been approaching inevitability, and therefore perhaps predetermination, for millennia. Perhaps that is what I touched during this hypnosis session.

Coming down to earth, I feel free will is our individual right of expression, but that the hint of predetermined destiny, which the clairvoyants sense, may be the overriding current of the evolution of mass consciousness, the strength of which can sometimes topple the strongest free will and carry it along in its tide.

From how to why

I cannot tell you scientifically how, as thought, we began. I can only tell you about the overlaps between my experiences, my experiments and the advances of modern science and how I explain these. I can only tell you that what we see is what we truly and emotionally believe, consciously and unconsciously, and that the mirror of life reflects those thoughts back to us, moment by moment. I can tell you that riding with the paradoxes, as science does, is the gateway to a new level of understanding. I can tell you that change exists in a timeless world, for timeless does not mean no time. It is rather a moment of layered simultaneous possibilities, those which you see in the outer world being those reflecting your strongest beliefs. All is out there and all is potential. All *is* in the same moment and the gap between the ultimate reality of what *is* and what we actually see is the reflection of the gap in our understanding. We live an illusion according to our strongest beliefs, but we are, in the same moment, all belief, so all reflections, all possibilities are ready to fall into focus depending on our moment of choice.

Have you seen the Magic Eye pictures which, at first glance, are simply two-dimensional colourful, patterns? As you look more deeply and focus your eyes beyond the surface of the picture, a three-dimensional world jumps into view. Reality is a three-dimensional Magic Eye picture containing, at a deeper level, an infinity of all possible worlds, four dimensional and perhaps beyond. Whichever one we focus on through belief is the one we see. With faith, all should be accessible. The picture and all possibilities within it exist in the one moment. The choice of depth of focus and belief also exist in the same moment. Is life simply reducible to a scientific mechanism, a kind of giant Magic Eye, with no greater purpose than existence? Or is there meaning behind the mirror?

part three

the soul
the soul searches for meaning
searches for
meaning

God: the painter 13 or the painting?

Stand back with me and view the painting: the great ocean of thought fills most of the canvas, topped with waves frozen in the now of the painter's brush. The wave patterns are you and I and the material world that we have each created according to our strongest thoughts. Above the ocean the sun shines, throwing our material world into patterns of light and shadow, defining edges and separateness. The sun is our consciousness which reinforces our current view of life.

Just below the materialised waves, the ocean waters are our individual unmaterialised thoughts. If you look very closely you can see the ghostly blueprint of your life: the shape of possible things to come etched by those thoughts which are gathering momentum. Here also our thoughts spread and intermingle with the unmaterialised thoughts of others. Water blends invisibly with water, being both separate and interconnected. Occasionally strong currents of resonating mass thought override and sweep us along in their frenzied rush towards expression of materialised mass consciousness.

At deeper levels in the ocean, where sunlight does not penetrate, our deepest unconscious thoughts merge and unite without interruption from splashing waves, rolling tides or rushing currents. Here, in stillness, we are close to the ocean bed, symbolically perhaps the birthplace of all that we are, as individual thought and as one ocean. Here, far from the sunlight of consciousness, far from our conscious existence as individuals atop an ocean wave, is the mystery of our origin, the true foundation of our being. Here is the unity of original thought.

Yet this painting is no snapshot in time, for time is an illusion. Pay closer attention and you will see the painter wields his brush with miraculous speed, portraying as you watch, the ever-reflecting now. Refocus your eyes and realise the sheer beauty of this painting, for it is not the two-dimensional canvas you created with your conditioned mind, but the multidimensional Magic Eye, where what you see depends on your depth of focus. The shape of things to come, the shape of things that are, and the shape of things that were, are ever present, simply lodged at different focal depths. All past, present and future are here, interchangeable within the blink of an eye.

We return to the focal point of the ever-reflecting now and see that the painting moves! See the rolling of the waves, the crumbling of the old, the birth of the new. See the blueprints intensify and dissolve, ever refining the shape of things to come, the shape of things that are. See the torrents of mass consciousness gather momentum and define the phases and ages of humanity: the domestication of animals, the rise of civilisation, the spread of Christianity, the fear of God, the fear of witches, belief in the Church, belief in science, the fear of communism, the fear of capitalism, the invention of flying machines, belief in racial superiority and so on.

This incredible painting is 'all that is' encapsulated. Pitched at the eye of the ever-reflecting now it appears to move, to record time, yet it is also the stillness of no time. It is all thought. It is you and I as individuals and it is you and I as one whole. Our thoughts create both material form and blueprint possibilities. We are the painting and we are the painter. We are miraculous in ways we cannot consciously comprehend.

The Eastern religions generally see the supreme being, Buddha, the God force, the divine, as an intrinsic part of the universe and the process of life, rather than as a ruler existing outside and looking on. The point of the various Eastern philosophies is to transcend the illusion of individual existence and realise the interconnectedness of all things: the ultimate unity of the universe. The idea is to work towards a state of consciousness which bursts the bubble of illusion. This is enlightenment and it can be seen clearly in our painting as a process of bringing sunlight to shine on the ocean floor, which in turn would reflect throughout the very ocean itself.

Western religion ascribes the creation of the world to a ruling God who is nonetheless omnipresent, all powerful and all knowing. We talk about 'divining' the future, just as we refer to God as being divine, reflecting our Western understanding that God exists beyond time as we know it. He gives us free will, yet our ultimate fate is in his hands. Faith and belief mark the pathway to his door and form our ultimate test, for if we show faith we will reside with God. Now our Western God begins to sound very much like our painting and our painter, which must mean that we are God and God is we. As all thought we are divine and we can divine. Our Western problem is that we have forgotten our divinity.

We have become so deluded by the 'reality' of the material world and the laws which seem to describe it that we have forgotten the umbilical cord which links us to our true self: one unity, one intrinsic creative God, one divinity. Caught up in the belief of the ticking clock notching finite time as we race to find meaning in physical existence, we opt for sculpting our material mark, our individual ego identity, our fingerprints in the world of form because it seems to offer more permanence than the world of thought alone. Have we become so focused on our need to matter that we have created, through the resonating shape and sound of the word, exactly that: a Western view dominated by matter?

And if we occasionally break through our illusion and feel the tug of the umbilical cord which connects us to all that is, are we so overawed by the implications of the experience that we run for the safety zone of denial? How often do we, poor deluded slaves of expectation, bury meaningful or true spiritual experience for fear of the regimented codes of organised religion, the waftiness of new age spirituality or the medicate-you-back-to-reality psychiatric system? How often do we embrace science and reasoning for the sake of public credibility while dissociating our spiritual experiences through the arts to be safely intellectualised as fantasy, history, fiction, creative expression or philosophy?

How much longer can science protect us from facing spiritual meaning? As we have seen, the arguments provided by modern physics have brought us closer to the spiritual realities described by both Eastern philosophies and Western religion. We find a world where each individual shares responsibility for the world we build through belief, not because the world is the sum of our individual parts, but because the whole is indeed much greater than this. What we think reverberates throughout the whole by resonating with the thoughts of like-minded individuals, increasing persuasive power by lending momentum. Resonance grows into the current of mass consciousness which has the power to tip the balance of outward expression, for better or for worse. We carry the responsibility and power of a creative God, but are we also answerable to a higher purpose?

The question of meaning is further compounded by the theory

of parallel universes which, according to quantum physics, may well exist. If they do, then you, as an individual, exist in multiple variations in an infinite number of alternative universes.

Every subatomic situation, according to quantum physics, has a variety of possible outcomes, each of which already exists. Which outcome *seems* to occur is determined by the observer since, according to modern physics, the observer's mind is always a part of the experimental outcome. However, since all possible outcomes exist, then so do all possible variations of the observer's expectations. The observer and the event exist in multiple parallel universes, each one featuring a different expected outcome.

In other words, according to the theory, every decision you have ever taken, and will ever take, exists, as do multiple copies of yourself, each occupying one of the infinite possibilities. Each universe will be different, some minimally so, some unrecognisably so.

Where would your boundaries as an individual lie, if you existed in infinite variations? Some variations would be almost indistinguishable from the you in this universe, and some would be remarkably different, since your material form would reflect your strongest thoughts which, between parallel universes, would be infinitely diverse. Apart from tracing common origins, could you distinguish between variations of yourself and other people? We can apply the same argument to the single universe we call our own and ask how we distinguish ourselves from others if we all share a common basis, a common origin, a common unity, a common divinity.

Some scientists argue that since we consciously sense ourselves as individuals we must not be aware of ourselves in parallel universes, while others argue that occasionally we might. If we did have that occasional awareness then our parallel universes would overlap in consciousness and we might find ourselves sharing, perhaps, thoughts and synchronicities with these parallel selves.

How often might our tuning in with other people be instead a resonance between us and their similar parallel selves? Suddenly infinite parallel universes reunite as one universe, or one 'multiverse' as some scientists have chosen to label totality.

As a child I experienced occasional déjà vu which intrigued me. By the age of ten I decided life was a pathway of options, a bit like a maze in a child's puzzle book, but one which we drew as we went along. Each decision became a junction on our path and wherever we turned right in one life (as I saw it then), we would find ourselves turning left in the next. My déjà vu experiences, I believed, were recognition of pathways previously travelled. The point, as I imagined it, was to ultimately experience all possible combinations of life and then stand in judgement of oneself at the end, richer for the learning. Life was, therefore, a serious game marked by oneself, after which one was ready for whatever came next. Parallel universe theory allows for all this to happen simultaneously. Multiverse theory allows for occasional, mystical experiences of overlap.

As an adult, no matter how seriously I take my life, I cannot rid myself of an underlying knowledge that it is a self-written drama, a big game, albeit one that carries meaningful responsibility. The game starts with a suspended belief in the greater reality, while the handicap is a perception of individual separate identity in a world of cause and effect. In such a way we gain compassion and understanding through walking in a multiplicity of shoes, through many parallel realities, seeing the game of life from an infinity of angles until all conscious experience is sum totalled as one divine consciousness. Through losing the ego in an infinity of selves, we finally acknowledge a unity of being. But if what we discover is our own divinity, where do we go from there?

Many find meaning in just being. It can be sufficient to know that if everyone is an aspect of oneself, a part of the whole unity, then compassion and caring is purpose enough. Some need a

God beyond the God: a higher purpose. Since nature delivers sensations of meaningfulness through synchronicity and oneness, the most sensible choice is surely to search for self-understanding through watching the reflection of our strongest thoughts in the outer world mirror, through observing synchronicities as signs of emerging breakthroughs of consciousness, to permit the sensation of oneness to encourage a shift in consciousness, to meditate, to watch our dreams and our visions and to regard everyone as aspects of ourself and, in so doing, learn compassion, empathy, caring and love. Use what you learn to peer as deeply into the Magic Eye ocean as you dare using your growing consciousness to shine a light into the depths until you see the ocean bed. Finally, conquering illusion, open your eyes in enlightenment and wake up from the dream into full consciousness of the greater reality.

I cannot tell you the whole story for I, like you, am a butterfly still encased in a pupa. When my wings unfold and give me flight I will know what it is to be transformed before the full sun. Until then our task is to grow towards the light of full consciousness, to free ourselves from the pupa, to break the bonds of illusion, to escape the dream and to wake up to all that truly is.

mirror, 14 mirror, who am I?

Life and all the people in it are our mirrors, because the outer world reflects our strongest thoughts. Through learning to read people closely associated with us, those who are our most magnified mirrors, we learn to know ourselves more objectively. It's much easier to recognise in others what we cannot see in ourselves.

When life overlaps through shared synchronicities with people close to us, intense mirroring is at work, providing us with the opportunity to predict our own shape of things to come through mutual observation.

Come, look into my mirror for a while. Today my fifteen-year-old son, Euan, is on a plane somewhere between Australia and New Zealand while my sixteen-year-old daughter, Rowan, is still in bed, sleeping off yesterday's physics exam and dreaming of freedom. Outside the misty weather has broken and winter sunshine lifts my spirit. And with the dawning of this sunshiny day, my writing agenda reveals the chapter heading I chose eight months ago: 'Mirror, Mirror, Who Am I?'

Euan's new zeal in life is a role as guest actor in a children's television drama, where he plays a cockney orphan pickpocketing his living in the goldfields of nineteenth-century Australia. One day he is befriended by a girl from the future who has reached the past by travelling through a magic mirror. Euan's character then crosses through the mirror into the twentieth century where, after several adventures, he is convinced by friends from both centuries to reunite with his long-lost adoptive parents. The series is called 'Mirror, Mirror 2'. As far as Euan's role is concerned, I think my chapter heading, 'Mirror, Mirror, Who Am I?', is more appropriate. My chapter was named five months before we knew anything about the television series. Euan hadn't acted professionally before and wasn't even registered with a casting agent when the opportunity to audition for the job came 'out of the blue'. My 'Mirror, Mirror' chapter title was a touch of precognition later acted out as a shared synchronicity.

Our shared synchronicities run deep at this time in our lives. This is Euan's third filming session in New Zealand for this series, while my own 'Mirror, Mirror' is found in Part Three of this book. I started writing *The Shape of Things to Come* the week Euan left home for his first month's work and by the time his filming is finished, I know my book will be too. I am writing about time, the future, precognition and discovering our identity through our greater reality. Euan is acting the same subject. I have been growing my hair for a few months to allow for a slight change in style. It feels a mess. A few weeks ago Euan's producer told him not to get his hair cut because it needed to be scruffy and waiflike. Two days ago, when I was wrestling with the previous chapter, Euan came in from the backyard and told me he had just discovered the meaning of life: 'To do whatever brings happiness.' He had no idea that I was writing a chapter about the meaning of life. And so it continues.

When he auditioned for the television series, I had no idea

(apart from through my dreams in retrospect!) that within a few weeks I would be hosting a television show. Euan has been on the radio and in and out of the newspapers over the years because of his award-winning art, poetry and writing. Whenever he appeared in the media, I did too, with no planning.

The point is that our mirroring has got to the stage where we can predict our personal futures or milestones by watching each other. When Euan heard that 'Mirror, Mirror 2' had been sold to a number of overseas countries, we both realised the potential of my book to do the same.

Euan and I are different people with overlapping lives. If this was a dream (which, until enlightenment, it is), my son would symbolise the male or Yang side of my life: that which is still growing and developing in the outer world. It is no surprise, therefore, that our overlaps occur in fields of work, contracts and outer world profile. No doubt in Euan's world, I symbolise the nurturing Yin (female) side of his creativity and our shared synchronicities underline his fulfilment in these areas.

My daughter, in my life's dream, symbolises the female or Yin side of myself: my inner world. Just as Rowan slept off her physics exam last night, so did I sign off from my last grapple with quantum physics. Rowan has a few months to go before she finishes school. She eagerly awaits the release of pressure and the increased freedom she will gain. During these months of book writing and exams we have shared the inner pains and pleasures of disciplined study, pressure and freedom.

Mirroring reflects what you need to know about yourself: the 'good' and the 'bad'. There is no need to blindly follow the life of your mirrored mate. You can choose at any time to apply your new insight on 'Who Am I?' to jump off the roundabout and make changes. The choice, ultimately, is always yours.

(*Postscript*: On 8 December 1997 Euan had a day's work acting in an international television commercial—his second professional acting role. He played the *pitcher* in a baseball game. During my third progression hypnosis in October 1996 [see page 118] I referred to 8 December 1997 and reported that on that day 'I am making a *documentary film*'. On 23 November 1997 I had been part of a team which *pitched* [the correct technical term] our *documentary* series idea to enthusiastic *international* reception. On 12 December 1997 I received confirmation of our success in this regard. So it seems that Euan mirrored the *international pitching aspects* of my own intentions. Although I received confirmation on 12 December, I later discovered that legal documents connected with this confirmation were officially registered by the other party on 8 December.)

Like Attracts Like, yet Opposites Attract!

'Like attracts like' yet 'opposites attract', or so the old adages tell us, referring to the friends who surround us as well as to the partners we choose in relationships or business. Paradox strikes again!

That like attracts like is easy to comprehend, since like thoughts resonate and materialise shared synchronicities. It is no surprise that we find ourselves in the same situations as many of those who surround us, since, as shared thoughts, we share worldly experience.

Yet it is also true that opposites attract. The giver and the receiver live or work in mutual dependency, as do the controller and the submissive, the aggressor and the victim, the shy and the extrovert, and the thinker and the doer. Each 'opposite' combination is really a polarity of likeness. The giver is at one pole, or one extreme, of the flow of exchange spectrum, while the receiver is the extreme at the opposite pole. Ideally the giving and the receiving for one person should be in balance.

The ancient Buddhists promoted the virtues of walking the Middle Way between extremes, a belief which the Chinese Taoists embrace through the circular Yin-Yang symbol: Yin and Yang, looking rather like two plump tadpoles, nestle together, each containing at its tail end a dot of the opposite's colour. Yin and Yang are opposites, and as we grow towards extreme Yang we find it peters out into a thin tail and gives way to Yin. As we grow towards the Yin extreme, we return to Yang. The dot in each tail symbolises the growing seed of Yin in the extreme Yang, and vice versa. In other words, the Taoists believe that as we approach the extreme in any issue, life ultimately serves the opposite lesson. The strong have often developed their strength to cover their weakness, but it is frequently that very weakness which eventually topples them and reveals their vulnerability. The weak hide from their own strength until they are finally forced by another's overbearing strength to retaliate. It is best, advise the Taoists, to find balance by walking that middle road between extremes. This is not achieved by taking a blinkered view or by shutting out emotion, but by actively resolving inner conflict.

Since our strongest thoughts manifest themselves, our hidden unresolved extreme thoughts, those in opposition to our outer world personality, materialise in the shape of partners and friends of the opposite extreme. In denial of our true selves we abhor their strength, their weakness, their aggression, their victimised attitude, their shyness, their loudness; yet in truth we manifest our opposites because they are a true reflection of our selves.

In terms of meaning, opposites attract to help us resolve our conflicts between extremes, to find balance, while like attracts like so that we can acknowledge ourselves more objectively. There is always meaning in the mirror. With practice, that reflection tells us all we need to know about who we are and the shape of things to come. All we need to do then is to take action according to what we see. In this way, we can be our own clairvoyants.

Life as a Mirrored Cliché

There is something magical about clichés. Much as we are taught to avoid them and to search for more creative linguistic expression instead, they often embody centuries of observation and conditioning. We still relate to 'carrying the weight of the world on one's shoulders' which perhaps evolved from the days when nomadic people did just that. Seldom do we carry real weights that way today, yet tense shoulder pain is one of the first physical manifestations of stress (carrying too heavy a load).

Clichés are repeated ready-made images which frequently register as conditioned thoughts, colouring our view of the world. If these thoughts are sufficiently strong, they manifest as outer world form, literally or symbolically. If you step back from your life with a sense of humour, you will notice how often you live out clichés or act out the alternative meanings of words, much as I did following some of the hypnosis experiments.

I like to exercise (workout: I like to work things out?) so I generally go to the gym several times a week. When my gym membership expired recently, I decided to change my routine temporarily to fit in with my writing. So three times a week, at the end of my working day, I went running in the dark. It worked well. I wasn't tied to a gym timetable so it suited my working style, and it also reminded me of the weeks when I was writing my first book when we lived in a more isolated place and I ended each day by running. Writing my first book was rather daunting, and I found the run a useful time to drum in the old cliché 'one step at a time'. I envisioned that as easily as I could run a distance by approaching it one step at a time, so could I write my book by approaching it one chapter at a time. So it was that each run put the day's writing to bed and refreshed my mind for the next.

This time running was a different proposition. We live in a hilly innercity area, and since I didn't really want to make my run that hard, I found a little stretch of flattish back alleys and did enough laps to make up the mileage. Towards the middle of the book when I was dealing with some of the tough stuff, it dawned on me that I was 'running around the block'. Since my outer world mirrors my strongest inner thoughts, I realised that I must have been blocked in my understanding and that I was going round and round the issue instead of overcoming it. The issue that I hadn't fully come to terms with was the last hypnosis session involving the Wright Brothers documentary. I was also running 'in the dark': lacking clarity. Several nights later as I prepared for my run, no one was at home so I went running clutching my door key. I hadn't done this before. It was only on the home straight that I caught onto the symbolism and laughed: I finally 'had the key'! A few days later I found my solution and finished Part Two. On the same day a long expected cheque arrived in the mail and I decided to celebrate by buying a membership to a new fitness centre. So I never did 'run around the block' any more, because the block was no longer there. I had moved on to new territory.

Now this may seem a silly story, but it is a simple illustration of how the outer world mirrors inner thoughts instantaneously. I didn't consciously go running because I had a block, just as I didn't know I had the key to understanding when I ran with the key. In each case, it was waking up to the cliché that alerted me to my corresponding inner thoughts. The 'block' realisation helped me to acknowledge that I had a block and to identify it, and the 'key' symbol gave me the confidence to let my unconscious solution write itself onto the computer, which it did.

It is not only the people in your life who are your mirrors. It is every aspect of your outer world. Your outer world is you. Look into the mirror when you need that extra insight and apply a little detective work. The answer may be there in cliché, or in the personalities of other people in your life, or in symbolism, but it will certainly be there. Clearly you will see the shape of things as they are and which actions, if any, you need to take to change the reflection in the mirror into the shape of things you would prefer.

responsibility
15 for the future

My quest to understand precognition has been an extraordinary experience, although I no longer know where the journey first began. As a child living on the south coast of England I was fascinated by Scotland, a country I had not visited. One year my primary school teachers were concerned because I always crayoned the same picture in art: a cottage with Scottish mountains in the background. I wore an enamelled highland dancer brooch, which I still have tucked away in a little treasure box. Years later the family moved to Scotland and I felt at home. I spent eleven years there, married a Scot and gave my children Scottish names. Yet as a tiny child I also recall digging in a hole in the back garden with an old dessert spoon, claiming I was tunnelling my way to Australia. I have lived here for fourteen years and have married an Australian. Were these childhood notions of the reality of the shape of things to come the true beginning of this quest for understanding precognition?

Perhaps I ignited the adventure as a child when I discovered that the best way to fall asleep was to close my eyes and imagine the beginning of time. I pictured myself floating in space looking at Earth, then orbiting round and round, backwards, through the years. I encountered coffins, which seemed to indicate death, yet still I orbited ever backwards. When I couldn't find the beginning, I'd circle in the opposite direction to search for time's end, but along the way I'd fall asleep and my dreams would take over the unresolved business of identifying the nature of time.

Was my inadvertently conscious choice of dream material the beginning of my journey? Or was it my first precognitive dreams and visions, or the day I fell from a mountain and thought my end had come until I had a preview of a future I wanted and vowed to live and accept it? Or was it the day I walked out of formal scientific research, knowing I was heading for something more relevant and just trusting that I would find it? Did acceptance and trust in my future mark the shape of things to come?

Or was it the day the elm tree in our back garden, which must have been over a hundred years old and which I admired every morning, mysteriously uprooted the week my first husband and I separated? Or the people and situations I subsequently met which reinforced the astounding clarity of life's symbolism. Was this the beginning of my journey?

Or did the real quest begin the day I made my interests public and professional, researching dreams, discussing dreams on the radio, meeting, interviewing and talking with people from all walks of life, each with their own extraordinary experiences to share? Or was it the moment I took a deep breath and sat in the hypnotist's chair, instantly redefining both my quest and the shape this book would take?

We can all look back over our lives and see the strange circum-stances, risks, trusts, insights and links which have led us to where we stand today. If we are happy with our progress we may look back in wonder, imagining that each event, each meeting along the way, was purposefully placed to bring us towards our destiny. If we are unhappy we may conjure up a picture of negative karma and atonement, or of a fixed destiny based on lack of personal choice. If our life experiences have included precognitive dreams, precognitive visions or clairvoyant readings which came true, then it is sometimes hard to believe that life is not predestined, at least in some aspects.

Yet for all the wonder, all the awe of apparent divine miraculous intervention to keep us on our predestined paths, my quest has revealed to me that it is we who are divine, we who are the magicians of synchronicity, dreams, visions, manifestations, mirrored meaning and, once we acknowledge the fact, total creation of the illusory world we each see. It is we who must take the final bow and accept responsibility for the drama that we, as both part and whole of the divine, have created. And when we open our eyes and awaken from the dream, we will finally know why we needed such experience.

The beauty of understanding that while we are individuals we are also interconnected as part of one whole unity is that we can draw on the collective wisdom of that greater part of our total being to help us make our individual choices. While some people prefer to rely on the authority of others through adhering to religious doctrines or by following codes laid down by cult gurus, freer spirits seek to absorb a greater sense of insight and empowerment without debt. Some call on God by name, some on Buddha, some on guardian angels, some on spirits and guides, some address Infinite Spirit, Divine Love or call upon the White Light. What works best for me is the sense of rejoining to a Divine Love from which I have separated. Each to their own.

If I know, should I tell?

Accurately foreseeing someone's death or an accident in great literal detail terrifies many first-time precognitive dreamers and visionaries. Living through a traumatic situation once in a dream (or more than once in a recurring dream) and then through the actual experience itself sends many people into exhausted spins of 'Why me?'

A natural reaction, for first-time experiencers, is to question whether the dream or the vision caused the situation. As experience grows, the dreamer generally becomes aware that previewing an event, even though they may not understand why it happens, helps them to be more prepared when the event occurs. Knowing that a person is likely to die at a particular time, or that the sickness which seems innocuous is likely to deliver a fast and fatal blow, allows the literal precognitive dreamer or visionary to spend quality time with the person, to say goodbye in their own way and to come to terms with the coming bereavement. Many dreamers feel spiritually uplifted by the experience, deeply sensing meaning and purpose through the demonstration of privileged preview.

This book has erased the question of cause and effect in such situations and replaced it with the picture of the ever-reflecting now, where the outer world mirrors our strongest inner thoughts. We have already dealt with dreams and visions of death as symbolic of change in the experiencer's inner world, and with how such people might expect to meet synchronicities in the shape of death and endings in their outer world mirror. However, it is important to realise that the person who is about to die or to have an accident is immersed in their own life process too.

Their accident or their passing out of materialised physical form is a reflection of their own inner thoughts. The person may be consciously unaware of the emerging unconscious thoughts which will express as death or accident, but as an individual they are totally responsible for their own drama, their own shape of things to come. The precognitive dreamer has simply overlapped, through the shared metaphor of death which symbolises change or endings, with that person.

The dreamer may be going through, for example, the death of old attitudes, whereas the person about to die is expressing endings in a different way. With accidents, the symbolic dreamer may be dealing with inner conflicts over direction, or the need to change direction, while the person involved in the accident has either remained consciously unaware of her own inner conflict or has chosen to ignore it. Either way, the unresolved conflict finally emerges into the outer world, screaming loudly via the physical pain of the accident.

Dreaming or having a vision of an accident at a certain location but involving unknown people is also a fairly common experience. Here the accident is, again, an outer world expression of the dreamer's inner world: it is a synchronicity. Without the inner conflict, the dream or vision would not have occurred. At the same time, however, the people involved in the accident were experiencing their own outer world dramas, reflecting their own inner thoughts. If the dreamer had not passed by at the time of the accident, or had not heard the news, the event would still have occurred and the dreamer may never have realised the dream was precognitive. It would have remained symbolic of her inner conflict.

Literal precognitive dreams and visions, or those believed to be conveyed by spirits and deceased family members, may also suggest, however, that the dreamer shares with genuine clairvoyants the ability to access the 'tuning fork' of the collective unconscious (see page 218): the ability to sense the subtle beyond the range of one's own matching thoughts.

Although we may not be responsible for the fate of others, if we are privileged to preview, should we warn them? My experiences, which I have always been able to match to my own inner processes, frequently reveal accurate details of a death but hide the exact identity. The person in the dream will either be a brother or sister of the person about to die, or will be someone else I know of the same name. In retrospect the connection is obvious, but at the time of the dream, even if I wanted to warn, I wouldn't know whom to inform! This has made my life easier and I believe it emphasises that our dreams highlight our responsibilities towards our own issues. Our dreams and our visions are primarily for us, they reflect our own thoughts and supply our own needs. Telling someone straight out to avoid a car journey because you have foreseen an accident may deter the event in the short run, but that person's thoughts will continue to be reflected back to him in his outer world. Without corresponding inner change, the accident is likely to re-present.

In all cases, start by analysing your dreams and visions and apply what you learn about yourself. If you feel that you have had a precognitive dream about a specific person who does not understand outer world symbolism, and you wish to warn them, use some detective work to deduce their possible inner thoughts which are on the verge of materialising, then gently test the issues in conversation. Acknowledgment may be all it takes to change their outer world reflection, but it is they who take ultimate responsibility for that change, not you.

Changing the World?

We each have total responsibility for the shapes of our lives, yet a tiny baby or child needs our love and support because, in human terms, he cannot take responsibility for himself. Within his spiritual domain the story may be quite different. He, too, is thought materialised as a physical body, implying that he existed as thought before he existed in human form. As he grows and learns about his environment he forms his own perceptions of his illusory world. He interacts with his parents and perceives his identity, his personality and his individuality, but these qualities are all measures of his own thoughts, just in the way that you and I are reflections of our strongest thoughts. His parents' actions may challenge his development along specific routes, but it is he who responds. He has the final response-ability.

So it is that we all have the ability to respond to the challenges of the world according to free will. It may be difficult sometimes to swim against the current of mass consciousness, but history lights the way with inspirational stories of pioneering thinkers and doers who have made the difference by breaking the mould. Just as the Yin and Yang pendulum eventually swings when we move into extremes of thought, so history has reflected the same readiness to change at critical points of overload. We are a part of the whole just as much as we are individuals and as such we hold responsibility for that whole, but we cannot exercise that response-ability by denying other individuals the freedom to respond in their own ways. Instead we must each be responsible for shaping our own inner worlds according to our wisdom, while allowing others to arrive at their own understanding.

Put aside your precognitive dreams of world disasters and concentrate on applying the symbolism to your own life. The way to change the world is to first change yourself. Take responsibility for your own emotional tidal waves, floods, earthquakes, wars, fires, droughts and famines, and watch your changed inner thoughts reflect in a changed outer world. Step by step, everything changes on the road towards waking from the dream.

Every Moment of Every Day?

We may be responsible for the shape of our lives in every single way, but it would be incredibly tedious to analyse and check each thought and word. It is enough to step back from time to time and take stock of the patterns of our lives and see how these relate to our inner worlds.

Everything we need to know is right there in front of us if we take the time to look. We can sit back and accept the future before us, or we can turn the tide and change the rules. The choice is up to us. Until now we have not known how to make that choice.

how to
16 develop precognition and make it work for you

Everything you need to know may well be right there in front of you, but where to start? This chapter is about practicalities. If you have flipped straight to this page without reading the rest of the book, you will find it totally baffling, so go back and read all about it first! These tips are based on the findings of my research and the tried and trusted methods I have used to predict the shape of things as they appear to be forming and to work out how to change them into the shape of things I prefer.

Keep a Synchronicity Dream Journal

To develop precognition and use it for positive change, you need to start by observing yourself and your life. Buy a large exercise book, preferably one you will take pleasure in owning to help instil a sense of self-nurturing and contemplation. Make the commitment to set aside time each day to dedicate to your journal and the improvements that it will bring into your life.

Use each right hand page to record your dreams, whether or not you understand them. Date each dream and give it a gut-reaction title, then keep a record of the titles and dates at the back of your journal for easy reference. If you have difficulty recalling dreams, simply start by writing down your waking emotions and thoughts each morning. In *Sleep On It*, my first book, I explain how to recall your dreams, how to interpret them and how to take correct action. To use precognition meaningfully and effectively in your life you will need to understand basic dream interpretation.

Divide each left-hand page into three columns. Head one 'Daily Journal' and use this to record in short note form general events, conflicts, thoughts or insights of the day. Listing these in point form only will help you keep it brief and easy to refer back to.

Head the second column 'Synchronicity' and use it to record, again in simple point form, any synchronicities which relate to either your dreams or your daily journal. You will find that synchronicities may occur a few days later than your dreams or may string out over a week or so. Simply go back and record each synchronicity, with its date, alongside the dream or daily journal entry it relates to.

Mark the third column 'Dream Interpretation' and use this to jot down in point form your understanding of each dream. In the early days it may take a while to get the hang of dream interpretation. In this case, record all your dreams, but interpret only one for each week; choose the most striking one, or a recurring theme.

You will note that there is no column for 'Precognition'. Since precognition is really a special case of synchronicity, I feel there is no need. If you have a burning desire to make predictions and test to see if they come true, set aside some pages towards the back of your journal and record the date, the prediction and the predicted date of the event. In this way you can check them off as they occur. However, I feel it is more instructive to record any visions or precognitive feelings in your 'Daily Journal' column, and then the events, when they occur, in your 'Synchronicity' column.

Most important of all, please allow yourself several weeks just to record your observations without analysis and brain work, to help cultivate a sense of peace and contemplation with this process. This is special time to dedicate to yourself. In this way you can establish the habit of keeping your journal without the pressure of the detective work.

Doing the Detective Work

After an allotted time, go back over your journal and look for patterns between the columns. Take the occasional double-page spread in your journal to record any overall patterns you see. These patterns will develop into insights about your life and the way in which your inner thoughts, through your dreams and daily journal notes, are reflecting in your outer world through daily events and synchronicities. Look specifically for the following clues.

MIRROR CLUES
Who is in your life or your dreams? Who symbolises 'like attracts like' and who represents dealing with balance and extremes through 'opposites attract'? Who appears and who disappears (in life or in your dreams), and how do these timings reflect your inner thoughts and changes? What do each of these people tell you about your own thoughts and attitudes?

Can you identify any clichés or sayings being acted out in your life or your dreams? These may be clues about your unconscious conditioning. If you don't like the effect they are having on your life, resolve to change them by understanding why you have been conditioned that way. Acknowledgment is usually all it takes to break the cycle.

Look for clues (predictions) in early pages which became events in later pages. Begin to see how you can use similar clues in the future to foresee the shape of things to come and how to act on these clues to accelerate or defuse your predicted outcome.

SYMBOLISM IN SYNCHRONICITIES

Look deeper than face value at the synchronicities which arise. This is easier when several synchronicities clump together, as in my 'Carol and Moving' series (page 178–81). Use your knowledge of dream symbolism and your own personal associations to crack the codes and identify the breakthrough emerging from your unconscious. Keeping the journal allows you to look back months later when the breakthrough has occurred, and then you will be able to see the obvious connection. This is a bit like getting stuck on the crossword puzzle and waiting for next week's paper to get the answers. With the solution in front of you, the clues are so clear! So it is with the symbolism of synchronicity: when the insight has broken through, the symbolism is obvious.

With practice you will learn to predict the shape of things to come by reading your synchronicities, then you can decide on your action according to what you see.

RECURRING DREAMS, LIFE CYCLES AND SYNCHRONICITIES

Which area of your life would you like to improve? Relationships, career, finances, leisure time? Whatever it is, you probably go through cycles of sheer frustration because things don't seem to go the way you want them to, no matter how many times you try.

There will be a pattern, a cycle, associated with this. Look through your journal and flip back through your memory until you identify what it is. If, for example, it's a new partner you seem unable to find, you may identify a cycle of, say, twelve weeks for each hopeful relationship, travelling from the heights of passion to carbon copy rejections that leave you totally mystified each time. Once you've found the repeating cycle, look through your journal for evidence of recurring dreams that cycle with the relationship, or whichever area it is you've elected to change. Look for evidence of repeating manifestations, of work situations, people or other issues that seem to cycle in the same way. With continued observation you will discover the unconscious thoughts which are barring you from the future you really want.

Synchronicities are the kick-start signs to look for: the ones that can get you out of the endless repeating grooves, if you know how to interpret them. Remember that synchronicities generally herald emerging breakthroughs related to change, overcoming previous limitations, realisation of wrong direction, death of the old, birth of the new and integration. They often present as travel, accident, death, birth and reunion. Remember that your symbolic dreams can be seen as the blueprints of the shape of possible things to come. When synchronicities are occurring, look for signs of change in the blueprints of your dreams. Determine whether the synchronicities are signs to follow or to avoid. Finally, in full awareness of the rumblings of your unconscious thoughts, select the blueprint you want and act on it to bring it into your life.

MEDITATION, DAYDREAMING, PRAYER, DREAM INCUBATION AND CONTEMPLATION
As the Hypnotism Project and dream incubation experiments showed, focusing conscious thoughts under conditions of

optimum access to the inner world challenges the unconscious to reveal its thoughts on the matter. Meditation, daydreaming, prayer and quiet contemplation can also provide ideal conditions for this process. Revealed unconscious thoughts take the shape of visions in meditation, symbolism within dreams, insights from prayer, or actual manifestation through synchronicity in the outer world. Remember that the unconscious responds symbolically, so while you may not get what you focus on, you will certainly challenge the unconscious to give you its symbolic version and all the added insight that endows.

Record any focused thoughts you deliberately introduce into these states and watch to see which synchronicities occur. Use symbolism and dream interpretation to crack your unconscious thoughts on your chosen subject and to understand how these have determined the shape of your life.

WORD PLAY

Listen to yourself as you talk with people. Notice words or phrases you use frequently. Hear your automatic reactions to certain topics. Take money, for example. How often do you hear yourself say 'I can't afford it' or 'My salary is just enough to put food on the table' or 'It all goes on bills' or 'There's never enough to go round'? Check back through your journal and look for evidence of your words manifesting in your life. How often are things priced just out of reach? How often do you eat well but have little cash left over?

Ask friends to alert you to words and phrases you use repetitively. Once you can clearly see the connection between your patterns of speech and the way your life works, you will realise how accurately you can make predictions for someone simply by listening to the way they express themselves. Remember that not all words and phrases are manifested literally. The right brain loves symbolism, so the predictable patterns of your life will often be right brain symbolic interpretations of your speech (unconscious thought patterns) rather than your conscious intentions.

Set aside the occasional double-page spread in your journal to record your 'old' speech patterns alongside examples of how these have shaped your 'old' life. Underneath each one, write out the 'new' words and phrases you choose to replace them with, alongside your prediction of the 'new' shape of things to come. Ask your family and friends to alert you if you fall back into the old expressions and enlist their help to prompt you with the new ones. Occasionally select one to reinforce aloud, as an affirmation, perhaps repeating it several times daily for a week. There is no need to think hard about affirmations. Just let the sound, resonance and shape of the words reprogramme your blueprint. Watch your life carefully for feedback in case your right brain has selected an alternative interpretation!

Examples:	Affirmation:	'I will be successful.'
	Likely outcome:	May occur, but future tense may delay success.
	Affirmation:	'I always try my best.'
	Likely outcome:	Plenty of trying, no achieving.
	Affirmation:	'I am successful.'
	Likely outcome:	Successful, but in which area?

As you can see, precision is vital. Remember that we generally get exactly what we ask for! Words, phrases and affirmations are powerful determinants of the shape of things to come whether we choose to use them or not. Awareness is infinitely better than sticking your head in the sand—even though that may stop you talking for a while!

Over To You

Your life has taken shape according to the guidelines you have set. Now that you know how to predict your future, you can turn the tide by changing your rules. Knowing that you alone are empowered to make those changes, the choice is entirely yours.

epilogue

epilogue

a dream:
déjà déjà vu

I stood on the paved walkway, where adults stroll for afternoon sea breath, and looked across the sand dunes onto the shore. The tide was so far out that it lay beyond the horizon, but the gaggle of little children over to my left hadn't noticed. They were too busy playing with their plastic sand trucks and toys, deeply absorbed in complex play.

Then I saw him. The lone two-year-old boy, silently watching, way over to my right. He couldn't play with the other kids because he didn't understand their game. In their eyes he was retarded, simple. In his eyes he was simply alone.

I climbed over the dunes and approached the simple boy. I held his hand and suggested we go over to join the sand truck game, but he declined and looked towards the exposed shore. He was right: why play with pretence when the whole mystery of the sandy bottom of the ocean is exposed before us?

Still holding hands we ran a huge semicircle across a few kilometres of wave-rippled wet sand, all the way out to the receded water's edge, and then continued to circle back to our starting point. The run was easy, joyous and I savoured every stride, smelling the touch of salt on my face and in my lungs. As we ran we saw tiny, white shells glistening in the sand, and as our footprints passed over them they transformed into white butterflies, lifting from the sand and flying skyward.

The circle completed, we sat together on the wet sand and laughed. I showed the simple boy the sky, not blue, but sandy yellow, also rippled and pebbled with shells, forming a backdrop to the fluttering white butterfly wings. 'Look,' I whispered, 'the sky is a mirror of the ocean floor!' I stared longer until I saw more: pitted and raised clumps of sand all over the sky. Suddenly I recognised them. 'Look again,' I encouraged the boy, 'those are the patterns you see when you look through an electron microscope. We are seeing the microscopic particles which form the universe.'

The simple boy turned and looked me straight in the eye. 'Do you think you're dreaming?' he asked. 'No!' I laughed, and continued to contemplate the sand-reflected sky. 'Jane, I think you're dreaming,' the little boy insisted. 'How could I possibly be dreaming?' I shouted. 'Watch!' I slapped my hands in the wet sand beside me. 'How could I be dreaming when we can hear that slap and smell and touch the sea water bubbling up and puddling around us? How could you be so stupid?'

'But Jane, I really think you're dreaming,' he persisted. To humour him I blinked my eyes in an effort to open them wider, and instantly he was gone. I lay in bed beside Glen and could not comprehend the infinitesimally small amount of time, perhaps indeed no time, in which I was transported from one reality to another. I moved from total faith in the dream reality to total belief in the waking reality in the blinking of an eye.

Are we really so blind to our illusion that reality is defined by faith alone? The simple boy was the only one who knew the truth.

I had this dream a few years ago, and it was only in the planning of this book that I realised how beautifully it told the same tale. I named it 'Déjà, Déjà Vu' in recognition of its muddling of realities and time, and its quality of paradoxical truth.

A friend who heard this tale came across a quote in a book shortly afterwards, which acted as a synchronicity experience for her. I'm unaware of having seen the quote before, but it closely resembles my dream and introduces the fish, which is a dream symbol of spirituality.

> *Time is but a stream I go fishing in. I drink at it, but while I drink I see the sandy bottom and detect how shallow it is. Its thin current slides away but eternity remains. I would drink deeper. Fish in the sky whose bottom is pebbly with stars.*
>
> Henry David Thoreau, *Walden*

All characters in dreams are aspects of the dreamer, so the little children on my left represented my left brain analytical self, dealing with modern ideas (toys) and forming complex concepts (complex games). Deeply engrossed in the illusion (game) of manipulating and explaining the false material world (plastic), I was blind to the greater reality offered by the right brain (the little boy on my right), with its much simpler yet wiser view. I had abandoned my right brain wisdom (it felt lonely).

In joyfully embracing the wisdom of the right brain, I came into contact with the ocean floor (the basis of the collective unconscious), discovering that a journey across such territory (the run) gives transformation (butterflies) through recognition of hidden thoughts (shells). In one run I saw the standing waves (rippled sand) related to the 'coffee cup' theory: the way in which the unconscious (sea) leaves its mark on the material world (sand), and yet also the way in which that material world is subject to change (sand shifts), with every ebb and flow of changed thought. The circle is a dream symbol of wholeness and completion, indicating that balancing right brain wisdom with left brain analysis gives a more holistic and complete view.

The sandy sky was the mirror of life, and so was the ocean floor. A hint of the importance of order of magnitude (quantum physics) was supplied with the symbolism of the microscopic imprint on the sky: as if I was experiencing reality from a different scale. The imbalance between left and right brain activity calls to mind the need for balance, so emphasised by the Taoists.

The simple truth is that our most trusted reality can change in the blinking of the waking eye and it is simplicity itself which leads us home.

sincerely
yours

The caged bird sits and watches the shadows march daily across
    her cage
Shadows long: child's laughter
Shadows short: heat and more heat
Shadows flip over: TV pictures flicker
All is shadow, all is dark: the bird counts time
Knowledge, predictable safety—tick, tock.

The cage door opens, the bird stretches,
flies beyond and watches
a glowing, golden orb crossing the sky.
The bird, transfixed,
never sees the shadows of the trees that count time,
caught in one wondrous moment
till all is shadow, all is dark,
When the confused bird counts time.

Liberated by her dreams
she flies alongside the golden orb

The bird, transfixed,
never sees the shadows cast by her flaming escort
dream-flying ever alongside
eternal light
until she wakes, in her cage.
Shadows long: child's laughter:
the confused bird counts time.

Tilting the mirror in her cage
She questions her reflected mate
'Have you too met the bird of light?'
In one blinding flash the mirror falls
sun's rays strike rebound the silvered surface
and so the bird knows
she and her mirror mate
are one with the light.
So why count time?

The bird lies still,
no shadows obscuring vision
no heart beat, no metronome,
nothing to count.
She is the silent flutter of a myriad wings.

And there had been no cage.
Tick, tock: the loud imaginary sound
measuring the illusionary bars
of no-risk bondage.
The choice was, is and always will be
In the same moment
Sincerely Yours.

Jane Anderson

appendix 1
precognitive
dreaming
questionnaire

Definition Box

'Literal' precognitive dreams are dreams which reveal the future exactly as it will later occur. When the waking-life experience happens, it is a blow-by-blow replica of the dream.

'Symbolic' precognitive dreams are dreams which give you precise information about future events in symbolic form. (It may only be after the event that you look back and recognise the dream as being precognitive.)

'Waking-Life Event' is the event which your dream predicted.

'Waking Dreams' are dreams that you experience while awake: in or out of bed! A **Precognitive Waking Dream** is one that comes true, either literally or symbolically.

A. A Literal Precognitive Dream

Please think of a LITERAL precognitive dream that you would like to share.

1. Briefly outline your dream.
2. When was your dream?
3. Briefly outline the waking-life event which later occurred.
4. How long after the dream did the waking-life event occur?
5. Did you know the dream was precognitive when you woke in the morning? *(Yes/No)*
   a) If **yes**, describe why (what was it about the dream?).
   b) If **no**, did you see anything unusual about your dream when you looked back on it after the waking-life event occurred (i.e. after you realised it was precognitive)?
6. How did you *feel* when the waking-life event began to occur, i.e. at the moment you realised that your dream was occurring in waking life?
7. Do you feel you handled the waking-life event differently because of the dream? In what way?
8. Any other comment on your experience?

B. A Symbolic Precognitive Dream

Please think of a SYMBOLIC precognitive dream that you would like to share.

9. Briefly outline your dream.
10. When was your dream?
11. Briefly outline the waking-life event which later occurred.
12. How long after the dream did the waking-life event occur?
13. Did you interpret your dream before the waking-life event occurred? *(Yes/No)*

If **yes**: *Sometimes, looking back, we see misunderstandings in our original interpretation of our symbolic precognitive dreams. Once the waking-life event occurs, we might look back and understand the dream more clearly. I am interested to look at these differences and the enlightenment which can occur looking back after the event.*

a) Did anyone help you with your original interpretation? Who? (E.g. friend, psychologist, dream interpreter.)

b) Briefly outline your original interpretation.

c) After the waking-life event, did you look back and see a different interpretation for your original dream? If **yes**, please outline your 'hindsight' interpretation.

14. Did you know your dream was precognitive when you woke in the morning? *(Yes/No)*

a) If **yes**, describe why (what was it about the dream that made you realise it was precognitive?).

b) If **no**, did you see anything unusual about your dream when you *looked back* at it after the waking-life event occurred (i.e. after you realised it was precognitive)?

15. How did you feel when the waking-life event began to occur, i.e. at the moment you realised that your dream was occurring in waking life?

16. Do you feel you handled the waking-life event differently because of the dream? In what way?

17. Any other comments?

C. General

Think now about all your precognitive dreams.

18. Are most of your dreams literal or symbolic?

19. How old were you when you had your first precognitive dream?

20. How do you feel about being a precognitive dreamer?

21. Do you talk about your precognitive dreams with (*pick from this list*):

    no one; partner or close relative; close friends;
    only other precognitive dreamers; friends; anyone who cares to listen

22. Do you feel you have precognitive dreams for other people? (*Yes/No*)

23. In general, do you know the difference, on waking, between a precognitive dream and a nonprecognitive dream? (*Yes/No*)
    a) If **yes**, how do you recognise a precognitive dream?

24. What is the usual time gap between a precognitive dream and the waking-life event?

25. Have you experienced precognitive dreams in any of the following areas? If so, which?

    major catastrophes; world events such as earthquakes, floods etc
    world events in general
    winning Lotto numbers, horses etc
    death of someone known to you at time of dream
    death of someone unknown to you at time of dream
    birth (before conception was announced)
    car, plane, bus (etc) crashes involving people you know
    car, plane, bus (etc) crashes involving people you don't know
    local events
    family events
    personal life

26. In general, which category do most of your precognitive dreams fall into? (*Choose from list in Question 25 or describe.*)

27. Do your precognitive dreams usually centre on what will happen to: a) you; b) people known to you; or c) people you don't know?

28. What do you believe is the cause of your precognitive dreams?
29. What do you believe is the purpose of your precognitive dreams?
30. I often refer to precognitive dreaming as 'time travel'. Does this term seem appropriate to you, or do you dislike it? Please outline your opinion.

D. Waking Dreams & Visions

31. Do you experience waking dreams which are precognitive *(Yes/No)*
    a) If **yes**, please outline one waking dream experience which was precognitive.
    b) Do you feel there is a difference between sleeping and waking precognitive dreams? If so, please outline.
32. Do you experience visions: either in dreams or while awake? (If you do not understand the question, your answer is 'No'.) *(Yes/No)*
    a) If **yes**, do you feel there is a difference between visions in dreams and visions while awake? *(Yes/No)*
    b) What do you feel is the difference between a vision and a dream? Please outline.
33. In your waking life, have you developed accuracy in any of the following abilities? If **yes**, which?
    clairvoyance *(seeing)*; clairaudience *(hearing)*; clairsentience *(feeling: e.g. body pain of another person)*; aura reading; past life reading; body scanning *(seeing disease)*; extraterrestrial/UFO communication; mediumship *(direct communication with spirit)*; channelling; other *(please describe)*.
34. Have you been aware of tuning into or using any of the abilities listed in Question 33 in your dreams? If **yes**, please outline.

appendix 2
clairvoyants'
questionnaire

1. What are your psychic abilities?
   e.g. clairvoyance, clairaudience, clairsentience, aura reading,
   past life reading, body scanning, UFO/extraterrestrial communication, mediumship, channelling, other.
2. How long have you been aware of these gifts?
   Did they develop in stages?
   Can you give an example?
3. Why do you think some people have these gifts and others
   don't?
4. Have you ever had a precognitive dream?
   Literal or symbolic?
   Example?
5. How often do you recall your dreams?
6. Do you use your dreams in any way for yourself?
7. Are you familiar with dream symbolism?
8. What do you feel is the difference between a vision and a
   dream?

9. How long have you been working in the field professionally?
   Full-time, part-time or occasionally?
   Type of venues?
10. What is the typical format for a reading?
11. Are some people easier to read than others?
    Why?
12. Can you see all things for some people, or do you only have access to some information?
    How do you explain this?
13. Responsibilities:
    Have you ever seen something and decided not to tell?
    How do you handle difficult or delicate information?
14. How do you see the future: fixed, partially fixed, changeable?
15. Do you think that, in some cases, to know our future gives us the choice to change it? To avoid it? To make it happen? To accept that it will happen (self-fulfilling prophecy), even if it is not desirable?
16. Do you feel you predict definite futures, probable futures, or possible futures?
17. Do you feel your most accurate skills lay in tuning in to the past, present or future of your clients?
18. How do you see time?
19. What do you think of the term 'time travel'?
20. What do you see as the most important aspect of your work?
21. How do you handle clients who can't relate to what you tell them?
22. Do you advertise? How do you market yourself and how do you decide what to charge?
23. If you use props (Tarot, tea, palms), how do you use them?
24. Do you make predictions beyond personal predictions; e.g. politics, earth changes etc? Would you like to make one now?
25. How would you summarise your personal belief in life and in afterlife?

26. Do you feel, in your readings, that you see things literally or symbolically?
27. What part do you feel the spirits of those passed away or guides help in your readings?
28. How do you use your gifts for yourself—or do you prefer not to?
29. Have you ever had a near death experience?
30. Are you able to work under test conditions?
31. What is your best experience in this work?
32. What is your worst experience in this work?
33. What advice would you give new readers starting out?
34. What advice would you give customers looking for an accurate reading?
35. Can a client do anything to prepare for a reading?
36. Do you prepare or protect yourself prior to a reading?

recommended reading

The following titles are either referred to in this book or were inspirational at some poing during its writing:

Anderson, Jane, *Sleep On It and Change Your Life*, Angus & Robertson/Harper Collins, 1994.

Anderson, Jane, *Dream It: Do It!*, Angus & Robertson/Harper Collins, 1995.

Capra, Fritjof, *The Tao of Physics*, Fontana Paperbacks, London, 1989.

Combs, Allan; and Holland, Mark, *Synchronicity*, Paragon House, 1990.

Davies, Paul, *About Time*, Viking, Penguin, 1995.

Davies, Paul, *Other Worlds*, Penguin Books, 1980.

Erbe, Peter, O., *God I Am*, Triad Publishers, 1991.

Godwin, Malcolm, *The Lucid Dreamer*, Element Books/Jacaranda Wiley, 1994.

Hawking, Stephen, *A Brief History of Time*, Bantam Books, 1988.

Jung, Carl, *Man and His Symbols*, Laurel Bantam/Doubleday Dell, 1964.

Way, Bruce, *How to Interpret a Psychic Reading*, Lothian Books, 1996.

index

postscript

Thanks for listening to my story so far.

As you read this I am contemplating new synchronicities, experiencing the latest unfoldings from the 1996 Hypnosis Project, making notes to postscript into the next edition of this book, scanning the signposts along the way for the best paths to take, for indications of the shape of things to come. As I dream the ever-reflecting mirror of life I continue to question, to learn, to puzzle, to act, to edge my way beyond the pupa stage, pausing to bathe in the shafts of light which sift through from the beginning/end point of this journey. Are you keen to accompany me further, to linger and find out what happens next?

How has this book affected your perception of life? Have your days been flooded with synchronicities and your nights drenched with meaningful dreams? Have sunlight and moonlight merged into one light through the insight they bring? Would you like to share your thoughts and your experiences with others who walk the same path?

In anticipation of your thirst and looking forward to your involvement, I have set up an interactive, informative web site. To find out more, to discover what's new and to join active discussion, tune in at:

http://www.janeanderson.com.au